A First Book of
DAILY READINGS
from the Works of
MARTYN LLOYD-JONES

A First Book of
DAILY READINGS
from the Works of
MARTYN LLOYD-JONES

Selected by
FRANK CUMBERS

WILLIAM B. EERDMANS PUBLISHING COMPANY
GRAND RAPIDS, MICHIGAN

This U.S. paperback edition published by special arrangement with
Epworth Press.
First U.S. edition published October 1970.
Printed in the United States of America.

Reprinted, December 1989

FOREWORD

I STOOD rather vaguely in a passage at Westminster Chapel, where I could see some friendly and active women busy with the arrangements for a tea. One of them, as she passed me, looked enquiringly and helpfully: 'I've got an appointment with Dr Lloyd-Jones,' I said. She beamed. 'Aren't you *lucky*!' she said. That seemed to express for me something of what the people of that historic church are still thinking of the beloved preacher who guided them for thirty years.

I agreed with her, and counted myself fortunate. The Doctor had graciously agreed to journey into Westminster so that we could plan the present book. It was my first personal encounter —though I had rejoiced to hear him in the great auditorium yonder. His immediate friendliness when he greeted me, the kind and full attention which he gave to my suggestions, were a benediction. I remembered reading, some time before, a newspaper description: 'His face is a frontier face, monolithic of brow, severely callipered about the mouth, and truculent of chin'—that face was all kindness as it considered the matter in hand. He spoke quietly, with an attractive lilt. I could understand Errol Hulse's word in the *Sunday Companion*: 'He starts slowly, his voice low. He cruises round the runway several times before taking off. Imperceptibly the message begins to grip and soon you are basking in the radiant sunshine of the Word preached with prophetic fire and unction. . . . The trumpets sound. The walls collapse. The citadel of the soul lies open to the conquest of truth. Once in full flight he is so vibrant spiritually, and reaches such peaks of eloquence, that even if you couldn't hear a word he said you would be impressed by the creative force of his gestures.' I could see, too, the force of another comment: 'On behalf of his faith he has no more modesty than an Old Testament prophet, and no hesitation in loosing bears on the children of darkness!'

I can remember even now the sensation when the young and successful Harley Street specialist, senior clinical assistant to

Lord Horder at Bart's, threw all this to the winds to become the leader of the Forward Movement Mission at Sandfields, Aberavon. The world for which money is everything noted his £225 stipend. He served there for twelve years. Such a ministry, such skill in opening the Scriptures, could not go unmarked; and although, as he told his people in his Centenary Sermon at Westminster Chapel (July 6, 1965) he was certain that he was called to minister in Wales, 'automatically' refusing every invitation that came from England, he did feel called to accept an invitation to a Bible Witness Rally in the Albert Hall. Dr Campbell Morgan was there—the man who had rescued the place which A. E. Garvie described as the 'white elephant of Congregationalism'—(Jowett compared it to Charing Cross Station!)—and it is evident that this encounter began the sequence of events which resulted in the invitation to become Campbell Morgan's associate pastor in 1938. Morgan was a troubled man a year later: 'I have brought you here, and this is what I have brought you to . . . we are almost certain to be bombed completely to the ground. We are so near to Buckingham Palace!' But even then, Martyn Lloyd-Jones had a strong conviction that 'this chapel will *not* be bombed!'—so strong that when, on May 11, 1940, following upon a tremendous raid upon Westminster, Nathaniel Micklem told him that he would announce him for the evening service at Mansfield College (in addition to the morning service which he was about to take)—since Micklem was certain that no Westminster Chapel could possibly still be standing. Lloyd-Jones insisted on coming back to London, guiding a sceptical taxi-driver past mountains of rubble—and taking his evening service as usual.

Many of us recall humbly, yet gratefully, how it created even firmer ties between our people and ourselves, to stand up under the assaults of war by their side, being with them and helping them through; and, perhaps equalled only by W. E. Sangster, his wife and he forged the bonds which hold so firmly between them and their people to this day. Yes—I *was* 'lucky' (though I suspect that that actual word is as much anathema to the Doctor as it is to me!).

His withdrawal from his pastorate came as a thunderbolt

when the people received his letter of May 30, 1968. He felt this to be under the Holy Spirit's guidance; it was not a consequence of the illness from which he had so triumphantly emerged, but rather the conviction that he must spend more time on writing. Those who benefit from the pages of this book will be thankful for the prospect of further writings such as these.

Many and deserved were the tributes at the time. 'End of a marathon ministry', said the *Methodist Recorder*, where A. E. Gould spoke of 'one of the most influential Free Church ministries of our time'.

Much could be added here concerning his preaching. He still preaches in Welsh, and the Welsh think of him as their preacher *par excellence*. He is known all over these islands, in Canada and in the States. He remembers the Hollywood church which did him the tribute of re-drafting the service order, this normally stressing the anthem more than the sermon, to give him greater opportunity! He is a pillar of the Evangelical Library; the Puritan Conference was a tiny group round a blackboard in 1955; nowadays it is wise to come in extra good time if you want a seat. There is another large and secret chapter of his activities. 'Was any minister of a large city church ever so accessible to his people?' a friend has asked, and spoke also of the 'stream of ministers, missionaries and secretaries of evangelical organizations' ever keen to receive his counsel. All this takes time.

Martyn Lloyd-Jones never pulls his punches; the presumptuous scientist straying beyond his sphere, the politician or publicist who infringes the Crown Rights of the Redeemer, will be answered in plain words. He is known as a sagacious conference chairman 'deflating the arrogant but uplifting the humble'—and *not* suffering fools gladly! When H. F. R. Catherwood published his *Christian Citizen in Industrial Society* I regarded this authoritative tome with awe and respect, for he is one of our leaders in today's industrial and economic scene. Then I noted that it was dedicated to Martyn Lloyd-Jones. Here, surely, is the preacher's role exemplified. Dr Lloyd-Jones would probably agree with me that his eminent son-in-law has written here of things which are as much a closed book to him as they are to me. But the writer had found inspiration from the preacher; having (under the preacher's guidance) put God first, he could write more truly of God's world.

Dr Lloyd-Jones told his hearers at the Centenary that he would sooner preach today than in 1865! and that is typical of the man. He was made for tough times.

Surely the final picture must be of those rapt occasions when up to two thousand hearers peopled the famous old chapel—and these so largely young thinking men and women, armed with Bible and notebook—or when some twelve hundred would attend the Friday evening Bible Schools. 'A notable feature', said A. E. Gould (the *Methodist Recorder*), 'has been the large numbers of young men and women, medical and other students, and youngsters earning their living in London, who have been consistently drawn to Westminster Chapel by simple, expository, Bible preaching, in a setting quite bare of liturgical ornament'.

'Tell me,' I said. 'Is it true that you preached on *Ephesians* every Sunday morning for two years?' 'I'm almost ashamed to tell you,' he said, smiling. 'It was *five*!' But when the well of truth is so deep, and the preacher has been gifted, through grace, so that he may draw, who will not rejoice? When in 1927 he married his beautiful young doctor-bride, Bethan, he asked for the complete works of Calvin and Owen as a wedding present! For Martyn Lloyd-Jones the Bible, and the great writings of the Christian centuries, are all that matters. May this firm, kind, eloquent man be given many more years in which to expound the Word, in fervent declamation and on the printed page!

FRANK CUMBERS

The glory of the gospel is that it is primarily an announcement of what God does, and has done, in the Person of Jesus Christ. That was the essence of Paul's gospel. . . . That was the gospel which was preached by all the apostles. They preached Jesus as the Christ. They made a proclamation, an announcement. Primarily, they called upon people to listen to what they called 'good news'. They did not in the first instance outline a programme for life and living. . . . They preached, not a programme, but a Person. They said that Jesus of Nazareth was the Son of God come from Heaven to earth. They said that He manifested and demonstrated His unique deity by living a perfect, spotless, sinless life of complete obedience to God, and by performing miracles. His death on the Cross was not merely the end of His life but the result of His rejection by His own countrymen, it had a deeper and more eternal significance. . . . 'God was in Christ reconciling the world to himself' and making 'him to be sin for us, who knew no sin; that we might be made the righteousness of God in him' (2 Corinthians 5:21). But that was not all. He had risen from the grave, had manifested Himself unto certain chosen witnesses, and then ascended into Heaven. From Heaven He had sent the gift of the Holy Spirit upon the early Church, and He had brought unto them . . . new life and power. Their lives had been entirely changed, and they now had life which was life indeed. That was the message. Its entire emphasis was upon what God had done. Its content was God's way of salvation and of making men righteous. Man had but to accept it and submit to it. Here indeed was something to be proud of as a message. Here was something which enabled one to face Stoics and Epicureans at Athens without a blush or an apology; here was a message which made the world's highest and greatest philosophies appear to be nothing but the prattling and babbling of babes.

The Plight of Man and the Power of God, pp. 82–3

You remember the famous story about William Wilberforce and the woman who went to him at the height of his campaign against slavery and said, 'Mr Wilberforce, what about the soul?' And Mr Wilberforce turned to the woman and said, 'Madam, I had almost forgotten that I had a soul' . . . with all due respect to him, the woman was right. Of course, she may have been a busy-body; but there is no evidence that she was. Probably the woman saw that here was a good and fine Christian man, doing a most excellent work. Yes, but she also saw and realized that the danger confronting such a man was that of being so absorbed in the question of anti-slavery that he might forget his own soul. A man can be so busy preaching in pulpits that he forgets and neglects his own soul. After you have attended all your meetings, and denounced Communism until you can scarcely speak, after you have dealt with your apologetics, and displayed your wonderful knowledge of theology and your understanding of the times, and your complete map of the next fifty years, and after you have read all the translations of the Bible, and have shown your proficiency in a knowledge of its mechanics, I still ask you: 'What about your relationship to the Lord Jesus Christ?' You know a great deal more than you did a year ago; but do you know Him better? You denounce many wrong things; but do you love Him more? Your knowledge of the Bible and its translations has become quite astounding, and you are an expert in apologetics; but are you obeying the law of God and of Christ increasingly? Is the fruit of the Spirit more and more manifest and evident in your life? Those are the questions . . . to 'know Him', and to 'be like' Him. If anything takes the place of that, we are on the wrong road. All these other things are means to bring us to a knowledge of Him, and if we stay with them they are robbing us of Him.

Studies in the Sermon on the Mount, ii, pp. 292–3

. . . God sitteth on the throne
And ruleth all things well!

Things do not just happen. Events are not just accidental, for there is a definite plan of history and everything has been pre-arranged from the beginning. God who 'sees the end from the beginning' has a purpose in it all, and knows 'the times and the seasons'. He knows when to bless Israel and when not to bless her. Everything is under His hand. It was 'when the fullness of the time was come' that God sent forth His Son. He allowed the great philosophers, with the clarification of thought, to come first. Then emerged the Romans, famous for ordered government, building their roads and spreading their wonderful legal system throughout the world. It was after this that God sent forth His Son. God had planned it all.

There is a purpose in history, and what is now happening in this twentieth century is not accidental. Remembering that the Church is at the centre of God's plan let us never forget the pride and arrogance of the Church in the nineteenth century. Behold her sitting back in self-satisfaction, enjoying her so-called cultured sermons and learned ministry, feeling just a little ashamed to mention such things as conversion and the work of the Holy Spirit. Observe the prosperous Victorian comfortably enjoying his worship. Note his faith in science and his readiness to substitute philosophy for revelation. . . . Yes, the Church needed chastisement, and it is not at all difficult to understand this twentieth century when we consider the story of the nineteenth. There is indeed a plan discernible in all these things.

God does not stop to consult us, and everything takes place according to 'the counsel of His own will'. God has His time; He has His own way; and He acts and works accordingly.

From Fear to Faith, pp. 22–3

[Blessed are the pure in heart: for they shall see God.] We come now to what is undoubtedly one of the greatest utterances to be found anywhere in the whole realm of Holy Scripture. Anyone who realizes even something of the meaning of the words, 'Blessed are the pure in heart: for they shall see God', can approach them only with a sense of awe and of complete inadequacy. . . .

It is, of course, the very essence of the Christian position and of the Christian teaching. 'Blessed are the pure in heart.' That is what Christianity is about, that is its message. . . . The Gospel of Jesus Christ is concerned about the heart: all its emphasis is upon the heart. Read the accounts which we have in the Gospels of the teaching of our blessed Lord, and you will find that all along He is talking about the heart. . . . Our Lord undoubtedly puts this emphasis here because of the Pharisees. It was His great charge against them always that they were interested in the outside of the pots and platters and ignored the inside. Looked at externally, they were without spot. But their inward parts were full of ravening and wickedness. They were most concerned about the external conjunctions of religion; but they forgot the weightier matters of the law, namely, love to God and the love of one's neighbour. So here our Lord puts this great emphasis upon it again. The heart is the whole centre of His teaching . . . He puts His emphasis upon the heart and not upon the head . . . He does not commend those who are intellectual; His interest is in the heart. . . . We must ever beware lest we stop at giving only an intellectual assent to the faith or to a given number of propositions. We have to do that, but the terrible danger is that we stop at that.

Studies in the Sermon on the Mount, i, pp. 106, 108–9

The Bible says quite plainly and frankly that man is totally incapable of arriving at a knowledge of truth by means of scientific theory, and that if he would arrive at a knowledge of truth, he must submit himself to revelation. In other words, he must admit that he cannot arrive at truth unaided. He must cease to have self-confidence; he must cease to trust his own intellect and his power of reason. . . .

The Bible starts by telling men just that. . . . Man has got to submit himself to revelation. For truth is a mystery, and if man would have any knowledge of it, he must submit in humility, and in reverence. . . .

I always think that one of the greatest statements [of this Bible teaching] is in that picture of Moses at the burning bush. With the typical scientific attitude Moses said when he saw that phenomenon, 'Ah! I will turn aside, and examine this curious phenomenon that I am seeing.' . . . He was about to advance and investigate when the voice came, saying, 'Draw not nigh hither: put off thy shoes from off thy feet, for the place whereon thou standest is holy ground' (Exodus 3:1–5). You do not investigate here, you worship, in reverence and in awe. . . . [Jesus] taught the same truth in His interview with Nicodemus, who was a very able and erudite teacher of the Jews, and who came along desiring to investigate, and wanting to understand. It was to him that Christ said: 'Verily, verily, I say unto thee, Except a man be born again, he cannot see the kingdom of God. . . . The wind bloweth where it listeth, and thou hearest the sound thereof, but canst not tell whence it cometh, and whither it goeth. . . .' (John 3:3–8).

The Approach to Truth: Scientific and Religious, pp. 21–3

What are the characteristics of the foolish man? The first is that he is in a hurry. Foolish people are always in a hurry; they want to do everything at once; they have no time to wait. How often does the Scripture warn us against this! It tells us that the godly, righteous man 'shall not make haste'. He is never subject to flurry and excitement and hurry. He knows God and he knows that the decrees and purposes and plan of God are eternal and immutable. But the foolish man is impatient; he never takes time; he is always interested in short cuts and quick results. . . . We are all familiar with this kind of person in ordinary life and quite apart from Christianity. He is the type of man who says, 'I must have a house at once; there is no time for foundations.' He is always in a hurry.

At the same time, because he has that mentality, he does not trouble to listen to instruction; he does not pay any attention to the rules that govern the construction of a house, [which] . . . is a serious matter, and a man who is anxious to build one should . . . realize that certain principles of construction should be observed if he is to have a satisfactory and durable edifice. . . . The wise man is anxious to know the right way to do things; and so he listens to instruction and is prepared to be taught. But the foolish man is not interested in such things; he wants a house; he cannot be bothered about rules and regulations. 'Put it up', he says. He is impatient, contemptuous of instruction and teaching, saying that he wants 'to get on with it'. . . .

Not only is he in too much of a hurry to listen to instruction, but this foolish man also considers it unnecessary. In his opinion his ideas are the best. He has nothing to learn from anybody. . . . He does not care what has been done in the past, but simply follows his own impulses and ideas.

Studies in the Sermon on the Mount, ii, p. 298
(*continued on January 7*)

Finally, it is a mentality that never thinks things right through, it never stops to envisage and consider possibilities and eventualities. The foolish man who built his house without a foundation, and on the sand, did not stop to think or to ask himself, 'Now what may happen? Is it possible that the river which is so pleasant to look at in the summer may, in the winter, suddenly become very swollen as the result of heavy rain or snow and I may be flooded out?' He did not stop to think of that; he just wanted a pleasant house in that particular position, and he put it up without considering any one of these things. And if someone had come along and said, 'Look here, my friend, it is no use putting up a house like that on the sand. Don't you realize what may happen in this locality? You don't know what that river is capable of doing. I have seen it like a veritable cataract. I have known storms here that bring down the best-built houses. My friend, I suggest that you dig deep. Get down to the rock'—the foolish man would have dismissed it all and persisted in doing what he considered best for him. In a spiritual sense, he is not interested in learning from Church history; he is not interested in what the Bible has to say; he wants to do something, and he believes it can be done in his way, and away he goes and does it. He does not consult the plans and the specifications; he does not try to look to the future and envisage certain tests that must inevitably come upon the house that is being built.

Studies in the Sermon on the Mount, ii, p. 299

(For the picture of the 'wise man', see p. 8.)

The wise man . . . has one great desire, and that is to build durably. So he starts by saying, 'I do not know much about this; I am not an expert in these matters; wisdom dictates therefore that I should consult people who do know. I want to have plans and specifications, I want some guidance and some instruction. I know men can build houses quickly, but I want a house that will last. There are many things that may happen, which will test my ideas of construction and my house.' That is the essence of wisdom. The wise man takes trouble to find out all he can; he holds himself in check, and does not allow his feelings and emotions or his enthusiasm to carry him away. He desires knowledge, truth and understanding; is ready to respond to the exhortations of the book of Proverbs which urges us to seek and to covet wisdom. . . . He is not prepared to take risks, and does not rush off in a hurry; he thinks before he acts. . . .

When the house is built it is already too late. The time for examination is at the very beginning. [The wise and the foolish builders] and their operations must be watched when they are prospecting and planning and choosing the site and location. The time to watch your jerry-builder is at the beginning, to see what he does as regards laying a foundation. It is not enough just to look at the house when it is completed. Indeed, [the house without foundations] may look better than the other . . . ultimately the most important thing about a house is the foundation. This is a truth which is frequently emphasized in the Bible. The foundation, which seems so insignificant and unimportant because it is out of sight, is nevertheless the most vital and important thing of all. If the foundation is wrong, everything else must be wrong.

Studies in the Sermon on the Mount, ii, pp. 299–300

This [the first Beatitude (Matthew 5:3)] is something which is not only not admired by the world; it is despised by it. You will never find a greater antithesis to the worldly spirit and outlook than that which you find in this verse. What emphasis the world places on its belief in self-reliance, self-confidence and self-expression! Look at its literature. If you want to get on in this world, it says, believe in yourself. That idea is absolutely controlling the life of men at the present time. . . . What, for instance, is the essence of good salesmanship according to modern ideas? It is giving the impression of confidence and assurance. If you want to impress your customer that is the way you must do it. The same idea is put into practice in every realm. If you want to succeed in a profession, the great thing is to give the impression that you are a success, so you suggest that you are more successful than you actually are, and people say, 'That is the man to go to.' . . . Self-confidence, assurance, self-reliance. And it is in terms of that fundamental belief that men think they can bring in the kingdom; it is the whole basis of the fatal assumption that by Acts of Parliament alone you can produce a perfect society. . . .

Now in this verse we are confronted by something which is in utter and absolute contrast to that. . . . You will remember the verse in which Charles Wesley says:

> I am all unrighteousness;
> Vile and full of sin I am . . .

[A few years ago, a man ridiculed this] and asked, 'What man desiring a post or job would dream of going to an employer and saying [that] to him . . .? Ridiculous!' . . . You see what a complete misunderstanding . . . that reveals . . . if one feels anything in the presence of God save an utter poverty of spirit, it ultimately means that you have never faced Him.

Studies in the Sermon on the Mount, i, pp. 44–5

Jesus warns us of . . . the awful grip and power of these earthly things upon us. . . . He says, 'Where your treasure is, there will your heart be also.' The heart! Then in [Matthew 6] verse 24 He talks about the mind. 'No man can serve two masters'—and we should notice the word 'serve'. These are the expressive terms He uses in order to impress upon us the terrible control that these things tend to exercise over us. Are we not all aware of them the moment we stop to think—the tyranny of persons, the tyranny of the world? . . . We are all involved in this; we are all in the grip of this awful power of worldliness which really will master us unless we are aware of it.

But it is not only powerful; it is very subtle. It is the thing that really controls most men's lives. Have you seen the change, the subtle change, that tends to take place in men's lives as they succeed and prosper in this world? It does not happen to those who are truly spiritual men; but if they are not, it invariably happens. Why is it that idealism is generally associated with youth and not with middle age and old age? Why do men tend to become cynical as they get older? Why does the noble outlook upon life tend to go? It is because we all become victims of 'treasures on earth', and if you watch you can see it in the lives of men. Read the biographies. Many a young man starts out with a bright vision, but . . . he becomes influenced, perhaps when he is at college, by an outlook that is essentially worldly. . . . He is still a very nice man and, moreover, just and wise; but he is not the man he was when he began. Something has been lost. Yes; this is a familiar phenomenon: 'Shades of the prison house begin to close upon the growing boy.' Do we not all know something about it? It is there; it is a prison house, and it fastens itself upon us unless we are aware of it.

Studies in the Sermon on the Mount, ii, pp. 91–2

In 2:13–16 [Paul] reminds these Ephesian Christians that they are people who have realized that all their own good works, all their good living, all their activities, their nationality, their religion, and everything they had before, are entirely useless, and that they are made Christian, and brought into this unity which is in the Church, entirely by the action of the Lord Jesus Christ, and particularly by the shedding of His blood upon the cross. . . . That is how these people have been brought into the unity. . . . These people are those who have been 'bought' into God's kingdom and family at the cost of 'the precious blood of Christ'. No one can ever belong to this family, and participate in its unity, unless he believes that.

The apostle then goes on to say that it is only because of this that we can pray. 'For through him we both have access by one Spirit unto the Father' (2:18). . . . Hebrews 10:19 teaches us the same thing. . . . It is only by relying upon the blood of Christ, by believing that His blood was shed for us and for our sins, that God 'made him to be sin for us, who knew no sin' (2 Corinthians 5:21) . . . that we have access to the Father.

The Apostle ends [chapter 2] by saying that the people whom he is exhorting to continue in this unity are those who, as the result of all this, are now fellow-citizens, and members together of the household of God, and are established together and 'built (together) upon the foundation of the apostles and prophets', which means the teaching and the doctrine of the apostles and prophets. And because they are on this foundation they have become 'a habitation of God', who dwells in them.

The Basis of Christian Unity, pp. 22–3

Both [God and mammon] make a totalitarian demand upon us. Worldly things really do make a totalitarian demand as we have seen. How they tend to grip the entire personality and affect us everywhere! They demand our entire devotion; they want us to live for them absolutely. Yes, but so does God. . . . Not in a material sense necessarily, but in some sense or other He says to us all, 'Go, sell all that thou hast, and come, follow me.' 'He that loveth father or mother more than me is not worthy of me: and he that loveth son or daughter more than me is not worthy of me.' It is a totalitarian demand. . . . It is 'either—or'; compromise is completely impossible at this point. 'Ye cannot serve God and mammon.'

This is something which is so subtle that many of us miss it completely. . . . Some of us are violent opponents of what we speak of as 'atheistic materialism'. But . . . let us realize that the Bible tells us that all materialism is atheistic. . . . So if a materialistic outlook is really controlling us, we are godless, whatever we may say. There are many atheists who speak religious language. . . . The man who thinks he is godly because he talks about God, and says he believes in God, and goes to a place of worship occasionally, but is really living for certain earthly things—how great is that man's darkness! . . . Study carefully 2 Kings 17:24–41. . . . The Assyrians conquered some area; then they took their own people and settled them in that area. These Assyrians of course did not worship [Jehovah]. Then some lions appeared and destroyed their property. 'This', they said, 'has happened to us because we do not worship the God of this particular land. . . .' So they found a priest who instructed them generally in the religion of Israel. . . . But this is what Scripture said about them: they 'feared the Lord, and served their graven images.' . . . Whom do you serve? That is the question, and it is either God or mammon.

Studies in the Sermon on the Mount, ii, pp. 94–5

The key to the history of the world is the kingdom of God. The story of the other nations mentioned in the Old Testament is relevant only as it bears upon the destiny of Israel. And ultimately history today is relevant only as it bears upon the history of the Christian Church. What really matters in the world is God's kingdom. From the very beginning, since the fall of man, God has been at work establishing a new kingdom in the world. It is His own kingdom, and He is calling people out of the world into that kingdom; and everything that happens in the world has relevance to it. . . . Other events are of importance as they have a bearing upon that event. The problems of today are to be understood only in its light. . . .

Let us not therefore be stumbled when we see surprising things happening in the world. Rather let us ask, 'What is the relevance of this event to the kingdom of God?' Or, if strange things are happening to you personally, don't complain, but say, 'What is God teaching me through this? . . . Where have I gone wrong and why is God allowing these things?' There is a meaning in them if only we can see it. We need not become bewildered and doubt the love or the justice of God. If God were unkind enough to answer some of our prayers at once, and in our way, we should be very impoverished Christians. Fortunately, God sometimes delays His answer in order to deal with selfishness or things in our lives which should not be there. He is concerned about us, and intends to fit us for a fuller place in His kingdom. We should therefore judge every event in the light of God's great, eternal and glorious purpose.

From Fear to Faith, pp. 23–4

How tragic it is that mankind should so long have been guilty of the foolish error of reversing the true order of religion and morality! For once they are placed in their right positions the situation is entirely changed. In precisely the same way as morality alone fails, the gospel of Christ succeeds. It starts with God and exists to glorify His holy Name. It restores man into the right relationship to Him, reconciling him to God through the blood of Christ. It tells man that he is more important than his own actions or his environment, and that when he is put right, he must then proceed to put them right. It caters for the whole man, body, soul, and spirit, intellect, desire and will, by giving him the most exalted view of all, and filling him with a passion and a desire to live the good life in order to express his gratitude to God for His amazing love. And it provides him with power, in the depth of his shame and misery as the result of his sin and failure, it restores him by assuring him that Christ has died for him and his sins, and that God has forgiven him. It calls him to a new life and a new start, promising him power that will overcome sin and temptation, and will at the same time enable him to live the life he believes and knows he ought to live.

There, and there alone, lies the only hope for men and for the world. Everything else has been tried and has failed. Ungodliness is the greatest and the central sin. It is the cause of all our other troubles. Men must return to God and start with Him. And, God be praised, the way for them to do so is still wide open in 'Jesus Christ and Him crucified'.

The Plight of Man and the Power of God, p. 40

People have often misunderstood this expression 'Take no thought' [Matthew 6:34] and . . . many have tripped and stumbled . . . the real meaning of 'Take no thought' has changed since the Authorized Version was introduced in 1611. If you consult the authorities, you will find that they give quotations from Shakespeare to show that 'taking thought' was then used in the sense of 'being anxious', or tending to worry. So that the real translation . . . should be, 'Be not anxious', or 'Have no anxiety', or if you prefer it, 'Do not worry', about your life, what you shall eat or what you shall drink . . . the actual word that was used by our Lord is a very interesting one; it is the word used to indicate something which divides, separates or distracts us, a word used very frequently in the New Testament . . . you will find [in Luke 12:29] the expression . . . 'neither be ye of doubtful mind'. It is a mind which is divided into sections and compartments, and which is not functioning as a whole. We cannot do better therefore than say that it is not 'a single eye'. There is a kind of double vision, a looking in two directions at one and the same time, and therefore not really seeing anything. . . .

A still better illustration of the meaning of the term is to be found in the story of Martha and Mary . . . (Luke 10:38–42). Our Lord turned to Martha and rebuked her. He said, 'Thou art careful and troubled about many things.' Poor Martha was 'distracted'—that is the real meaning of the expression; she did not know where she was nor what she really wanted. Mary, on the other hand, had a single purpose, a single aim; she was not distracted by many things. What our Lord is warning us against, therefore, is the danger of thus being distracted from the main objective in life by care, by this anxiety about earthly, worldly things, by looking so much at them that we do not look at God.

Studies in the Sermon on the Mount, ii, p. 110

What shall we say of this phrase: 'The peace of God that passeth all understanding'? (Philippians 4:7). You cannot understand this peace, you cannot imagine it, you cannot even believe it in a sense, and yet it is happening and you are experiencing it and enjoying it. It is God's peace that is in Christ Jesus. What does he mean by that? He is telling us that this peace of God works by presenting the Lord Jesus Christ to us and reminding us about Him. To put it in terms of the argument of the Epistle to the Romans: 'If while we were enemies we were reconciled to God by the death of his Son, much more, being reconciled, we shall be saved by his life' (Romans 5:10). [See also Romans 8:28, 32]. 'I am persuaded that neither death, nor life, nor angels, nor principalities, nor powers, nor things present, nor things to come, nor height, nor depth, nor any other creature, shall be able to separate us from the love of God, which is in Christ Jesus our Lord' (Romans, 8:38-9). The argument is that if God has done that supreme thing for us in the death of His Son upon the Cross He cannot forsake us now, He cannot leave us half way, as it were. So the peace of God that passeth all understanding keeps our hearts and minds through, or in, Christ Jesus. In that way God guarantees our peace and our freedom from anxiety.

Spiritual Depression, pp. 270-1

There was never a man whose preaching, with its mighty emphasis upon grace, was so frequently misunderstood [as Paul]. You remember the deduction some people had been drawing in Rome and in other places. They said, 'Now then, in view of the teaching of this man Paul, let us do evil that grace may abound, for, surely, this teaching . . . leads to that conclusion and to no other. Paul has just been saying, "Where sin abounded grace did much more abound"; very well, let us continue in sin that more and more grace may abound.' 'God forbid', says Paul; and he is constantly having to say that. To say that because we are under grace we therefore have nothing at all to do with law and can forget it, is not the teaching of the Scriptures. . . . We are not under the law in the sense that it condemns us; it no longer pronounces judgement or condemnation on us. No! but we are meant to live it, and we are even meant to go beyond it. The argument of the Apostle Paul is that I should live, not as a man who is under the law, but as Christ's free man. Christ kept the law, He lived the law; as this very Sermon on the Mount emphasizes, our righteousness must exceed that of the scribes and Pharisees. Indeed, He has not come to abolish the law; every jot and tittle of the law has to be fulfilled and perfected.

Studies in the Sermon on the Mount, i, p. 12

The Gospels were written with a definite and deliberate objective in view. They were not just written as records or as mere collections of facts. No. . . . They all present the Lord Jesus Christ as the Lord, as this final Authority.

The message of John the Baptist was essentially the same. There he stands by himself after preaching and baptizing the people at the Jordan . . . they say, 'Surely this must be the Christ. We have never heard preaching like this before . . . This must be the Messiah that we have been expecting'. But John turns upon them . . . and says, 'I am not the Christ'. . . (Luke 3:16f.) '. . . I am the forerunner, the herald. He is the authority. He is yet to come'. How careful these Gospels are to put that claim repeatedly forward!

Then there is something else. . . . It is their report of what happened at the baptism of our Lord. There He submits to baptism by John. . . . But . . . . the Holy Spirit descends upon Him as a dove. Still more important is that Voice . . . 'This is my beloved Son, in whom I am well pleased' (Matthew 3:17). . . . At the Mount of Transfiguration similar language is used, but there is a most significant and important addition . . . '. . . hear ye him' (Matthew 17:5). . . .'This is the one to listen to. You are waiting for a word. You are waiting for an answer to your questions. You are seeking a solution to your problems. You have been consulting the philosophers; you have been listening; and you have been asking, "Where can we have final authority?" Here is the answer from Heaven, from God: "Hear *Him*".' Again, you see, marking Him out, holding Him before us as the last Word, the ultimate Authority, the One to whom we are to submit, to whom we are to listen.

Authority, pp. 16–17

*Even so let your light shine before men,
that they may see your good works, and
glorify your Father which is in heaven*

The Christian life is always a matter of balance and
poise. It is a life that gives the impression of being self-
contradictory. . . . We read the Sermon on the Mount and we
come across something like this: 'Let your light so shine before
men, that they may see your good works, and glorify your
Father which is in heaven.' Then we read, 'Take heed that ye
do not your righteousness before men, to be seen of them:
else ye have no reward with your Father which is in heaven.'
And a man looking at that says, 'Well, what am I to do? If I
am to do all these things in secret . . . how can men know I am
doing these things, and how can they possibly see this light
which is shining in me?'

But, of course, this is only a superficial contradiction . . . we
are called to do both these things at one and the same time. The
Christian is to live in such a way that men looking at him, and
seeing the quality of his life, will glorify God. He must always
remember at the same time that he is not to do things in order
that he may attract attention to himself. He must not desire
to be seen of men, he is never to be self-conscious. But, clearly,
this balance is a fine and delicate one; so often we tend to go
to one extreme or the other. . . . But here we are called to avoid
both extremes. It is a delicate life, it is a sensitive life; but if
we approach it in the right way, and under the leading of the
Holy Spirit, the balance can be maintained. . . . Let us never
forget this, the Christian at one and the same time is to be
attracting attention to himself, and yet not attracting attention
to himself.

Studies in the Sermon on the Mount, ii, pp. 12–13

The case against this modern teaching [of self-expression] is not yet complete . . . it ignores recklessly the ultimate destiny of this self of ours . . . it does so from a merely earthly and human standpoint. . . . But there is a higher standpoint, and an infinitely more important one, which it also entirely ignores. Our Lord said, 'It is better for thee to enter into life halt or maimed rather than having two hands and two feet to be cast into everlasting fire.' . . . On the purely human plane . . . this talk of self-expression is utterly degrading to the true self. But, over and above that, there is God's view of us, which is of infinitely greater consequence, as we are in His hands and He is the Judge eternal. That it is His view of self that matters is made abundantly clear in the Bible. . . . God gave man a nature and a being like His own. He created man in His own image. He breathed into man the breath of life and made of him a living soul. That soul is God's gift to us. It is the treasure which He has committed to our charge and keeping. It is the self He asks us to express and expects us to express. And at the end of life and of time He will test our performance. The standard of judgement will be the moral law as given to Moses, the teachings of the prophets, the Sermon on the Mount, and, above all, our believing knowledge of Himself and our approximation to the life lived by our Lord and Saviour, Jesus Christ. For true self-expression has been revealed perfectly once and for all in Him. The question we shall all have to face therefore is, What have you made of the self? How have you expressed it? The consequences are eternal—life or death, heaven or hell.

Truth Unchanged, Unchanging, pp. 28–30

We are always in the presence of God. We are always in His sight. He sees our every action, indeed our every thought . . . He is everywhere . . . He sees it all. He knows your heart; other people do not. You can deceive them, and you can persuade them that you are quite selfless; but God knows your heart. . . . When we wake up in the morning we should immediately remind ourselves and recollect that we are in the presence of God. It is not a bad thing to say to ourselves before we go any further: 'Throughout the whole of this day, everything I do, and say, and attempt, and think, and imagine, is going to be done under the eye of God. He is going to be with me: He sees everything: He knows everything. There is nothing I can do or attempt but God is fully aware of it all. "Thou God seest me".' It would revolutionize our lives if we always did that . . . the many books which have been written on the devotional life all concentrate on this. . . . This is the fundamental thing, the most serious thing of all, that we are always in the presence of God. He sees everything and knows everything, and we can never escape from His sight [see Psalm 139]. . . . If we only remembered that, hypocrisy would vanish, self-adulation and all we are guilty of by way of feeling ourselves above others, would immediately disappear. . . .

If we were all to practise this it would be revolutionary. I am quite certain a revival would start at once. What a difference it would make to church life, and the life of every individual. Think of all the pretence and sham, and all that is unworthy in us all! If only we realized that God is looking at all, and is aware of it all, and is recording it all! . . . the man who starts with a true realization of that is soon to be seen flying to Christ and His cross, and pleading to be filled with the Holy Spirit.

Studies in the Sermon on the Mount, ii, pp. 15–16

Forgetting the things which are behind . . .
I press on toward the goal unto the prize of the
high calling of God in Christ Jesus

If you really do bemoan the fact that you have wasted so much time in the past, the thing to do is to make up for it in the present. Is not that common sense? Here is a man who comes in utterly dejected and saying: 'If only—the time I have wasted!' What I say to him is this: 'Are you making up for that lost time? Why are you wasting this energy in telling me about the past which you cannot undo? Why don't you put your energy into the present?' I speak with vehemence because this condition has to be dealt with sternly and the last thing to do with such people is to sympathize with them. If you are suffering from this condition take yourself in hand and examine yourself from an ordinary common sense point of view. You are behaving like a fool, you are irrational, you are wasting your time and your energy. You do not really believe what you are saying. If you bemoan a wasted past, make up for it in the present, give yourself entirely to living at this present moment. That is what Paul did. He says: 'And last of all He was seen of me also as of one born out of due time.' He says in effect: I have wasted a lot of time, others have got ahead of me. But he is able to go on and to add: 'I laboured more abundantly than they all, yet not I, but the grace of God which was with me.'

Spiritual Depression, pp. 83–4

It is most important for us to realize that there is such a thing as 'the discipline of the Christian life'. It is not enough to say . . . that, whatever may happen to us, we have just to 'look to the Lord' and all will be well. . . . It is unscriptural teaching. Were that the only thing we have to do, many of these scriptures would be quite unnecessary . . . the Epistles need never have been written; but they have been written . . . by men inspired by the Holy Spirit . . . what they tell us . . . is that there is an essential *discipline* in the Christian life.

One of the saddest features in the lives of certain types of Christian at the present time is that they seem to have lost sight of this aspect of the faith. This is, alas, especially true of those who are evangelical. . . . First and foremost there was a reaction against Roman Catholic teaching. In the Roman Catholic system they make a great deal of a certain type of discipline. They have many handbooks and manuals on the subject. In fact, some of the greatest masters in this kind of teaching have been Roman Catholics as, for instance, Saint Bernard of Clairvaux, or the well-known Fénélon, whose famous *Letters to Men* and *Letters to Women* were very popular at one time.

Now Protestants have reacted against all that, and to some extent very rightly. . . . But to deduce from its misuse that there is no need for discipline at all in the Christian life is quite wrong.

In fact, the really great periods in Protestantism have always been characterized by the realization of the need for such discipline. . . . Why were men like the two Wesley brothers and Whitefield called Methodists? They were so called because they were methodical in their living. They were Methodists because they had method in their meetings. . . . The very term Methodist . . . emphasizes the fact that they believed in discipline and in the importance of disciplining one's life and of knowing how to deal with oneself and how to handle oneself in the various circumstances and situations that we meet in the world we live in.

Faith on Trial, pp. 23–4

Is it not true to say of many of us that in actual practice our view of the doctrine of grace is such that we scarcely ever take the plain teaching of the Lord Jesus Christ seriously? We have so emphasized the teaching that all is of grace and that we ought not to try to imitate His example in order to make ourselves Christians, that we are virtually in the position of ignoring His teaching altogether and of saying that it has nothing to do with us because we are under grace. Now I wonder how seriously we take the gospel of our Lord and Saviour Jesus Christ. The best way of concentrating on that question is, I think, to face the Sermon on the Mount. What is our view, I wonder, of this Sermon? Supposing that at this point I suggested that we should all write down on paper our answers to the following questions:

> What does the Sermon on the Mount mean to us?
> Where does it come in our lives and what is its place in our thinking and outlook?
> What is our relationship to this extraordinary Sermon that has such a prominent position in these three chapters in the Gospel according to St. Matthew?

I think you would find the result would be very interesting and perhaps very surprising. Oh, yes, we know all about the doctrine of grace and forgiveness, and we are looking to Christ. But here in these documents, which we claim to be authoritative, is this Sermon. Where does it come in our scheme?

Studies in the Sermon on the Mount, i, pp. 12–13

[The Christian life] is not a life which at first is fairly broad, and which as you go on becomes narrower and narrower. No! The gate itself, the very way of entering into this life, is a narrow one. . . . Too often the impression is given that to be a Christian is after all very little different from being a non-Christian, that you must not think of Christianity as a narrow life, but as something most attractive and wonderful and exciting, and that you come in in crowds. It is not so according to our Lord. The gospel of Jesus Christ is too honest to invite anybody in that way. It does not try to persuade us that it is something very easy, and that it is only later on that we shall begin to discover it is hard. The gospel of Jesus Christ openly and uncompromisingly announces itself as being something which starts with a narrow entrance, a strait gate. . . .

We are told at the very outset of this way of life, before we start on it, that if we would walk along it there are certain things which must be left outside, behind us. There is no room for them, because we have to start by passing through a strait and narrow gate. I like to think of it as a turnstile. It is just like a turnstile that admits one person at a time and no more. And it is so narrow that there are certain things which you simply cannot take through with you. It is exclusive from the very beginning, and it is important that we should look at this Sermon in order to see some of the things which must be left behind.

The first thing we leave behind is what is called worldliness. We leave behind the crowd, the way of the world. . . . The Christian way of life is not popular. . . . You cannot take the crowd with you into the Christian life; it inevitably involves a break.

Studies in the Sermon on the Mount, ii, pp. 220–1

Before we begin to talk about freedom for self-expression we must discover whether or not we have that true self which God has desired for all men. If we lack it, we cannot express it, and we shall not be able to hand it back to Him and give an account of it at the dread Day of Judgement. The one urgent question therefore confronting every man is the question, What of your self? Do you possess your soul? Is the true self still in existence? Are the vision and the divine faculty still there? Is your soul alive? . . . Man cannot rehabilitate his true self. He cannot find God. Man can lose his own soul, but he can never find it again. He can kill and destroy it but he cannot create it anew. . . . But . . . 'The Son of Man is come to seek and to save that which was lost' (Luke 19:10). Jesus of Nazareth, the Son of God, came down to earth and lived and died and rose again in order to save. He has borne the punishment that we deserve on account of sin and for spoiling and marring the image of God upon us. But more, He restores our soul to us. He gives us a new nature and fills us with power that will enable us to express this new and true self even as He expressed it Himself. This self-expression expresses man as a son of God, well-pleasing in the sight of his Heavenly Father, and as an heir to eternal life. . . .

The Bible, therefore, calls upon us to give up the pleasures of sin for a season and to find our true selves in Jesus Christ. It calls upon us to this end to deny ourselves, to cut off hand or foot, to pluck out eye, to do anything that may be necessary in order to serve the best and the highest interests of this true self, for it tells us that 'it is better to enter into life halt or maimed rather than having two hands or two feet to be cast into hell fire'.

Truth Unchanged, Unchanging, pp. 30–1

Do not announce to others in any shape or form what you are doing.... Do not even announce it to yourself.... Note that our Lord does not stop at saying you must not sound a trumpet before you and announce it to the world; you do not even announce it to yourself... having done it in secret you do not take your little book and put down: 'Well, I have done that. Of course I haven't told anybody else that I have done it.' ... In effect our Lord said: 'Don't keep these books at all; don't keep spiritual ledgers; don't keep profit and loss accounts in your life; don't write a diary in this sense; just forget all about it. ...'

And what is the result of all this? It is glorious. This is how our Lord puts it. He says, 'You must not keep the account. God does that. He sees everything and He records it all, and do you know what He will do? He will reward you openly.' ... If we just forget all about it and do everything to please Him, we shall find that God will have an account. Nothing we have done will be forgotten, our smallest act will be remembered. Do you remember what He said in Matthew 25? 'When I was in prison you visited me. ...' And they will say, 'When did we do all this? We were not aware we have done this.' 'Of course you have done it,' He will reply, 'it is there in the Book.' He keeps the books. We must leave the account to Him. 'You know,' He says, 'you did it all in secret; but I will reward you openly. I may not be rewarding you openly in this world, but as certainly as you are alive, I will reward you openly at the Great Day ... when the great Book shall be opened ... and I will say, "Well done, thou good and faithful servant; ... enter thou into the joy of thy lord".'

Studies in the Sermon on the Mount, ii, pp. 19–20

Let . . . no man put a stumbling-block in his brother's way (Romans 14:13)

[The Psalmist] tells us [Psalm 73:15] that he was still not clear about, and still could not understand, the difficulty that had shaken him and tempted him so severely. . . . So he stopped trying to solve it, saying to himself, 'Well, I must leave this main problem for the time being. I will say nothing about it because I can see that if I express my thoughts it will cause me to offend against the generation of God's people. And I cannot do that. Very well; I will take my stand on what I am certain of, and be content not to understand the other matter for the present.'. . .

How simple his method is, and yet how vital is every single step . . . our speech must always be essentially positive. I mean that we should never be too ready to express our doubts and to proclaim our uncertainties. . . . I remember a young man coming to me years ago. He was a student who had gone to his college grounded in the Christian faith and believing it. A Professor in that college who prided himself on being an unbeliever, and who had nothing positive to give that young man, would ridicule him and his position, not only in his lectures but in private, laughing at all his beliefs and pouring scorn upon his faith. It had landed this young man in a very grievous and unhappy condition. There are not many things worse than the action of such a Professor who, having nothing himself by which to live, tries to take away and to destroy the faith of a young man, speaking against it and trying to undermine it. This, of course, was a malicious and intentional attack. . . . But we, too, can be guilty of the same thing, although we may not be aware of it. Though we may be assailed by doubts and uncertainties, we ought not to proclaim our doubts, or voice our uncertainties. . . . If we can say nothing helpful we should say nothing at all. That was what this man did.

Faith on Trial, pp. 27–8

First and foremost among the causes of depression I would
not hesitate to put—temperament. There are, after all, certain
different types of people. . . . I wonder whether anybody wants
to say: When you are talking about Christians you must not
introduce temperament or types. Surely Christianity does away
with all that . . . ? Now that is a very important objection, and
it must be answered . . . temperament, psychology and make-
up do not make the slightest difference in the matter of our
salvation. That is, thank God, the very basis of our position as
Christians. It does not matter what we are by temperament;
we are all saved in the same way, by the same act of God in
and through His Son, our Lord and Saviour Jesus Christ. . . . It
does not matter what your background is, it does not matter
what temperament you may happen to have been given in this
world, all that does not make the slightest difference in the
matter of salvation. . . . We glory in the fact that the history of
the Church proves abundantly that every conceivable type of
temperament has been found, and is still to be found today, in
the Church of the living God. But while I emphasize . . . the
matter that temperament does not make the slightest difference
in the matter of our fundamental salvation, I am equally
anxious to emphasize the fact that it does make a very great
difference in actual experience in the Christian life. There is
nothing which is quite so important as that we should . . . get
to know ourselves . . . though we are all Christians together,
we are all different, and the problems . . . that we are likely to
meet are in a large measure determined by the difference of
temperament and of type. We are all in the same fight, of course,
as we share the same common salvation, and have the same
common central need. But the manifestations of the trouble
vary from case to case and from person to person. There is
nothing more futile, when dealing with this condition, than to
act on the assumption that all Christians are identical in every
respect. They are not, and they are not even meant to be.

Spiritual Depression, pp. 14–15

January 30 *The perfect picture of the life of the Kingdom of God*

There is nothing . . . so dangerous as to say that the Sermon on the Mount has nothing to do with modern Christians . . . it is something which is meant for all Christian people. It is a perfect picture of the life of the kingdom of God . . . that is why Matthew put it in his Gospel at the beginning. It is agreed that Matthew was writing his Gospel especially for the Jews. That was his set desire. Hence all this emphasis upon the kingdom of heaven. And what was Matthew out to emphasize? Surely it was this. The Jews had a false, materialistic conception of the kingdom. They thought the Messiah was one who was coming to give them political emancipation. They were looking forward to someone who would deliver them from the bondage and yoke of the Roman Empire. They always thought of the kingdom in an external sense, a mechanical, military, materialistic sense. So Matthew puts the true teaching concerning the kingdom in the very forefront of his Gospel, for the great purpose of this Sermon is to give an exposition of the kingdom as something which is essentially spiritual. The kingdom is primarily something 'within you'. It is that which governs and controls the heart and mind and outlook. Far from being something which leads to great military power, it is to be 'poor in spirit'. In other words, we are not told in the Sermon on the Mount, 'Live like this and you will become Christian'; rather we are told, 'Because you are Christian live like this'. This is how Christians ought to live; this is how Christians are meant to live.

Studies in the Sermon on the Mount, i, pp. 16–17

Before the problems of life and of man can be solved we must first of all realize the true nature of the problem. . . . We must be prepared for honest thought, and a thoroughgoing examination and analysis, which will probe us to the very depths and search our motives as well as our actions. Where are such examination and analysis to be found? . . . they are to be found alone in the Bible. . . . According to this Book, man's troubles are due to the fact that he has sinned and rebelled against God. He was created in a state of happiness which depended upon his relationship to God and his obedience to God's laws and God's will. But man rebelled against God's will and therefore broke the law of his own nature . . . happiness follows health. Nowhere is this succession seen more than in the spiritual and moral realms. Man has become unhealthy. A disease called sin has ravaged his being. Man refuses to recognize his corruption and resorts to various expedients . . . in an attempt to find happiness and peace. But invariably he fails, for the trouble is not only within himself and in his surroundings, but also in his relationship to God. Man is fighting against the only One who can give him what he needs and desires. God has said, 'There is no peace to the wicked' (Isaiah 57:21). Man, therefore, by fighting God, by resisting and disobeying Him, is robbing himself of the very prize that he covets. And whatever he may do, until a relationship of obedience to God is restored, he will never know health and happiness. He may multiply his wealth and possessions, he may perfect his educational facilities, he may gain the whole world of wealth and knowledge; but to do so will profit him nothing so long as his relationship to God is not right.

Truth Unchanged, Unchanging, pp. 49–50

If this picture [Matthew 6:5–8]* does not persuade us of our own utter sinfulness, of our hopelessness as well as our helplessness, if it does not make us see our need of the grace of God in the matter of salvation, and the necessity of forgiveness, rebirth and a new nature, then I know of nothing that ever can persuade us of it. Here we see a mighty argument for the New Testament doctrine about the absolute necessity of being born again, because sin is a matter of disposition, something that is so profound and so vitally a part of us that it even accompanies us into the presence of God. But follow that argument beyond this life and world, beyond death and the grave, and contemplate yourself in the presence of God in eternity for ever and ever. Is not the rebirth something which is a bare essential? Here, then, in these instructions about piety and the conduct of the religious life, we have implicit in almost every statement this ultimate New Testament doctrine of regeneration and the nature of the new man in Christ Jesus. Indeed we can go on even beyond that and say that even if we are born again . . . we still need these instructions. This is our Lord's instruction to Christian people, not to the non-Christian. It is His warning to those who have been born again; even they have to be careful lest in their prayers and devotions they become guilty of this hypocrisy of the Pharisees.

Studies in the Sermon on the Mount, ii, p. 23

*'And when you pray, you must not be like the hypocrites; for they love to stand and pray in the synagogues and at the street corners, that they may be seen by men. Truly, I say to you, they have their reward. But when you pray, go into your room and shut the door and pray to your Father who is in secret; and your Father who sees in secret will reward you.
'And in praying do not heap up empty phrases as the Gentiles do; for they think that they will be heard for their many words. Do not be like them, for your Father knows what you need before you ask him.' (Matthew 6:5–8).

The biblical view of sin ... starts by saying that sin is not to be explained merely as a part of the process in man's development. For sin is something which is outside man, something which can exist and which did exist apart from man. It is something which has entered human nature from without. No view therefore which regards it in purely human terms can possibly be adequate or sufficient. This it explains further by showing how actual experience points that way. We are aware of a power other than ourselves acting upon us, and influencing us, a power with which we can struggle and fight, a power which we can overcome and dismiss. This is seen supremely, of course, in the temptation of our Lord. No temptation could or did arise within Him, or from His nature, because He was perfect. The temptation, the incitement to sin, was entirely external.

But it is not enough just to say that sin is a power which has independent existence. It is a mighty power, a terrible power. It has a fiendish quality, a malignity which is truly terrifying. It is a definite spirit, a positive attitude, active and powerful. Furthermore, it is a power which man has allowed to enter his life and which affects him profoundly and vitally. It is not something light and comparatively trivial. It does not belong to the order of vestigial remains. It does not merely affect one part of man and his nature. It is so deep-seated and so much a part of us that the entire man is affected—the intellect, the desires and therefore the will. Indeed, it constitutes such a terrible problem that God alone in Christ can deal with it.

The Plight of Man and the Power of God, pp. 46–7

... we must never forget our relationship to one another. The thing that held this man [Psalm 73] at first was not anything that he discovered about God's way with respect to himself but his recollection of his relationship to other people. That is marvellous, I think. That is the thing that held this man.... The apostle Paul puts that in a striking verse in Romans 14. He says, 'None of us liveth to himself, and no man dieth to himself.' He goes on to elaborate it, and in doing so analyses the question of the weaker brother. He does the same in 1 Corinthians 8 and 10. He puts it like this in a most remarkable phrase, 'Conscience, I say, not thine own, but of the other' (10:29). In other words, you as a strong Christian must not decide this in terms of yourself. What about your weaker brother for whom Christ died? You must not offend his conscience. No man 'liveth unto himself'; we are all bound up together, and if you cannot check yourself for your own sake, you must check yourself because of your weaker brother. When you are next tempted, when the devil makes you forget that you are not an isolated case, when he suggests that this is something that concerns you alone, think of the consequences, remember the other people, remember Christ, remember God. If you and I fall, it is not an isolated fall, the whole Church falls with us. This man realized that he was bound in the bundle of life with these other people. Say then to yourself, 'I see that all these others are going to be involved. We are children of a heavenly kingdom, we are individual members, in particular, of the one Body of Christ. We cannot act in isolation.' So if nothing else checks you when you are about to do something wrong, remember that fact, remember your family, remember the people to whom you belong, remember the Name that is on your forehead, and if nothing else will hold you, let that hold you. It held this man.

Faith on Trial, pp. 28–9

We all agree that we should examine ourselves, but we also agree that introspection and morbidity are bad. But what is the difference between examining oneself and becoming introspective? I suggest that we cross the line from self-examination to introspection when, in a sense, we do nothing but examine ourselves, and when such self-examination becomes the main and chief end in our life. We are meant to examine ourselves periodically, but if we are always doing it, always, as it were, putting our soul on a plate and dissecting it, that is introspection. And if we are always talking to people about ourselves and our problems and troubles, and if we are forever going to them with that kind of frown upon our face and saying, 'I am in great difficulty,' it probably means that we are all the time centred upon ourselves. That is introspection, and that in turn leads to the condition known as morbidity.

Here, then, is the point at which we must start. Do we know ourselves? Do we know our own particular danger? Do we know the thing to which we are particularly subject? The Bible is full of teaching about that. The Bible warns us to be careful about our strength and about our weakness. Take a man like Moses. He was the meekest man, we are told, the world has ever known; and yet . . . his great failure was in connexion with that very thing. He asserted his own will, he became angry. We have to watch our strength and we have to watch our weakness. . . . If I am naturally an introvert I must always be careful about it, and I must warn myself about it lest unconsciously I slip into a condition of morbidity. The extrovert must in the same way know himself and be on his guard against the temptations peculiar to his nature. Some of us by nature, and by the very type to which we belong, are more given to this . . . spiritual depression than others. We belong to the same company as Jeremiah and John the Baptist and Paul and Luther and many others. A great company! Yes . . . but you cannot belong to it without being unusually subject to this particular type of trial.

Spiritual Depression, pp. 17–18

Some say . . . 'Doesn't our Lord say, "If ye forgive not men their trespasses, neither will your Father forgive your trespasses"? Is not that law? Where is grace there? To be told that if we do not forgive, we shall not be forgiven, is not grace.' Thus they seem to be able to prove that the Sermon on the Mount does not apply to us. But if you say that, you will have to take almost the whole of Christianity out of the gospel. Remember also that our Lord taught exactly the same thing in His parable, recorded at the end of Matthew 18, of the steward who committed an offence against his master. This man went to his master and pleaded with him to forgive him; and his master forgave him. But he refused to forgive an underling who was likewise in debt to him, with the result that his master withdrew his forgiveness and punished him. Our Lord comments on this: 'So likewise shall my heavenly Father do also unto you, if ye from your hearts forgive not every one his brother their trespasses.' That is exactly the same teaching. But does it teach that I am forgiven only because I have forgiven? No, the teaching is, and we have to take this teaching seriously, that if I do not forgive, I am not forgiven . . . the man who has seen himself as a guilty, vile sinner before God knows his only hope of heaven is that God has forgiven him freely. The man who truly sees and knows and believes that, is one who cannot refuse to forgive another. So the man who does not forgive another does not know forgiveness himself. If my heart has been broken in the presence of God I cannot refuse to forgive; and, therefore, I say to any man who is imagining fondly that his sins are to be forgiven by Christ, though he does not forgive anybody else, 'Beware, my friend, lest you wake up in eternity and find Him saying to you "Depart from me; I never knew you".' . . . The man who is truly forgiven and knows it, is a man who forgives. That is the meaning of the Sermon on the Mount at this point.

Studies in the Sermon on the Mount, i, p. 17

What is the nature of faith? . . . Faith, obviously, is not a mere matter of feeling . . . if faith were a matter of feelings only, then when things go wrong and feelings change, faith will go. But faith is not a matter of feelings only, faith takes up the whole man including his mind, his intellect and his understanding. It is a response to truth, as we shall see. . . .

Faith is not something that acts automatically . . . magically. . . . Many people conceive of faith as if it were something similar to those thermostats which you have in connexion with a heating apparatus. You set your thermostat at a given level . . . and it acts automatically. . . . Now there are many people who seem to think that faith acts like that. They assume that it does not matter what happens to them, that faith will operate and all will be well. Faith, however, is not something that acts magically or automatically. If it did, [the disciples, during the storm on Galilee—Luke 8:22–5] would never have been in trouble, faith would have come into operation and they would have been calm and quiet and all would have been well. But faith is not like that. . . .

What is faith? Let us look at it positively. The principle taught here is that faith is an activity, it is something that has to be exercised. It does not come into operation itself, you and I have to put it into operation. . . . That is exactly what our Lord said to these men. He said: 'Where is your faith?' which means, 'Why are you not taking your faith and applying it to this position?' . . . Faith is a refusal to panic. . . . Does that seem to be too earthy and not sufficiently spiritual? It is of the very essence of faith.

Spiritual Depression, pp. 142–3

We can say of sincerity what is said of fire. . . . 'Fire is a good servant but a bad master.' So long as it is under control, nothing is more valuable than fire. . . . But once fire ceases to be under control and itself becomes the master, it leads to nothing but destruction and havoc. Or we may take the illustration of a well-bred, powerful, spirited horse. Nothing is more enjoyable than to be seated on such a horse as long as one is firmly in the saddle, and has a solid grip on the reins. But should such a horse take the bit between his teeth and bolt, the position would become precarious and the incident end in disaster. Now, the case is precisely the same with sincerity. Given knowledge in the saddle, given knowledge and truth in control, nothing is finer or more important than sincerity. But if we hand over the control to sincerity itself it may well lead us hopelessly astray and land us in disaster. That is what had happened to St Paul before his conversion. . . . Given knowledge and right direction, there is nothing that is so essential as sincerity. But when one relies upon the pressure of steam in the engine rather than on the compass for the right direction there can be but one result, shipwreck. At the present time masses of people are steaming ahead in this supposedly great quest for truth and reality . . . but in the name of God we ask them, 'Where are you going? Have you the knowledge? Is your compass working? Are you still keeping your eye on the north star? Do you not think it is time for you to take your bearing and to discover your exact position? Are you not aware of certain grave dangers which are liable to meet you at any moment . . . ? Stop for a moment. Realize the danger of trusting only to power. Realize the all-importance of knowledge and truth, of information and direction.'

Truth Unchanged, Unchanging, pp. 62–4

*From the world of sin, and noise
And hurry I withdraw;
For the small and inward voice
I wait with humble awe.*

To make sure that I realize that I am approaching God I have to exclude certain things. I have to enter into that closet. [Matthew 6:6.] Now what does this mean?

. . . The principle is that there are certain things which we have to shut out whether we are praying in public or whether we are praying in secret. Here are some of them. You shut out and forget other people. Then you shut out and forget yourself. That is what is meant by entering into thy closet. You can enter into that closet when you are walking alone in a busy street, or going from one room to another in a house. You enter into that closet when you are in communion with God and nobody knows what you are doing. But if it is an actual public act of prayer the same thing can be done. . . . What I try to do when I enter a pulpit is to forget the congregation in a certain sense. I am not praying to them or addressing them; I am not speaking to them. I am speaking to God, I am leading in prayer to God, so I have to shut out and forget people. Yes; and having done that, I shut out and forget myself. That is what our Lord tells us to do. There is no value in my entering into the secret chamber and locking the door if the whole time I am full of self and thinking about myself, and am priding myself on my prayer. I might as well be standing at the street corner. No; I have to exclude myself as well as other people; my heart has to be open entirely and only to God. I say with the Psalmist: 'Unite my heart to fear thy name. I will praise thee, O Lord my God, with all my heart.' This is of the very essence of this matter of prayer. When we pray we must deliberately remind ourselves that we are going to talk to God. Therefore other people, and self also, must be excluded and locked out.

Studies in the Sermon on the Mount, ii, pp. 29–30

Much of the argument against belief in the doctrine of the wrath of God has been presented in a more or less utilitarian manner. The older type of preaching, we are told, would drive people away from our churches; whereas if we emphasized and stressed the love of God it would appeal to the people. The simple answer to that is that the facts indicate the exact opposite. It is as the idea of judgement and the wrath of God have fallen into the background that our churches have become increasingly empty. The idea has gained currency that the love of God somehow covers everything, and that it matters very little what we may do, because the love of God will put everything right at the end. The more the Church has accommodated her message to suit the palate of the people, the greater has been the decline in attendance at places of worship.

But still more serious and ominous is the fact that at the same time belief in God has also declined. As men cease to believe in God as the Lord of all the earth, and as the Judge Eternal before whom we shall all appear to render an account of ourselves, and as the impression is given more and more that God is just some benign being who smiles indiscriminately upon all, so men have ceased to believe in Him and to relate their lives to Him.

It is simply not true to say that if only we emphasize constantly the love of God men will believe in Him, whereas if we preach His wrath and justice and righteousness they will be antagonized from Him. It is only as men know something of the meaning of 'the fear of the Lord' that they continue to believe in God.

The Plight of Man and the Power of God, p. 64

You and I are people who have been called by God out of this present evil world. We have been purchased at the cost of the shed blood of the only begotten Son of God on a cross on Calvary's hill, not merely that we may be forgiven and go to heaven, but that we may be delivered from all sin and iniquity, and that He may 'purify unto himself a peculiar people, zealous of good works' (Titus 2:14) . . . whenever any perplexity arises or anything that tends to shake you, take it and put it in the light of that. . . . It does not matter at what level we stand against this enemy of our souls, it does not matter how low the level, so long as we stand . . . this man [Psalm 73] stood at a very low level. He simply stood on one principle, 'If I do thus, I shall harm these people.' . . . I do not care how low the level is. So long as you can find anything that will hold you, use it. . . . Stand on any point you can. . . . For it comes to this, when your feet are slipping the one thing you need is to be able to stand. Stop slipping and sliding. Get your feet firm for a moment and take anything that offers itself for that purpose; stand on that and stay on that. We are engaged in spiritual mountaineering. The slopes are like glass, and you can slip into that terrible ravine and lose yourself. I say, therefore, that if you see anything, however small a twig, clutch at it, hold it, put your feet in the slightest hole, or on the narrowest ledge, anything to steady yourself and to enable you to stop for the moment. Once you have stopped the downward slipping and sliding you can begin to climb again.

It was because the Psalmist found that small foothold and planted his feet in it, that he stopped slipping. And from that moment he began the wonderful process of climbing again until eventually he found himself able to rejoice once more in the knowledge of God and to understand even the problem that had perplexed him.

Faith on Trial, pp. 30–1

[a cause of spiritual depression]—physical conditions. Is anyone surprised? Does someone hold the view that as long as you are a Christian it does not matter what the condition of your body is? Well, you will soon be disillusioned if you believe that. Physical conditions play their part in all this . . . there are certain physical ailments which tend to promote depression. Thomas Carlyle, I suppose, is an outstanding illustration of this. Or take that great preacher who preached in London for nearly forty years in the last century—Charles Haddon Spurgeon—one of the truly great preachers of all time. That great man was subject to spiritual depression, and the main explanation in his case was undoubtedly the fact that he suffered from a gouty condition which finally killed him. . . . And there are many, I find, who come to talk to me about these matters, in whose case it seems quite clear to me that the cause of the trouble is mainly physical . . . tiredness, overstrain, illness. You cannot isolate the spiritual from the physical for we are body, mind and spirit. The greatest and the best Christians when they are physically weak are more prone to an attack of spiritual depression than at any other time and there are great illustrations of this in the Scriptures.

Let us give a word of warning at this point. We must not forget the existence of the devil, nor allow him to trap us into regarding as spiritual that which is fundamentally physical. But we must be careful on all sides in drawing this distinction; because if you give way to your physical condition you become guilty in a spiritual sense. If you recognize, however, that the physical may be partly responsible for your spiritual condition and make allowances for that, you will be better able to deal with the spiritual.

Spiritual Depression, pp. 18–19

Why should we study [the Sermon on the Mount]? Why should we try to live it? . . . The Lord Jesus Christ died to enable us to live the Sermon on the Mount . . . He has made this possible for me.

The second reason for studying it is that nothing shows me the absolute need of the new birth, and of the Holy Spirit and His work within, so much. . . . These Beatitudes crush me to the ground. They show me my utter helplessness. Were it not for the new birth, I am undone. Read and study it, face yourself in the light of it. It will drive you to see your ultimate need of the rebirth and the gracious operation of the Holy Spirit. . . .

Another reason is this. The more we live and try to practise this Sermon on the Mount, the more shall we experience blessing. Look at the blessings that are promised to those who do practise it. The trouble with much holiness teaching is that it leaves out the Sermon on the Mount, and asks us to experience sanctification. That is not the biblical method. If you want to have power in your life and to be blessed, go straight to the Sermon on the Mount. Live and practise it and give yourself to it, and as you do so the promised blessings will come. 'Blessed are they which do hunger and thirst after righteousness: for they shall be filled.' If you want to be filled, don't seek some mystic blessing; don't rush to meetings hoping you will get it. Face the Sermon on the Mount and its implications and demands, see your utter need, and then you will get it. It is the direct road to blessing.

Studies in the Sermon on the Mount, i, p. 18

February 13   *He comes to us . . . as of old by the lakeside . . .*
He speaks to us the same words, 'Follow Me', and
sets us the task which He has to fulfil for our time
and . . . [those who obey Him] shall learn in their
own experience who He is

Jesus is walking along one day and He sees a man called Matthew sitting at the receipt of custom. He does not hesitate to confront that man in the middle of transacting his business and say, 'Follow *me*'. And Matthew rose up, left everything and went after Jesus. He goes to the children of Zebedee and says the same thing. They too leave their boats, fishing nets, father and everything else. Here is One who does not hesitate to speak in a kind of totalitarian manner when He commands them, 'Follow me'. And they went and they followed Him. That is the gospel in action. That is evangelism. That is how the Church comes into being. That is the way in which the work of God is carried on.

But He went even beyond that! He does not hesitate to claim that He has power to forgive sin. And He got into much trouble for claiming it. 'Who can forgive sins, but God alone?' said the people. But He *does* forgive sins. He asserts that He possesses the authority and power, and He is going to prove it. So He tells the man, 'Take up thy bed and walk', as a sign that He has power to forgive sins also. . . . So often when we ministers preach through the Gospels we take these things, and turn them into parables, accompanied by nice, soothing little messages. But we are really missing the point. We should be preaching the Lord Jesus Christ and asserting His authority. . . . Why are people expected to want to accept Christianity? Because . . . it does this or that. It promises you happiness. It gives you peace and joy . . . this is *false* evangelism. Our one business is to preach the Lord Jesus Christ, the final Authority. . . . The cults can give you 'results'. Christian Science can tell you that if you do this and that you will sleep well at night, you will stop worrying, you will feel healthier. . . . We are not to do that. We are to declare *Him*, and to bring people face to face with *Him*.

Authority, pp. 20–1

Those who ignore God's word; who refuse to consider the gospel, with its light and its knowledge; who keep away from God's house and every form of instruction with respect to these matters; who argue that all that is necessary is that one should be sincere, that one should pay one's twenty shillings in the pound, give to charity, be friendly and affable—they are trusting to their own zeal, and to their own ideas and are refusing to be enlightened as to what God really demands. To them we must say what Paul said to his contemporaries, that having done all, they are simply establishing their own righteousness. We are not questioning their sincerity or their honesty. . . . But the vital question is, What is the value of it all? It is not God's way. It is not God's idea of righteousness, but simply their own. Surely the essence of wisdom is that before we begin to act at all, or to attempt to please God, we should discover what it is that God has to say about the matter. We must first learn His idea of righteousness, His demands. But the men and women of today, like the Jews of old, take their orders everywhere except from God's word. They rely upon the statements of certain modern writers, and live lives according to their own ideas rather than according to the teachings of Jesus of Nazareth, the Son of God. But let them go on. . . . Let them establish their own righteousness and refuse the Gospel of Jesus Christ, and the day will surely come when they will discover that 'that which is highly esteemed among men is abomination in the sight of God' (Luke 16:15). The vital question to ask, therefore, is, Whom are we really pleasing? Is it ourselves or God? Have we yielded to His way? Can we say that we have submitted our wills and surrendered them to Him?

Truth Unchanged, Unchanging, pp. 66–8

. . . we must realize that we are in the presence of God. What does that mean? It means realization of something of who God is and what God is. Before we begin to utter words we always ought to do this. We should say to ourselves: 'I am now entering into the audience chamber of that God, the almighty, the absolute, the eternal and great God with all His power and His might and majesty, that God who is a consuming fire, that God who is "light and in whom is no darkness at all", that utter, absolute Holy God. That is what I am doing.' . . . But above all, our Lord insists that we should realize that, in addition to that, He is our Father. . . . O that we realized this! If only we realized that this almighty God is our Father through the Lord Jesus Christ. If only we realized that . . . whenever we pray it is like a child going to its father! He knows all about us; He knows our every need before we tell Him. . . . He desires to bless us very much more than we desire to be blessed. He has a view of us, He has a plan and a programme for us, He has an ambition for us, I say it with reverence, which transcends our highest thought and imagination. . . . He cares for us. He has counted the very hairs of our head. He has said that nothing can happen to us apart from Him.

Then we must remember what Paul puts so gloriously in Ephesians 3. He 'is able to do exceeding abundantly above all that we ask or think'. That is the true notion of prayer, says Christ. You do not go and just turn a wheel. You do not just count the beads. You do not say: 'I must spend hours in prayer, I have decided to do it and I must do it.' . . . We must get rid of this mathematical notion of prayer. What we have to do first of all is to realize who God is, what He is, and our relationship to Him.

Studies in the Sermon on the Mount, ii, pp. 30–1

It is good for a man that he bear the yoke in his youth

The argument that the modern man refuses to be coerced into living the good life by the fear of God, but will respond to appeals, is entirely falsified by the facts . . . as men have ceased to believe in the wrath of God, and have discarded the idea of law and righteousness, so their moral standards have gradually deteriorated and conduct has become lax and loose. . . .

As men ceased to recognize God as the One to whom they are responsible, and under whose eye they live, so a sense of discipline and order gradually began to disappear from all the relationships of life. A man who does not live a life of obedience himself soon ceases to be concerned about the fact that his own children should obey him. The result is that discipline in the home has been sadly neglected, children no longer respect their parents as they should, and quite frequently these children have become the tyrants of the home. The fact is that those who were brought up under the stern and strict, and often hard discipline of former times, had actually a deeper regard as well as a greater respect for their parents. . . . As man's sense of responsibility to God has declined, and as he has ceased to believe that God has ordained the whole of life, including the natural orders of society, so the ideas of the family and home, of marriage and parenthood, and, indeed, of law and order in general, have become looser and looser, and men have regarded themselves as being laws unto themselves. And what real hope can there be of international peace and concord unless nations are prepared to recognize and acknowledge a law above themselves and outside themselves—a law which has sanctions and power, a law the breaking of which will lead to suffering and punishment?

The Plight of Man and the Power of God, pp. 65–6

For [unbelievers] Jesus Christ was only a man who was born and laid in a manger, lived, ate and drank like other men and worked as a carpenter. Then He was crucified in utter weakness upon a cross. 'There are the facts', they say, 'and am I asked to believe that that is the Son of God? It is impossible.' . . . They are thinking only on the rational level. . . . That is rational thinking. You talk to them about the doctrine of the rebirth, and they say, 'Of course things like that don't happen, there is no such thing as a miracle . . . once you talk about miracles you are violating the laws of nature.' As Matthew Arnold said, 'Miracles cannot happen, therefore miracles have not happened.' That is rational thinking.

. . . before a man can become a Christian he has to cease to think like that. He has to have a new type of thinking, he has to begin to think spiritually . . . when we become Christian . . . we find that we are thinking in a different way. We are on a different level . . . miracles are no longer a problem, the rebirth is no longer a problem, the doctrine of the atonement is no longer a problem. We have a new understanding, we are thinking spiritually. Our Lord was visited by Nicodemus, who . . . said, 'Master, I have watched your miracles; you must be a Teacher sent from God, for no man can do the things you do except God be with him.' And he was clearly on the point of adding, 'Tell me how you do it. . . .' But our Lord looked at him and . . . what He was saying to Nicodemus was really this, 'Nicodemus, if you think that you can understand this thing before it has happened to you, you are making a real mistake. You will never become a Christian in that way . . . you are trying to understand spiritual things with your natural understanding. But you cannot. Though you are a master of Israel you must be born again . . . you have to realize the nature of this new type of thinking which is spiritual.'

Faith on Trial, pp. 35–6

In the last analysis . . . [there is only one] cause of spiritual depression—it is the devil, the adversary of our souls. He can use our temperaments and our physical condition. He so deals with us that we allow our temperament to control and govern us, instead of keeping temperament where it should be kept. There is no end to the ways in which the devil produces spiritual depression. We must always bear him in mind. The devil's one object is so to depress God's people that he can go to the man of the world and say, 'There are God's people. Do you want to be like that?' Obviously the whole strategy of the adversary of our souls, and God's adversary, is to depress us and to make us look as this* man looked when he was passing through this period of unhappiness.

Indeed I can put it, finally, like this; the ultimate cause of all spiritual depression is unbelief. For if it were not for unbelief even the devil could do nothing. It is because we listen to the devil instead of listening to God that we go down before him and fall before his attacks. This is why this psalmist keeps on saying to himself: 'Hope thou in God: for I shall yet praise Him. . . .' He reminds himself of God. Why? Because he was depressed and had forgotten God, so that his faith and his belief in God and in God's power, and in his relationship to God, were not what they ought to be. We can indeed sum it up by saying that the final and ultimate cause is just sheer unbelief.

Spiritual Depression, pp. 19–20

---

*(The Psalmist, as recorded in Psalm 42.)

February 19
'I will believe in your Redeemer
when I see the redeemed' (Nietzshe)

A one-time Law Minister in the Indian Government was a great man called Dr Ambedkar, an out-caste himself and a leader of the out-castes in India. At the time of which I am speaking he was taking a great interest in the teachings of Buddhism, and attended a great Conference of twenty-seven countries in Ceylon which had met together to inaugurate a world fellowship of Buddhists.... He said at the Conference, 'I am here to find out to what extent there is dynamic in the Buddhist religion so far as the people of this country are concerned.' There was the leader of the out-castes turning to Buddhism, and examining it. He said, '. . . Has it something to give to these masses of my fellow out-castes?' . . . But the real tragedy about this able, learned man is that he had already spent much time in America and Great Britain studying Christianity. And it was because he had found it was not a live thing, because he had found an absence of dynamic in it, that he was now turning to Buddhism.... That is the challenge that comes to you and to me. We know Buddhism is not the answer. We claim to believe that the Son of God has come into the world and has sent His own Holy Spirit into us, His own absolute power that will reside in men and make them live a quality of life like His own. . . .

If only all of us were living the Sermon on the Mount, men would know that there is dynamic in the Christian gospel; they would know that this is a live thing; they would not go looking for anything else. They would say, 'Here it is.' . . . it has always been when men and women have taken this Sermon seriously and faced themselves in the light of it, that true revival has come. And when the world sees the truly Christian man, it not only feels condemned, it is drawn, it is attracted.

Studies in the Sermon on the Mount, i, pp. 19–20

It is a rule of the Scriptures, and a rule which is confirmed by and exemplified in the long history of the Church and her saints, that when God has a particularly great task for a man to perform, He generally does try him. I care not which biography you pick up, you may take the life of any man who has been signally used by God, and you will find that there has been a severe time of testing and of trial in his experience.... So one may have to pass through this kind of experience because of some great task ahead. Look at Joseph.... Can you imagine a more dismal kind of life? Everybody seemed to be against him.... But in all this God was only preparing the man for the great position that He had in store for him. And it is the same with all the great men of the Bible. Look at the suffering of a man like David. ... The Apostle Paul was no exception (2 Corinthians, 11 and 12). ...

God sometimes prepares a man for a great trial ... by giving him some lesser trials. It is there that I see the love of God shining out so gloriously. There are certain great trials that come in life, and it would be a terrible thing for people suddenly to be plunged into a great trial from the undisturbed and even tenor of their ways. So God sometimes, in His tenderness and love, sends lesser trials to prepare us for the greater ones. 'If need be' (1 Peter 1:6)—if such proves needful, if God, in looking upon us as our Father, sees that this is just what we need at that moment. So we start with this great principle, that God sees and knows what is best for us and what is needful. We do not see, but God always does, and, as our Heavenly Father, He sees the need and He prescribes the appropriate trial which is destined for our good.

Spiritual Depression, pp. 225–6

Paul reminded his contemporaries that Moses in giving the
law to the Jews had said, 'The man which doeth those things
shall live by them' (Romans 10:5). That may be translated
thus: 'Anyone who can perform it shall live by it.' God . . . had
said, in effect, 'If you keep all that, you will have followed my
commandments. That is what I demand. That is the only way
of pleasing me.' What is that way? Look at it. Consider it
deeply . . . consider what we should have to do. Can man atone
for his own past sins and misdeeds? Can he blot out his own
transgressions? Can he sharpen his conscience and cleanse his
memory? More than these, can he live in the present in a
manner that truly satisfies himself? Can he withstand temptation? . . . Can he control his thoughts, his desires, inclinations,
and imaginations as well as his every action? . . . By his very
greatest efforts can he, and does he, succeed in really living up
to his own standard of life? Then consider God's standard.
Read the law as given to the children of Israel, the Ten Commandments and the moral law which St Paul, with all his zeal,
could not keep when once he saw their true meaning. Then
read the Sermon on the Mount and our Lord's various statements about the holiness of God. Then ponder His own perfect
life. That is what we have to do. . . . Can any man do it? Can
all the good intentions, and all the sincerity, and all the zeal
of which anyone is capable, ever provide sufficient power to
scale such heights? That is the mount which we should have
to climb—the mount of the holiness of God. . . . Is there anyone
who is capable of producing such holiness? Is the power in
the little engine of our life sufficient to take us to such a height?
Ask St Paul. Ask Augustine, Luther, John Wesley. Ask all the
noblest souls that the world has ever seen . . . with one accord
they answer saying, 'Not the labours of my hands Can fulfil
Thy law's demands. . . .' And if they have failed, who are we
to succeed? . . . Our best, our all is not enough.

Truth Unchanged, Unchanging, pp. 68–70

We must come [to prayer] with the simple confidence of a child. We need a child-like faith. We need this assurance that God is truly our Father, and therefore we must rigidly exclude any idea that we must go on repeating our petitions because it is our repetition that is going to produce the blessing. God likes us to show our keenness, our anxiety and our desire over a thing. He tells us to 'hunger and thirst after righteousness' and to seek it; He tells us to 'pray and not to faint'; we are told to 'pray without ceasing'. Yes; but that does not mean mechanical repetitions; it does not mean believing that we shall be heard for our 'much speaking.' . . . It means that when I pray I know that God is my Father, and that He delights to bless me, and that He is much more ready to give than I am to receive and that He is always concerned about my welfare. . . . I must see God as my Father who has purchased my ultimate good in Christ, and is waiting to bless me with His own fullness in Christ Jesus.

So . . . in confidence we make our requests known to God, knowing He knows all about it before we begin to speak. . . . But we must not come with doubtful minds; we must know that God is much more ready to give than we are to receive . . . O the blessings that are stored at the right hand of God for God's children. Shame on us for being paupers when we were meant to be princes; shame on us for so often harbouring unworthy, wrong thoughts of God in this matter. It is all due to fear, and because we lack this simplicity, this faith, this confidence, this knowledge of God as our Father. If we but have that, the blessings of God will begin to fall upon us, and may be so overwhelming that with D. L. Moody we shall feel that they are almost more than our physical frames can bear, and cry out with him, saying, 'Stop, God!' God is able to do for us exceeding abundantly above all that we can ask or think. Let us believe that and then go to Him in simple confidence.

Studies in the Sermon on the Mount, ii, pp. 31-2

I have often listened to Christian people who are in some perplexity and, even as they have been stating their problem, I have realized that their trouble was wholly due to the fact that they had dropped back to the rational [i.e., human] level of thinking. For instance, when something happens to you that you do not understand, the moment you begin to feel a sense of grudge against God you may be sure that you have already dropped back to that rational level. When you complain that what is happening to you does not seem to be fair, you are at once bringing God down to your own level of understanding. . . . But everything in the Christian life must be regarded from the spiritual angle. The whole of this life is spiritual. Everything about us must therefore be considered spiritually, every phase, every stage, every interest, every development . . . we must think in a spiritual way and leave the other mode of thinking behind. . . . That was [Psalm 73] this man's problem. Why does God allow these things, he says. Why are the ungodly allowed to prosper? . . . That was the problem, trying to understand God's ways . . . there is only one answer to that. It is found in Isaiah 55:8, 'For my thoughts are not your thoughts, neither are your ways my ways, saith the Lord.' . . . The first thing you have to realize, God says to us, is that when you come to consider Me and My ways, you must not do so on that low level to which you have been accustomed . . . are we not constantly guilty here? We will persist in thinking as natural men and women in these matters. We see that the matter of salvation calls for spiritual thinking, but in the things that happen to us our thinking is prone to become rational thinking again, and we must not be surprised therefore if we do not understand God's ways, for they are altogether different from ours. The difference between the two outlooks is the difference between heaven and earth.

Faith on Trial, pp. 36–7

Large numbers of people . . . are always asking the same question. 'Why cannot I get there? Why cannot I be like that?' They read books which are meant to give instruction about the Christian way of life, they attend meetings and conferences, always seeking this something which they do not find. And they are cast down, their souls are cast down and disquietened within them.

Now it is all-important . . . to be quite certain that they are clear in their minds about the primary and most fundamental principles of the Christian faith . . . I would not say that they are not Christians but I am suggesting that they are what I would call miserable Christians, simply because they have not understood the way of salvation, and for that reason all their beliefs and efforts have been more or less useless. They often concentrate on the question of sanctification, but it does not help them because they have not understood justification. . . . It is an interesting theological point as to whether such people are Christians or not. For myself I would say they are. The classic example is of course John Wesley. I would hesitate to say that John Wesley was not a Christian until 1738; but I am certain . . . that [he] had not understood the way of salvation as justification by faith only, until 1738. He had in a sense sub-scribed to the full teaching of the Bible, but he had not under-stood it, nor fully apprehended it . . . it was only as the result of his meeting with the Moravian brethren, and in particular the conversation he had with one called Peter Böhler . . . that he was truly made to understand this vital doctrine. . . . *There* was a man who had been trying to find happiness in his Christian life by doing things, preaching to the prisoners in Oxford, giving up his fellowship of his college, and facing the hazards of crossing the Atlantic in order to preach to pagans in Georgia. He was trying to find happiness by living life in a given way.

Spiritual Depression, pp. 25–6

The reason, then, why I believe it is important for us to take the Sermon [on the Mount] as a whole before we come to the details, is this constant danger of 'missing the wood because of the trees'. We are all of us ready to fix on certain particular statements, and to concentrate on them at the expense of others. The way to correct that tendency, I believe, is to realize that no part of this Sermon can be understood truly except in the light of the whole. Some good friends have already said to me, 'I am going to be most interested when you come to state exactly what is meant by "Give to him that asketh thee",' etc. That is a betrayal of a false attitude to the Sermon on the Mount. They have jumped to particular statements. There is a great danger at this point. The Sermon on the Mount, if I may use such a comparison, is like a great musical composition, a symphony if you like. Now the whole is greater than a collection of the parts, and we must never lose sight of this wholeness. I do not hesitate to say that, unless we have understood and grasped the Sermon on the Mount as a whole, we cannot understand properly any one of its particular injunctions. I mean that it is idle and useless and quite futile to confront anybody with any particular injunction in the Sermon on the Mount unless such a person has already believed, and accepted, and has indeed already conformed to, and is living, the Beatitudes.

Studies in the Sermon on the Mount, i, p. 22

Peter and John go up to the temple at the hour of prayer and they see an impotent man sitting at the Beautiful gate of the temple. . . . You remember their formula, 'In the name of Jesus Christ of Nazareth rise up and walk.' And he arose, and the people came and were full of wonder and amazement. They began praising the apostles. But Peter said, 'Do not look at us. It is not by our own words or power that we have made this impotent man to walk. His name, through faith in his name, has given this man this perfect soundness in the presence of you all' (Acts 3:1–16). Again, in Acts 4 when the disciples are arraigned before the authorities and are told never again to preach in this name, there is only one answer to be given: 'There is none other name under heaven given among men, whereby we must be saved.' This is the only name. The translation should be, 'There is no second.' Jesus Christ is not one in a series, He does not represent one authority among a number of authorities. He stands alone. In the New Testament He is the sole Authority.

And so it continues right through the book [of Acts]. In preaching to Cornelius and his household Peter says again, 'Jesus Christ is Lord of all' (see Acts 10:36). The same stands out in the ministry of the Apostle Paul, who, being arrested in his career of violent opposition to, and persecution of, the Christian Church on the road to Damascus, and discovering to his amazement that the Jesus whom he had so despised and hated is none other than the Lord of glory, cries out asking, 'Lord, what wilt thou have me to do?'

Authority, pp. 26–7

The Apostle Paul . . . had known what it was to trust to his own zeal and sincerity, and to his own efforts. He knew all about the striving and the sweating, the fasting and all the mighty efforts. But he knew also the feeling of hopelessness. He knew the failure to find satisfaction. And then he had experienced that glorious release which had come to him with the knowledge of the gospel. But here were his fellow country-men still going on in the old way . . . still striving to do the impossible. . . . 'How sad,' he cried, 'how tragic. They have the zeal and the sincerity, but it is of no value. They are trying to justify themselves, but they never can; and while they are thus trying and failing they are deliberately refusing the knowledge which could give them in reality everything they desire and more.' It was bad enough that all that energy and effort should be a sheer waste; but the tragedy was heightened and made infinitely greater by the contemplation of what they might have been if they had but accepted the gospel. They not only failed, but they utterly refused to be made successful. They preferred to trust to themselves and their own zeal and their own efforts and fail, rather than trust themselves to Jesus Christ and be saved. They were so anxious to do things them-selves that they refused God's offer of eternal salvation as a pure gift. . . . They had but to believe that Jesus of Nazareth was the Son of God, that He had died to atone for their sins, and had risen again from the grave in order to justify them, and they would find themselves righteous in the sight of God and receive forgiveness of their sins. They said they wanted to be right with God; yet they deliberately refused the one way of being put right with God.

Truth Unchanged, Unchanging, pp. 70–2

When a man is speaking to God he is at his very acme. It is the highest activity of the human soul, and therefore it is at the same time the ultimate test of a man's true spiritual condition. There is nothing that tells the truth about us as Christian people so much as our prayer life. Everything we do in the Christian life is easier than prayer. It is not so difficult to give alms . . . you can have a true spirit of philanthropy in people who are not Christian at all. . . . The same applies also to the question of self-discipline—refraining from certain things and taking up particular duties and tasks. God knows it is very much easier to preach like this from the pulpit than it is to pray. Prayer is undoubtedly the ultimate test, because a man can speak to others with greater ease than he can speak to God. Ultimately, therefore, a man discovers the real condition of his spiritual life when he examines himself in private, when he is alone with God . . . have we not all known what it is to find that, somehow, we have less to say to God when we are alone than when we are in the presence of others? It should not be so; but it often is. So that it is when we have left the realm of activities and outward dealings with other people, and are alone with God, that we really know where we stand in a spiritual sense. It is not only the highest activity of the soul, it is the ultimate test of our true spiritual condition.

Studies in the Sermon on the Mount, ii, p. 46

What a wonderful place God's house is. Often you will find deliverance by merely coming into it. Many a time have I thanked God for His house. I thank God that He has ordained that His people should meet together in companies, and worship together. The house of God has delivered me from 'the mumps and measles of the soul' a thousand times and more—merely to enter its doors. How does it work? I think it works like this. The very fact that there is a house of God to come to at all tells us something. How has it come into being? It is God who has planned and arranged it. To realize that in itself puts us immediately into a more healthy condition. Then we begin to go back through history, and remind ourselves of certain truths. Here am I at this present time with this terrible problem, but the Christian Church has existed all these long years. (I am already beginning to think in an entirely different way.) The house of God goes back through the centuries to the time of our Lord Himself. What is it for? What is its significance? And the cure has begun.

Again, we go to the house of God, and to our amazement we find other people there before us. We are rather surprised at that, because in our private misery and perplexity we had come to the conclusion that perhaps there was nothing in religion at all, and that it was not worth continuing with it. But here are people who think it is worth continuing with; and we feel better. We begin to say: Perhaps I may be wrong; all these people think there is something in it; they may be right. The healing process is going on; the cure is being continued.

Faith on Trial, p. 39

Then we go a step farther. We look round the congregation and suddenly find ourselves looking at someone whom we know has had an infinitely worse time than we have been having. We thought our problem was the most terrible problem in the world, and that no one had ever before suffered as we had. Then we see a poor woman, a widow perhaps, whose only child has died or has been killed. But she is still there. It puts our problem into a new perspective immediately. The great Apostle Paul has a word for this, as for all things. 'There hath no temptation taken you', he reminds us, 'but such as is common to man' (1 Corinthians 10:13). Where the devil gets us is just there. He persuades us that nobody has ever had this trial before; no one has ever had a problem like mine, no one else has been dealt with like this. . . . We are always helped in our suffering by hearing that somebody else is suffering too! . . . The realization that we are not alone in this helps to put the thing in the right perspective. I am one of a number; it seems to be something that happens to God's people—the house of God reminds us of all that.

Then it reminds us of things that go still farther back. We begin to study the history of the Church throughout the ages, and we remember what we read years ago, perhaps something in the lives of some of the saints. And we begin to understand that some of the greatest saints that have ever adorned the life of the Church have experienced trials and troubles and tribulations which cause our little problem to pale into insignificance. The house of God, the sanctuary of God, reminds us of all that. And immediately we are beginning to climb, we are going upwards, we have our problem now in its right setting. The house of God, the sanctuary of the Lord, teaches us all these lessons. . . . My experience in the ministry has taught me that those who are least regular in their attendance are the ones who are most troubled by problems and perplexities. There is something in the atmosphere of God's house.

Faith on Trial, pp. 39–40

March 2   *When he had sat down,* his disciples *came unto him, and he opened his mouth and taught* them . . .

There is a kind of logical sequence in this Sermon. Not only that, there is certainly a spiritual order and sequence. Our Lord does not say these things accidentally; the whole thing is deliberate. Certain postulates are laid down, and on the basis of those, certain other things follow. Thus I never discuss any particular injunction of the Sermon with a person until I am perfectly happy and clear in my mind that that person is a Christian. It is wrong to ask anybody who is not first a Christian to try to live or practise the Sermon on the Mount. To expect Christian conduct from a person who is not born again is heresy. The appeals of the gospel in terms of conduct and ethics and morality are always based on the assumption that the people to whom the injunctions are addressed are Christian.

Now that is obvious in any one of the Epistles, and it is equally obvious here. Take any Epistle you like. You will find that the subdivision in each one of them is the same; always doctrine first, then deductions from doctrine. The great principles are laid down and a description is given of the Christians to whom the letter is written. Then, because of that, or because they believe that, 'therefore' they are exhorted to do certain things. We always tend to forget that every New Testament letter was written to Christians and not to non-Christians; and the appeals in terms of ethics in every Epistle are always addressed only to those who are believers, to those who are new men and women in Christ Jesus. This Sermon on the Mount is exactly the same.

Studies in the Sermon on the Mount, i, pp. 23–4

Let us follow [Habbakuk] as he applies this method* to the two major problems that troubled him. . . .

(*a*) *God is eternal*. After stating his difficulty the prophet declares, 'Art thou not from everlasting?' (1:12). You see, he is laying down a proposition. He is forgetting for a moment the immediate problem, and asking himself what it was he was sure of about God. . . . He had just said (1:11) that the Chaldeans, flushed with success, imputed their power to their god; and . . . he began to think, 'Their god—what is their god? Just something they have made themselves (cf. Isaiah 46). God . . . the everlasting God . . . is not like the gods whom men worship . . . He is God from eternity to eternity . . . He has preceded history; He has created history. His throne is above the world and outside time. He reigns in eternity, the everlasting God.'

(b) *God is self-existent* . . . the eternal I AM. . . . The name 'I AM that I AM' means, 'I am the Absolute, the self-existent One'. Here is a second vital principle. God is not in any sense dependent upon anything that happens in the world. . . . Not only is He *not* dependent upon the world, but He need never have created it had He not willed to do so. The tremendous truth concerning the Trinity is that an eternally self-existent life resides in the Godhead—Father, Son, and Holy Spirit. Here again is wonderful reassurance. . . . The problem begins to fade.

(c) *God is holy* . . . utterly, absolutely righteous and holy, 'a consuming fire'. 'God is light and in him is no darkness at all.' And the moment you consider Scriptures like that you are forced to ask, 'Can the Lord of the earth do that which is unrighteous?' Such a thing is unthinkable.

(d) *God is almighty* . . . The God who created the whole world out of nothing, who said, 'Let there light' and there was light, has absolute power; He has illimitable might. He is 'The Rock'.

From Fear to Faith, pp. 28–30

(*continued on March 4*)

   *December 20, pp. 25–28.

(e) *God is faithful* . . . God is the God of the Covenant. Though He is independent and absolute, eternal, mighty, righteous and holy, nevertheless He has condescended to make a covenant with men. . . . It was this covenant that entitled Israel to turn to God and say, 'My God, mine Holy One'. [Habakkuk] remembers that God has said, 'I will be their God and they shall be my people.' For those saintly men, the prophets, and all who had spiritual understanding in Israel, this fact was more significant than anything else. While believing in the eternal attributes of God they might have been chilled by the thought that such a God might be far away in the heavens and oblivious to their need. But what linked Him to them was the knowledge that He was a faithful, covenant-keeping God. God had given His word and He would never break it. . . . Whatever the Chaldean army might do it could never exterminate Israel, because God had given certain promises to Israel which He could never break. . . .

The prophet now proceeds to bring his problem into the context of those absolute and eternal principles. . . . He reaches his answer to this question about the Chaldeans by reasoning like this: 'God must be raising them up for Israel's benefit: of this I can be absolutely certain. It is not that the Chaldeans have taken the law into their own hands; it is not that God is incapable of restraining them. These things are impossible in view of my propositions. God is just using them for His own purposes . . . and He is carrying out those purposes. I do not understand it fully, but I am quite sure that we are not going to be exterminated . . . although . . . there are apparently going to be very few of us left, and we are going to be carried into captivity. But a remnant will remain, because the Almighty is still God, and He is using the Chaldeans to do something within the purpose of the covenant. God . . . is not being defeated . . . He is doing this and doing it for His own grand end and object.'

From Fear to Faith, pp. 31–2

What are the characteristics of the true Christian? . . . it is that he 'doeth the will of my Father which is in heaven'. . . .

The first part of the answer is to make clear what it does not mean. . . . Obviously it does not mean 'justification by works' . . . the first statement [in the Beatitudes] is, 'Blessed are the poor in spirit'. We can try from now until we are dead, but we shall never make ourselves 'poor in spirit', and we can never make ourselves conform to any of the Beatitudes. . . .

Neither is it a teaching of sinless perfection. Many people read these pictures at the end of the Sermon on the Mount, and say that they mean that the only man who is allowed or able to enter into the kingdom of heaven is the man, who, having read the Sermon on the Mount, puts each detail into practice, always and everywhere. This again is obviously impossible. If that were the teaching, then we could be quite certain that there never has been and there never will be a single Christian in the world. . . .

What then is it? It is none other than the doctrine which James, in his Epistle, summarizes in the words, 'Faith without works is dead.' It is simply a perfect definition of faith. Faith without works is not faith, it is dead. The life of faith is never a life of ease; faith is always practical. The difference between faith and intellectual assent is that intellectual assent simply says, 'Lord, Lord', but does not do His will. In other words, though I may say 'Lord, Lord' to the Lord Jesus Christ, there is no meaning in it unless I regard Him as my Lord, and willingly become His bondslave. My words are idle words, and I do not mean 'Lord, Lord' unless I obey Him. Faith without works is dead.

Studies in the Sermon on the Mount, ii: pp. 308–10

*We praise Thee for the radiance
That from the hallowed page,
A lantern to our footsteps,
Shines on from age to age*

The authority of the Scriptures is not a matter to be defended, so much as to be asserted. . . . I am reminded of what the great Charles Haddon Spurgeon once said in this connexion: 'There is no need for you to defend a lion when he is being attacked. All you need to do is to open the gate and let him out' . . . it is the preaching and exposition of the Bible that really establish its truth and authority. I believe that this is more true today, perhaps . . . than it has been for the last two centuries. . . . There is nothing that really explains the whole world situation, as it is today, except the Bible. Take even the question of the origin of the world, and the very nature and character of the world itself. We know that there have been certain scientists in this present century who . . . have been forced to come to the conclusion that there must be a great Mind, a great Architect behind the universe. . . . The Bible has always asserted this, but at long last some of these men are coming to admit it.

But when you come to consider the state and condition of the world this particular point is still more evident. When you look at the average individual man as he is today, in spite of all the advance of learning and culture and knowledge . . . what are you to say? When you are confronted by the fact of two major world wars in this present century . . . the only adequate explanation is that which is given in the Bible: the biblical doctrine of sin. Nothing else really gives an adequate explanation. . . . It is only in the light of this teaching that you can understand the whole process of history. Now it is of great interest and real significance to observe that the critics themselves are now beginning to say this. They used to deny it. . . . They hated the whole notion of sin. Man was developing and improving. He was getting better and better. But now they have been forced to admit the truth of the biblical teaching and they are coming back to it.

Authority, pp. 41–2

Is not [modern man] trusting for salvation to himself, his own sincerity and his own efforts? Why is it that he still refuses the gospel concerning Jesus Christ and His atoning death and glorious Resurrection? Think again of the utter folly and futility of that position. Contemplate once more the task which faces us, and what is demanded of us. It is all utterly impossible for man in his own effort. Try to think of being in the presence of God; and if you realize to any extent what that means you will be compelled to agree with him* who said,

> Eternal light! Eternal light!
>   How pure the soul must be,
> When, placed within Thy searching sight,
> It shrinks not, but, with calm delight,
>   Can live, and look on Thee!
>
> Oh, how shall I, whose native sphere
>   Is dark, whose mind is dim,
> Before the Ineffable appear,
> And on my naked spirit bear
>   That uncreated beam?

How can one rise to perfect purity? How can all our zeal and sincerity get us there? The one way is outlined in the third stanza:

> There is a way for man to rise
>   To that sublime abode:
> An offering and a sacrifice,
> A Holy Spirit's energies,
>   An Advocate with God.

The Son of God came to die for us and for our sins. He now offers to clothe us with His righteousness, and to present us faultless before God in eternity. There is no need for us to exhaust ourselves further in futile efforts. There is no need for heroics. . . . Our all is not enough. But He is all sufficient . . . 'if thou shalt confess with thy mouth the Lord Jesus, and shalt believe in thine heart that God hath raised him from the dead, thou shalt be saved' (Romans 10:9).

Truth Unchanged, Unchanging, pp. 72–3

*Thomas Binney.

March 8
          O the pure delight of a single hour
          That before Thy throne I spend,
          When I kneel in prayer, and with Thee, my God,
          I commune as friend with friend

The outstanding characteristic of all the most saintly people that the world has ever known has been that they have not only spent much time in private prayer, but have also delighted in it. . . . The more saintly the person, the more time such a person spends in conversation with God. Thus it is a vital and all-important matter. . . .

This has been true in the experience of God's people throug out the centuries. We find it recorded in the Gospels that John the Baptist had been teaching his disciples to pray. They obviously had felt the need of instruction, and they had asked him. . . . And John had taught them how to pray. Our Lord's disciples felt exactly the same need. . . . 'Lord, teach us how to pray.' Undoubtedly the desire arose in their hearts because they were conscious of this kind of natural, instinctive, initial difficulty of which we are all aware; but it must also have been greatly increased when they watched His own prayer life. They saw how He would arise 'a great while before dawn' and go up into the mountains to pray, and how He would spend whole nights in prayer. And sometimes, I have no doubt, they said to themselves, 'What does He talk about? What does He do?' They may also have thought, 'I find after a few minutes in prayer that I come to the end of my words. What is it that enables Him to be drawn out in prayer? What is it that leads to this ease and abandonment?' 'Lord,' they said, 'teach us how to pray.' They meant by this . . . 'We wish we knew God as You know Him. Teach us how to pray.' Have you ever felt that? Have you ever felt dissatisfied with your prayer life, and longed to know more and more what it is truly to pray? If you have, it is an encouraging sign.

Studies in the Sermon on the Mount, ii, p. 47

68

It is only in the light of God's hatred and abhorrence of sin that we can really see His love, and appreciate the wonder and the glory of the gospel. The measure of His anger against sin is the measure of the love that is prepared to forgive the sinner and to love him in spite of the sin. In spite of all the talk and writing about the love of God during the past century, there has been much less evidence of true appreciation of the love of God and less readiness to surrender all to it. The idea of love has been so sentimentalized that it has become little more or better than a vague general benevolence. The love of God is a holy love. It expresses itself not by condoning sin or compromising with it; it deals with it, and yet does so in such a way that the sinner is not destroyed with his sin, but is delivered from it and its consequences. . . .

But there is no real ground at all for the objection to this teaching concerning 'the wrath of God'. For the way of escape is wide open. There is no need for anyone to remain under the wrath of God. And surely that fact settles the matter. Were there no escape, the position would be very different. But what can happen to anyone who deliberately refuses to accept that offer of salvation, save to suffer the consequences of that refusal? And that is the explanation of the note of urgency in the preaching of Paul and the other Apostles, and of all the greatest preachers ever since. That is why the gospel is good news. The wrath of God already revealed. But now the way to escape that wrath is also revealed in the gospel of Christ.

The Plight of Man and the Power of God, pp. 72–3

There are certain simple principles about which we must be quite clear before we can ever hope to enjoy this Christian salvation. The first is conviction of sin. We must be absolutely clear about our sinfulness. Here I follow the method of the Apostle Paul and raise an imaginary objection. I imagine someone saying at once: 'Are you going to preach to us about sin, are you going to preach about conviction of sin? You say your object is to make us happy but if you are going to preach to us about conviction of sin, surely that is going to make us still more unhappy. Are you deliberately trying to make us miserable and wretched?' To which the simple reply is, Yes! That is the teaching of the great Apostle in these chapters.* It may sound paradoxical—the term does not matter—but beyond any question that is the rule, and there are no exceptions. You must be made miserable before you can know true Christian joy. Indeed the real trouble with the miserable Christian is that he has never been truly made miserable because of conviction of sin. He has by-passed the essential preliminary to joy, he has been assuming something that he has no right to assume.

Let me put it again in a Scriptural statement. You remember the aged Simeon standing with the infant Lord Jesus Christ in his arms? He said a very profound thing when he said, 'This Child is set for the fall and for the rising again of many in Israel.' There is no rising again until there has been a preliminary fall. This is an absolute rule, and yet this is the thing that is being so sadly forgotten by so many today, and assumed by as many more. But the Scripture has its order, and its order must be observed if we are to derive the benefits of the Christian salvation. Ultimately the only thing which is going to drive a man to Christ and make him rely upon Christ alone, is a true conviction of sin.

Spiritual Depression, pp. 27–8

*Romans 1–4.

70

The whole of [Matthew] chapter 6, I suggest, relates to the Christian as living his life in the presence of God, in active submission to Him, and in entire dependence upon Him. . . . Take, for instance, the first verse: 'Take heed that ye do not your alms before men, to be seen of them: otherwise ye have no reward of your Father which is in heaven.' It continues like that from beginning to end. . . . 'Therefore take no thought, saying, What shall we eat? . . . or, Wherewithal shall we be clothed . . . your Heavenly Father knoweth that ye have need of these things. But seek ye first the kingdom of God, and his righteousness; and all these things shall be added unto you.' There, I say, is a description of the Christian as a man who knows he is always in the presence of God, so that what he is interested in is not the impression he makes on other men, but his relationship to God. Thus, when he prays, he is not interested in what other people are thinking, whether they are praising his prayers or criticizing them; he knows he is in the presence of the Father, and he is praying to God. Also, when he does his alms, it is God he has in mind all along. Furthermore, as he meets problems in life, his need of food and clothing, his reaction to external events, all are viewed in the light of this relationship which he bears to the Father. This is a very important principle with regard to the Christian life.

Then chapter 7 can be regarded in general as an account of the Christian as one who lives always under the judgement of God, and in the fear of God. 'Judge not, that ye be not judged.' 'Enter ye in at the straight gate.' 'Beware of false prophets.' 'Not every one that saith unto me, Lord, Lord, shall enter into the kingdom of God; but he that doeth the will of my Father which is in heaven.' Moreover, the Christian is likened to a man who builds a house which he knows is going to be tested.

Studies in the Sermon on the Mount, i, pp. 25–6

If a knowledge of the truth were really dependent upon man's capacity, man's reason, man's sense-perception, man's intellectual intuition, and all that the scientific method postulates, then it follows that a knowledge of truth . . . would be possible only to a very select number of V.I.P.s who can follow the arguments of the philosophers. . . . But what a few! The vast majority would never have any hope at all for any knowledge of truth . . . for any solution to their pressing problems.

But when you come to the Christian method there is hope for all. Why? Because all are inadequate, all are insufficient, all are failures. Here the position depends not upon man's capacity but upon his incapacity . . . it does not depend upon my capacity to understand or to discover, but upon God's power to give. And He can give to all; therefore there is a chance and a hope for all. . . . When 'the world by wisdom knew not God', when all the philosophers could get no further, then the unknown God sent His own Son into the world. God came into the world in the Person of His Son, yes, from outside, wherever it may be, 'up above', or 'out there', or from the depths, for He is omnipresent. . . . Here is truth being revealed to us, coming to us [John 1:18; 14:9 and 6]. . . . The great story of the Christian Church is the story of thousands upon thousands of men and women, once hopeless in ignorance and sin, debauchery and iniquity, entirely renewed and transformed through the simple belief of this message, and becoming new creatures, knowing that God is their Father, and that they are forgiven. They have a new life, a new orientation, new desires, new power, and are enabled to live in this world in a triumphant manner, to the astonishment of those who knew them as they once were.

That is the Christian method. It is the very antithesis of the scientific method; but it is God's method, and, thank God, it really does work.

The Approach to Truth: Scientific and Religious, pp. 25–7

. . . all teaching and all truth and all doctrine must be tested in the light of the Scriptures. Here is God's revelation of Himself, given in parts and portions in the Old Testament with an increasing clarity and with a culminating finality, coming eventually 'in the fulness of the times' to the perfect, absolute, final revelation in God the Son. He in turn enlightens and reveals His will and teaching to these apostles, endows them with a unique authority, fills them with the needed ability and power, and gives them the teaching that is essential to the well-being of the Church and God's people. We can build only upon this one, unique, authority.

The choice for us today is really as simple as it was for those first Christians in the early days. We either accept this authority or else we accept the authority of 'modern knowledge', modern science, human understanding, human ability. It is one or the other. . . .

For us . . . there is no real choice. On the one hand, trusting to human ability and understanding, everything is flux and change, uncertain and insecure, ever liable to collapse. On the other is not only 'the impregnable Rock of Holy Scripture', but there is the Light of the world, the Word of God, the Truth itself. . . .

The Lord of the Church has declared: 'Heaven and earth shall pass away, but my word shall not pass away.' It is a word that abides in time; it is a word that abides in death; it is a word that shall confront us in eternity.

Authority, pp. 60–1

The unity itself is inevitable among all those who have been quickened by the Holy Spirit out of spiritual death and given new life in Christ Jesus . . . it is a unity which is produced by the Holy Spirit and by Him alone. Man cannot produce this, try as he may. Because of the nature of this unity, because it is a spiritual unity, it can be brought into being only as a result of the operation of the Holy Spirit. The Apostle rejoices in this staggering fact, that these people who were once Jews and Gentiles are now one in Christ Jesus. They not only share the same life, they are agreed about their doctrine. They believe the same things, they are trusting to the same Person, and they know that He has saved them all in the same way. The 'middle wall of partition' has gone. The Jews no longer pride themselves on the fact that they are Jews, and that they had the law given to them, whereas the Gentiles were ignorant, and were not in the unique position of being the people of God. All these differences have gone, and they are one in seeing their lost estate and condition, their utter hopelessness and helplessness. They are united in their common trust in the Lord Jesus Christ, the Son of God, who has purchased them at the cost of His own precious blood. So they are ready to listen to this exhortation which urges them to maintain with great diligence, to preserve and to guard, this unity into which they have been brought by the operation of the Holy Spirit of God.

The Basis of Christian Unity, p. 25

March 15 One thing I know, that, whereas I was blind, now I see.

. . . there are large numbers of people outside the Church, and outside Christ, at the present time solely because . . . they seem to have determined not to allow the gospel to work on their lives until they understand the gospel itself. . . . They say that they do not desire to commit intellectual suicide and to submit themselves passively to what they do not understand. The fear of passivity is a genuine and a good one. . . . The gospel places no premium on our ignorance. Indeed, it teaches that we must use the mind and the powers with which God has endowed us. But . . . [they] are guilty of a fallacy and are behaving in an unreasonable and irrational manner. Let me illustrate. It is clear, is it not, that we know much more about light and heat than we know about the sun itself? In other words, we understand a great deal about the functions and the working of the sun while the sun itself in its essential nature and constitution remains a mystery to us. Or take electricity as an example. Here again, we know a great deal more about its use than we do about the nature of electricity itself. There is nothing unreasonable about availing ourselves of the benefit offered by electricity even though we do not understand the thing itself . . . there are many laws which have been discovered. . . . We may know a great deal about these laws without understanding the essential nature of electricity itself. We are saved, for instance, from the danger of putting our hand on a live current by this knowledge. . . . In the religious and the theological realm it is much the same. The mystery of godliness remains a mystery, and will ever remain so. . . . But that is not the case with regard to the effects and the results and the working out of the gospel . . . . [which] is characterized above all else . . . by this essential directness and simplicity . . . the gospel, on the one hand, has ever baffled, and is still baffling, the greatest philosophers the world has ever known, and yet can save a little child.

Truth Unchanged, Unchanging, pp. 75–7

[The Lord's Prayer] is undoubtedly a pattern prayer. The very way in which our Lord introduces it indicates that . . . it really covers everything in principle. There is a sense in which you can never add to the Lord's Prayer; nothing is left out. That does not mean, of course, that when we pray we are simply to repeat the Lord's Prayer and stop at that, for that . . . was not true of our Lord Himself . . . He spent whole nights in prayer; many times He arose a great while before day and prayed for hours. You will always find in the lives of the saints that they have spent hours in prayer. John Wesley used to say he held a very poor view of any Christian who did not pray for at least four hours every day. . . .

[The Lord's Prayer] really does contain all the principles. . . . What we have is a kind of skeleton. . . . The principles are all here and you cannot add to them. You can take the longest prayer that has ever been offered by a saint, and you will find that it can all be reduced to these principles. . . . Take our Lord's High Priestly prayer [John 17]. If you analyse it in terms of principles, you will find that it can be reduced to the principles of this model prayer.

The Lord's Prayer covers everything; and all we do is to take these principles and employ and expand them and base our every petition upon them. . . . I think you will agree with St Augustine and Martin Luther and many other saints who have said that there is nothing more wonderful in the entire Bible than the Lord's Prayer. The economy, the way in which He summarizes it all, and has reduced everything to but a few sentences, is something that surely proclaims the fact that the speaker is none other than the very Son of God Himself.

Studies in the Sermon on the Mount, ii, pp. 48–9

There was a time when it was true to say of the masses of the people that . . . they recognized the truth of the Gospel . . . but failed to put it into practice. They may have gone further and objected to its stringent ethical and moral demands. But even then they were paying tribute to it, and merely putting up defences for their own sin and weaknesses. The gospel in those days was recognized as presenting the highest and the best way of life. . . . That was once the position. But it is no longer so. . . . The general attitude towards the gospel has changed completely . . . today it is being actively attacked and opposed. Indeed, we have even reached a stage beyond that; it is being ridiculed and dismissed. The claim today is that it is something which no educated, reasonable person can possibly accept and believe. It is placed in the category of folk-lore and superstition. . . . All this can be proved, it is contended, by the advance of knowledge, the result of scientific discovery, and the light which psychology has thrown on human nature and its strange behaviour. Certain aspects of the moral teaching of the gospel are accepted and praised, though some would even reject that, but as for the central claims of the gospel . . . all these things are rejected with contempt and sarcasm. . . . Salvation is to be found, according to the modern man, in the full use of the human capacities and powers which can be trained by knowledge and education. Man must save himself; man can save himself. . . . And if anyone ventures . . . to say that the gospel is the only hope for mankind . . . he would be roared at as a lunatic or a fool.

Nevertheless, that is precisely and exactly what we assert today, as Paul did so long ago. . . . We do not hesitate to state that the only hope for men is to believe the gospel of Christ.

The Plight of Man and the Power of God, pp. 76–9

It is just here that the devil causes confusion. It suits him well that people should be concerned about sanctification and holiness and various other things, but they can never be right until they are right here, and that is why we must start with this . . . great doctrine [of justification]. This confusion is an old trouble. In a sense it is the masterpiece of Satan. He will even encourage us to be righteous as long as he has us confused at this point. That he is doing so at the present time is clear from the fact that the average person in the Church seems to regard men as Christian simply because they do good works, even though they may be entirely wrong about this preliminary truth. . . . It is what our Lord was continually saying to the Pharisees, and it certainly was the major argument which the Apostle Paul had with the Jews. They were entirely wrong with regard to the whole question of the Law, and the main problem was to show them the right view of it. The Jews believed that the Law was made by God in order that man might save himself by keeping it. They said that all one had to do was to keep the Law . . . and that if you led your life according to the Law, God would accept you and you would be well-pleasing in his sight. And they believed that they could do that, because they had never understood the Law. They put their own interpretation on it and made of it something that was well within their reach. And so they thought that all was well. That is the picture of the Pharisees given in the Gospels and everywhere in the New Testament . . . and it is still the essence of the problem with many people. We have to realize that there are certain things about which we must be perfectly clear before we can really hope to have peace, and to enjoy the Christian life.

Spiritual Depression, pp. 26–7

The Christian is a man who of necessity must be concerned about keeping God's law. . . . We are not 'under the law' but we are still meant to keep it; the 'righteousness of the law' is meant to be 'fulfilled in us', says the Apostle Paul in writing to the Romans. . . . So the Christian is a man who is always concerned about living and keeping the law of God. Here he is reminded how that is to be done.

Again one of the most essential and obvious things about a Christian is that he is a man who lives always realizing he is in the presence of God. The world does not live in this way; that is the big difference between the Christian and the non-Christian. The Christian is . . . not, as it were, a free agent. He is a child of God, so that everything he does, he does from this standpoint of being well-pleasing in His sight. That is why the Christian man, of necessity, should view everything that happens to him in this world entirely differently from everybody else. . . . The Christian is not worried about food and drink and housing and clothing. It is not that he says these things do not matter, but they are not his main concern, they are not the things for which he lives. The Christian sits loosely to this world and its affairs. Why? Because he belongs to another kingdom and another way. He does not go out of the world; that was the Roman Catholic error of monasticism. The Sermon on the Mount does not tell you to go out of life in order to live the Christian life. But it does say that your attitude is entirely different from that of a non-Christian, because of your relationship to God and because of your utter dependence upon Him.

Studies in the Sermon on the Mount, i, pp. 26–7

March 20   *Not by might, nor by power, but by my Spirit, saith*
              the Lord

We often quote, 'Not by might, nor by power, but by my
spirit, saith the Lord', and yet in practice we seem to rely upon
the 'mighty dollar' and the 'power of the press' and advertising.
We seem to think that our influence will depend on our tech-
nique and the programme we can put forward, and that it will
be the numbers, the largeness, the bigness, that will prove
effective! We seem to have forgotten that God has done most
of His deeds in the Church throughout its history through
'remnants'. We seem to have forgotten the great story of
Gideon, for instance, and how God insisted on reducing the
thirty-two thousand men down to three hundred, before He
would make use of them. We have become fascinated by the
idea of bigness, and we are quite convinced that if we can only
'*stage*' (yes, that is the word!) something really big before the
world, we will shake it, and produce a mighty religious awakening. That seems to be the modern conception of authority.

All that, I suggest, is nothing but the old error into which the
Church has fallen so repeatedly. For Hegel's dictum about
history is as true of the church as it is of the world: 'History
teaches us that history teaches us nothing.' We seem
determined to go on repeating in this way the same errors, and
falling into the same pitfalls as our forefathers have ever
done . . . the Bible teaches plainly and clearly that God's own
method is always through the Spirit and His authority and
power.

Authority, pp. 70–1

*March 21   By two wings man is lifted from the things of earth—
simplicity and purity* (Thomas à Kempis)

As life in general becomes more and more complex, so
religion tends to be affected in the same way. In the secular
world, life today has become involved and sophisticated; in
every direction one sees increased organization and multi-
plicity of machinery. Bustle and business, conferences and con-
ventions are the order of the day. Never has the life of the world
been so complicated. . . . The simple truths are being ignored,
and men spend their time in holding conferences to explore
their difficulties. The same tendency is seen in the world of
religion. It seems to be assumed that if the affairs of men are so
difficult and complicated, the affairs of God should be still
more complicated, because they are still greater. Hence comes
the tendency to increase ceremony and ritual, and to multiply
organizations and activities . . . the argument is that it is ridiculous to assert that the vast problems of life today can be solved
in the apparently simple manner suggested by those who
preach the gospel in the old evangelical manner. . . .

The fact is, that as we get further away from God life becomes more complicated and involved. We see this not only in
the Bible, but also in subsequent history. The Protestant
Reformation simplified not only religion, but the whole of life
and living in general. . . . The truly religious life is always
simple . . . there is nothing which is so characteristic of God's
work in every realm as its essential simplicity and order. Look
where you will, you see that God ever works on an uncompli-
cated design. See how He repeats the seasons year by year—
spring, summer, autumn, winter. Examine a flower . . . you will
find that the basic pattern of nature is always simple. Simplicity is God's method. Is it, then, reasonable to believe that
in the most vital subject of all, the salvation of man and the
ordering of his life, God should suddenly jettison His own
method and become involved and complex?

Truth Unchanged, Unchanging, pp. 78–80

. . . we remind ourselves of the vital importance of the right approach, for this is the key to the understanding of successful prayer. People so often say, 'You know, I prayed and prayed, but nothing happened. I did not seem to find peace. I did not seem to get any satisfaction out of it.' Most of their trouble is due to the fact that their approach to prayer has been wrong. . . . We tend to be so self-centred in our prayers that when we drop on our knees before God, we think only about ourselves and our troubles and perplexities. We start talking about them at once, and of course nothing happens. . . . That is not the way to approach God. We must pause before we speak in prayer.

The great teachers of the spiritual life throughout the centuries, whether Roman Catholic or Protestant, have been agreed . . . that the first step in prayer has always been what they call 'Recollection'. There is a sense in which every man when he begins to pray to God should put his hand upon his mouth. That was the whole trouble with Job. . . . He felt that God had not been dealing kindly with him, and he had been expressing his feelings freely. But when . . . God began to deal with him at close quarters, when He began to reveal and manifest Himself to him, what did Job do? . . . He said, '. . . I will lay mine hand upon my mouth'. And, strange as it may seem to you, you start praying by saying nothing; you recollect what you are about to do.

I know the difficulty in this. We are but human, and we are pressed by the urgency of our position, the cares, the anxieties, the troubles, the anguish of mind. . . . And we are so full of this that, like children, we start speaking at once. But if you want to make contact with God, and if you want to feel His everlasting arms about you, put your hand upon your mouth for a moment. Recollection! Just stop for a moment and remind yourself of what you are about to do.

Studies in the Sermon on the Mount, ii, pp. 51–2
(*continued on March 23*)

Do you know that the essence of true prayer is found in the two words in [Matthew 6] verse 9, 'Our Father'? . . . If you can say from your heart, whatever your condition, 'My Father', in a sense your prayer is already answered. . . .

There are people who believe it is a good thing to pray because it always does us good. They adduce various psychological reasons. That of course is not prayer as the Bible understands it. Prayer means speaking to God, forgetting ourselves, and realizing His presence. Then again, there are others . . . who rather think that . . . one's prayer should be very brief and pointed, and one should just simply make a particular request. That is something which is not true of the teaching of the Bible concerning prayer. Take any of the great [Bible] prayers. . . . None of them is simply what we might call this 'business-like' kind of prayer which simply makes a petition known to God and then ends. Every prayer recorded in the Bible starts with invocation. . . . We have a great and wonderful example of this in the ninth chapter of Daniel. There the prophet, in terrible perplexity, prays to God. But he does not start immediately with his petition; he starts by praising God. A perplexed Jeremiah does the same thing . . . he does not rush into the presence of God for this one matter; he starts by worshipping God. And so you will find it in all the recorded prayers. Indeed, you even get it in the great High-Priestly prayer of our Lord Himself which is recorded in John 17. You remember also how Paul put it in writing to the Philippians. He says, 'in nothing be anxious; but in everything by prayer and supplication with thanksgiving let your requests be made known unto God' (Philippians 4:6 RV.). That is the order. We must always start with invocation.

Studies in the Sermon on the Mount, ii, pp. 52–3

[Lack of conviction of sin] is in particular the problem of all those who have been brought up in a religious or Christian manner. Their chief trouble often is their wrong idea of sin. I remember . . . a woman who had been brought up in a very religious home, who had always attended a place of worship and been busily and actively engaged in the life of the Church. She was then a member in a church where a number of people had been converted suddenly from the world and from various kinds of evil living—drunkenness and such like things. I well remember her saying to me: 'You know, I almost wish that I had not been brought up in the way I have been brought up. I could wish that I had been living their kind of life in order that I might have their marvellous experience.' What did she mean? What she was really saying was that she had never seen herself as a sinner. Why not? There are many reasons. That kind of person thinks of sin only in terms of action, in terms of sins. Not only that, but in terms of certain particular actions only. So their tendency is to think that because they have not been guilty of these particular things, that they are not really sinners at all. Indeed, sometimes they put it quite plainly and say: 'I have never really thought of myself as a sinner; but of course that is not surprising as my life has been sheltered from the beginning. I have never been tempted to do these things, and it is not surprising therefore that I have never felt myself to be a sinner.' Now there we see the very essence of this fallacy. Their thinking is in terms of actions, particular actions, and of comparisons with other people and their experiences, and so on. For this reason they have never had a real conviction of sin, and because of that they have never plainly seen their utter absolute need of the Lord Jesus Christ. They have heard it preached that Christ has died for our sins and they say that they believe that; but they have never really known its absolute necessity for themselves.

Spiritual Depression, pp. 28–9

The Christian is a man who always walks in the fear of God —not craven fear, because 'perfect love casteth out' that fear. Not only does he approach God in terms of the Epistle to the Hebrews, 'with reverence and godly fear', but he lives his whole life like that. The Christian is the only man in the world who does live always with and under this sense of judgement. He must do so because our Lord tells him to do so. He tells him his building is going to be judged, the test of life is going to come. He tells him not to say, 'Lord, Lord', nor to rely upon his activities in the Church as being of necessity sufficient, because judgement is coming, and judgement by One who sees the heart. . . . These New Testament people lived in the fear of God. They all accepted the teaching of the Apostle Paul when he said, 'We must all appear before the judgement seat of Christ; that every one may receive the things done in his body, according to that he hath done, whether it be good or bad' (2 Corinthians 5:10). That is addressed to Christians. Yet the modern Christian does not like that; he says he will have nothing to do with it. But that is the teaching of the apostle Paul as it is the teaching of the Sermon on the Mount. 'We must all appear before the judgement seat of Christ'; 'Knowing, therefore, the terror of the Lord. . . .' Judgement is coming and it is going to 'begin at the house of God', where it should begin, because of the claim we make. It is all impressed upon us here in the final section of the Sermon on the Mount. We should always be living and walking, distrustful of the flesh, distrustful of ourselves, knowing we have to appear before God and be judged by Him. It is a 'strait gate', it is a 'narrow way', this way that leads to life which is life indeed.

Studies in the Sermon on the Mount, i. pp. 27–8

[Nicodemus] is a master of Israel, but here he is confronted by Someone who clearly has more than he has himself. But he thinks. . . . 'It is only a more advanced stage than that which I have already reached.' . . . He is on the point of saying, 'What do I need *in addition*?' And our Lord turns upon him and says, '. . . You are all wrong. . . . What you need is to be born of water and of the Spirit. . . . You need the illumination and power of the Spirit. You cannot do this thing for yourself. . . .'

You see the same thing in practice in the Acts of the Apostles. The first Christian convert on the continent of Europe . . . was a woman called Lydia. . . . How was she converted? Was she carried away by the personality of the Apostle Paul? . . . This is not what the record says. In Acts 16:14 we read, 'Whose heart the Lord opened, that she attended unto the things which were spoken of Paul.' Even Paul could not save a soul, mighty man that he was. The Lord the Holy Spirit alone can open the heart and enable us to receive the truth. . . . [See 1 Corinthians 12:3]. If you need something further, you need only go to Ephesians 2 and there you will find that there is only one hope for those who are 'dead in trespasses and sins', those who are 'the children of wrath' and who walk 'according to the prince of the power of the air, the spirit that now worketh in the children of disobedience' and are slaves to lusts and passions of the mind as well as of the flesh and the body. There is only one hope for them. 'You hath he quickened.' 'We are his workmanship.' Without the work and authority and power of the Holy Spirit there would never be a single believer in our Lord and Saviour Jesus Christ.

Authority, pp. 74–6

86

In the days of the Psalmist they did not have God's Word as you and I have it today. It is not only in the sanctuary, it is available everywhere. Turn to it in the home or in the church, it does not matter where, and it will immediately make you think spiritually. . . . One of the reasons why God has given us this Word is in order to help us to deal with this problem that we are considering. . . . Take a Psalm like this one [73] and its story. Merely to read what this man went through puts me right, and all the histories do the same. . . . Begin to read your Bible and its great teaching and doctrines and you are again reminded of God's gracious purposes for man. . . .

Then it has explicit teaching on the question of the suffering of the godly. Paul writes to Timothy, who was ready to whimper and complain when things went wrong, and he says to him, 'Yea, and all that will live godly in Christ Jesus shall suffer persecution' (2 Timothy 3:12). . . . Again, Paul speaking to the early Christian churches told them that it is 'through much tribulation' that we must enter into the kingdom of God. If we grasp Paul's teaching to the early Christian churches we shall not be surprised at the things that happen to us. Indeed, instead of being surprised at them we almost get to the stage in which we expect them, in which we feel like saying, 'If I am not having troubles, what is wrong with me? Why are things going so well with me?' In other words, the whole atmosphere of the Bible is spiritual, and the more we read it, the more we shall be delivered from the rational level and raised to that higher level where we see things on the spiritual plane.

Faith on Trial, pp. 40–1

You remember what brought [John Wesley] to a conviction of sin? It began when he saw the way in which some Moravian Brethren behaved during a storm in mid-Atlantic.* John Wesley was terrified by the storm and afraid to die; the Moravians were not. They seemed to be as happy in the hurricane and in the midst of the storm as they were when the sun was shining. John Wesley realized that he was afraid of death, he somehow did not seem to know God as these people knew Him. In other words he began to feel his need, and that is always the beginning of a conviction of sin . . . the way to know yourself a sinner is not to compare yourself with other people; it is to come face to face with the Law of God. . . . Would you like to know what the Law of God is? Here it is—'Thou shalt love the Lord thy God with all thy heart, and with all thy soul and with all thy mind and with all thy strength. . . .' Forget all about drunkards and their like, forget all the people you read about in the press at the present time. Here is the test for you and me: Are you loving God with all your being? If you are not, you are a sinner. That is the test. 'All have sinned and come short of the glory of God.' God has made us and He has made us for Himself. He made man for His own glory and He intended man to live entirely for Him. Man was to be His representative, and was to dwell in communion with Him. He was to be the lord of the universe, he was to glorify God. As it is put in the Shorter Catechism: 'The chief end of man is to glorify God and to enjoy Him for ever', and if you are not doing so you are a sinner of the deepest dye, whether you know it and feel it or not.

Spiritual Depression, p. 30

*See p. 295.

There was a time when the designation applied to the Christian was that he was a 'God-fearing' man. I do not think you can ever improve on that. . . . It does not mean craven fear, it does not mean 'the fear that hath torment', but it is a wonderful description of the true Christian. He is of necessity, as we are reminded very forcibly in the seventh chapter of this* Gospel, a man who lives in the fear of God. We can say of our blessed Lord Himself that His Life was a God-fearing life. . . . So often modern Christians, who may be able to give very bright and apparently thrilling testimonies of some experience they have had, do not suggest that they are God-fearing people, but give the impression of being men of the world, both in dress and appearance, and in a kind of boisterousness and easy confidence. . . .

Here is the life to which we are called, and I maintain again that if only every Christian in the Church today were living the Sermon on the Mount, the great revival for which we are praying and longing would already have started. Amazing and astounding things would happen; the world would be shocked, and men and women would be drawn and attracted to our Lord and Saviour Jesus Christ.

May God give us grace to consider this Sermon on the Mount and to remember . . . that we ourselves are under judgement, and that the building we are erecting in this world and in this life will have to face His final test and the ultimate scrutiny of the eye of the Lamb of God that once was slain.

Studies in the Sermon on the Mount, i, pp. 30–1

*Matthew.

[People who do not believe the Scriptures] do not seem to realize fully what our Lord did on the Cross on Calvary's Hill. They do believe in His sacrificial, atoning death, but they do not work out its implications. . . . They know enough to be saved . . . but they are in a state of depression because they do not realize fully what this means. They forget that the angel announced to Joseph at the very beginning that He should 'save His people from their sins' (Matthew 1:21). The angel did not say that He shall save from all sins except this one sin that you have committed. No! 'He shall save His people from their sins.' . . . There is no qualification there, no limit. Or listen to the words of the Apostle Paul when he says, 'He hath made him to be sin for us who knew no sin' (2 Corinthians 5:21). They were all put there, every one, there is no limit, there is nothing left. All the sins of His people are there, every one of them. Indeed, He said it Himself, did He not, on the Cross? He said, 'It is finished', absolutely finished. . . . It is finished in the sense that not only all the sins committed in the past were dealt with there, but all the sins that could ever be committed were also dealt with there. It is one sacrifice, once and forever. He would never come back to the Cross again. All the sins were dealt with there finally and completely, everything. Nothing was left undone—'It is finished'. What we remind one another of as we take the bread and the wine, and what we proclaim, is that completed finished work. There is nothing left undone, there is no qualification concerning particular sins. All the sins of those who believe on Him, every one, have been dealt with and God has blotted them out as a thick cloud. All the sins you may ever commit have been dealt with there, so that when you go to Him it is 'the Blood of Jesus Christ' His Son, that is going to cleanse you.

Spiritual Depression, pp. 73–4

We say [that the only hope for men is to believe the gospel of Christ] knowing full well all the talk about science and learning and culture. We say so knowing that, at the end of this war* the world, in exactly the same way as at the end of the last war, will announce with confidence its plans and schemes for a new world, without taking any account of what the gospel has to say. Why do we say so? For precisely the same reasons adduced by St Paul [Romans 1:16] . . . he is proud of the gospel *because it is God's way of salvation.* . . . At once we see that it possesses an authority which is quite unique. For all other ideas with respect to life and its problems are man-made. At their best and highest, they never get beyond the realm of speculation and supposition. . . . The great minds and the profoundest thinkers . . . end by admitting that the ultimate problems of life are shrouded in mystery. . . . The very fact that there are so many different and differing schools of thought bears eloquent testimony to this uncertainty and inability. . . . But there was another fact . . . which proved how inadequate all the schools were finally. And that was the endless number of religions that were to be found. . . . We see a perfect picture of this in Acts 17 as regards Athens. The same was true of Rome and all other great cities. . . . Paul had something essentially different to offer and to preach. He knew of the other systems. But he also knew their limits and their inability to solve the problems. He could not make his boast in men and their systems. Before he could boast of a system it must have authority; it must have certainty. The gospel Paul preached was not speculation; it was a revelation from God Himself [Gal. 1:11, 12]. There was no need to be ashamed of such a message. And it is precisely the same today.

The Plight of Man and the Power of God, pp. 79–81

---

*Written in 1942.

The true Christian realizes . . . God's way of salvation in
Christ. This is the great good news. 'This is the thing I am
preaching,' says Paul, in effect, to the Romans, 'this righteousness that is of God, that is in Jesus Christ, His righteousness.'
What is he talking about? It can be put in the form of a question if you like. What is your view of Christ? Why did He come
into the world? What has God done in Christ? Is He merely a
teacher, an example, and so on? . . . No, this is something
positive, this righteousness of God in Jesus Christ. Salvation is
all in Christ, and unless you feel yourself shut up to Christ with
everything else having failed, you are not a Christian, and it is
not surprising that you are not happy. 'The righteousness of
God in Jesus Christ' means that God sent Him into the world
in order that He might honour the Law and so men might be
forgiven. Here is One who gave perfect obedience to God.
Here is One, God in the flesh, who has taken human nature
unto Himself, and, as man, has rendered perfect homage to
God, perfect allegiance, perfect obedience. God's law He kept
fully and absolutely without a failure. But not only that. . . .
Before man can be reconciled to God . . . this sin of his must
be removed. God has said that He will punish sin, and that the
punishment of sin is death and banishment from the face of
God . . . God has set Him forth as a propitiation . . . [this]
means that God has made Him responsible for our sins. They
have been placed upon Him and God has dealt with them and
punished them there, and therefore . . . He can justly forgive
us. . . . It is a daring thing for the Apostle to say, but it has to
be said. . . . God, because He is righteous and holy and eternal,
could not forgive the sin of man without punishing it. He said
He would punish it, so He must punish it, and, blessed be His
Name, He has punished it. He is just, therefore, and the
justifier of them that believe in Jesus.

Spiritual Depression, pp. 32–3

92

Our Lord says, 'Our Father which art in heaven'; and Paul says, 'The God and Father of our Lord Jesus Christ.' . . . It is vital when we pray to God, and call Him our Father, that we should remind ourselves . . . of His majesty and of His greatness and of His almighty power . . . remember that He knows all about you. The Scripture says, 'all things are naked and opened unto the eyes of him with whom we have to do'. . . . It is not surprising that, when he wrote Psalm 51, David said in the anguish of his heart, 'Thou desirest truth in the inward parts.' If you want to be blessed of God you have to be absolutely honest, you have to realize He knows everything, and that there is nothing hidden from Him . . . as the wise man who wrote the book of Ecclesiastes put it, it is vital when we pray to God that we should remember that 'He is in heaven and we are upon the earth.'

Then remember His holiness and His justice, His utter, absolute righteousness . . . whenever we approach Him we must do so 'with reverence and godly fear: for our God is a consuming fire' [Hebrews 12:19].

That is the way to pray, says Christ . . . never separate these two truths. Remember that you are approaching the almighty, eternal, ever-blessed holy God. But remember also that that God, in Christ, has become your Father, who not only knows all about you in the sense that He is omniscient, He knows all about you also in the sense that a father knows all about his child. . . . Put these two things together. God in His almightiness is looking at you with a holy love and knows your every need. . . . He desires nothing so much as your blessing, your happiness, your joy and your prosperity. Then remember this, that He 'is able to do exceeding abundantly above all that we ask or think'. As your 'Father which is in heaven' He is much more anxious to bless you than you are to be blessed. There is also no limit to His almighty power.

Studies in the Sermon on the Mount, ii, pp. 55–6

'Now we can all live like this!'
(Olive Schreiner)

. . . *all Christians are to be like this.* Read the Beatitudes, and there you have a description of what every Christian is meant to be. It is not merely the description of some exceptional Christians. Our Lord does not say here that He is going to paint a picture of what certain outstanding characters are going to be and can be in this world. It is His description of every single Christian. . . .

[It is a] fatal tendency to divide Christians into two groups —the religious and the laity, exceptional Christians and ordinary Christians, the one who makes a vocation of the Christian life and the man who is engaged in secular affairs. That tendency is not only utterly and completely unscriptural; it is destructive ultimately of true piety, and is in many ways a negation of the gospel of our Lord Jesus Christ. There is no such distinction in the Bible. There are distinctions in offices —apostles, prophets, teachers, pastors, evangelists, and so on. But these Beatitudes are not a description of offices; they are a description of character. And from the standpoint of character, and of what we are meant to be, there is no difference between one Christian and another. . . .

Read the introduction to almost any New Testament Epistle and you will find all believers addressed as in the Epistle to the Church at Corinth, 'called to be saints'. All are 'canonized', if you want to use the term, not some Christians only. The idea that this height of the Christian life is meant only for a chosen few, and that the rest of us are meant to live on the dull plains, is an entire denial of the Sermon on the Mount, and of the Beatitudes in particular. . . . Therefore let us once and for ever get rid of that false notion. This is not merely a description of the Hudson Taylors or the George Müllers or the Whitefields or Wesleys of this world; it is a description of every Christian. We are all of us meant to conform to its pattern and to rise to its standard.

Studies in the Sermon on the Mount, i, pp. 33–4

God accepts this righteousness of Christ, this perfect righteousness face to face with the Law which He honoured in
every respect. He has kept it and given obedience to it, He has
borne its penalty. The Law is fully satisfied. God's way of
salvation, says Paul, is that. He gives to us the righteousness
of Christ. If we have seen our need and go to God and confess
it, God will give us His own Son's righteousness. He imputes
Christ's righteousness to us who believe in Him, and regards
us as righteous, and declares us and pronounces us to be
righteous in Him. That is the way of salvation, the Christian
way of salvation, the way of salvation through justification by
faith. So that it comes to this. That I see and I believe and I
look to nothing and to no one except to the Lord Jesus Christ.
I like Paul's way of putting it. He asks: 'Where is boasting
then? It is excluded. By what law? of works? Nay, but by the
law of faith' [Romans 3:27]. You foolish Jews, says Paul.
you are boasting about the fact that . . . you have the oracles of
God and that you are God's people. You must cease to do
that. You must not rest upon the fact that you have this
tradition and that you are children of your forefathers. There
is no boasting, you have to rest exclusively upon the Lord
Jesus Christ and His perfect work. The Jew is not superior to
the Gentile in this respect. . . . We look to Christ and to Christ
alone, and not to ourselves in any respect whatsoever.

Spiritual Depression, p. 33

Let us now see what the gospel has to say about life. The first principle is that face to face with the problems of life there is only one thing that needs to be examined—namely, the eye, the centre, the soul . . . the light of the body is the eye, the only thing that needs to be examined is the eye, for if the eye is single the whole body will be full of light. But if the eye is evil the whole body will be full of darkness . . . our Lord goes on to add the solemn warning [Luke 11:35], 'Take heed therefore that the light which is in thee be not darkness.' . . . How direct is [the gospel] in its approach! . . . it comes at once to the heart of the matter.

This direct simplicity is perfectly illustrated . . . in an incident which followed immediately after our Lord had spoken the above words. He went in at the request of a certain Pharisee to dine in his house, and at once sat down to meat. The Pharisee observing His act was surprised, marvelling that Christ had not first washed before dinner. . . . [Our Lord] turned to him and delivered a stern denunciation of the Pharisees and their ways and views. They who were so careful about the outside of the cup and the platter forgot the inside, which was infinitely more important. . . . They kept rules and regulations. . . . They were experts in minutiae. . . . They knew all about the things that were on the circumference of the law, but they were ignorant of its very object, which was to glorify God. . . . This may be used as a typical example of the way in which the gospel examines the problem of man. It is concerned about one thing only, the soul. Though a man may be right in many respects, as the Pharisees most certainly were, it is all of no avail if he is wrong in the centre, in the eye, in the soul. It is the eye alone that matters. The gospel has but one test to apply.

Truth Unchanged, Unchanging, pp. 82–4

We should all have a consuming passion that the whole world might come to know God [as the ever-present One who will never leave us nor forsake us]. . . . The Psalmist in Psalm 34 invites everybody to join him in 'magnifying' the Lord. What a strange idea! . . . At first sight that appears to be quite ridiculous. God is the Eternal, the self-existent One, absolute and perfect in all His qualities. How can feeble man ever magnify such a Being? How can we ever make God great or greater (which is what we mean by magnify)? . . . And yet, of course, if we but realize the way in which the Psalmist uses it, we shall see exactly what he means. He does not mean that we can actually add to the greatness of God, for that is impossible; but he does mean that he is concerned that this greatness of God may appear to be greater amongst men. Thus it comes to pass that amongst ourselves in this world we can magnify the name of God. We can do so by words, and by our lives, by being reflectors of the greatness and the glory of God and of His glorious attributes.

That is the meaning of this petition [of the Lord's Prayer (Matthew 6:9)]. It means a burning desire that the whole world may bow before God in adoration, in reverence, in praise, in worship, in honour and in thanksgiving. Is that our supreme desire? Is that the thing that is always uppermost in our minds whenever we pray to God? . . . When you come to God, says our Lord, in effect, even though you may be in desperate conditions and circumstances, it may be with some great concern on your mind and in your heart; even then, He says, stop for a moment and just recollect and realize this, that your greatest desire of all should be that this wonderful God . . . should be honoured, should be worshipped, should be magnified amongst the people. 'Hallowed be thy Name.'

Studies in the Sermon on the Mount, ii, p. 61

I know a number of Christian people who have a universal answer to all questions. It does not matter what the question is, they always say, 'Pray about it.' . . . What a glib, superficial and false bit of advice that can often be, and I am saying that from a Christian pulpit. You may ask, 'Is it ever wrong to tell men to make their problems a matter of prayer?' It is never wrong, but it is sometimes quite futile. . . . The whole trouble with this poor man [Psalm 73] . . . was that he was so muddled in his thinking about God that he could not pray to Him. If we have muddled thoughts in our mind and heart concerning God's way with respect to us, how can we pray? We cannot. Before we can pray truly we must think spiritually. There is nothing more fatuous than glib talk about prayer, as if prayer were something which you can always immediately rush into.

. . . Let me quote one of the greatest men of prayer the world has ever known . . . George Müller, in lecturing to ministers . . . told them this. He said that for many years the first thing he did every morning of his life was to pray. He had now long since discovered that this was not the best way. He had found that in order to pray truly and spiritually, he had to be in the Spirit himself, and that he must prepare himself first. He had discovered that it was good and most helpful, and he now strongly recommended it to them, always to read a portion of Scripture and perhaps some devotional book before they began to pray. In other words, he found it was necessary to put himself and his spirit right, before he could truly pray to God. . . . We must take time with prayer. We do not begin to pray to God until we realize His presence. . . . So the steps are perfectly right—the house of God, the Word of God, prayer to God and communion with God.

Faith on Trial, pp. 41–2

If you tarry till you're better
You will never come at all!

There is a very simple way of testing yourself to know whether you believe that [we must look to Christ and Christ alone]. We betray ourselves by what we say. . . . I have often had to deal with this point with people, and I have explained the way of justification by faith and told them how it is all in Christ and that God puts His righteousness upon us. I have explained it all to them, and then I have said, 'Well, now are you quite happy about it, do you believe that?' And they say, 'Yes'. Then I say, 'Well, then, you are now ready to say that you are a Christian.' And they hesitate. And I know that they have not understood. Then I say, 'What is the matter, why are you hesitating?' And they say, 'I do not feel that I am good enough.' At once I know that in a sense I have been wasting my breath. They are still thinking in terms of themselves; their idea still is that they have to make themselves good enough to be a Christian, good enough to be accepted with Christ. They have to do it! 'I am not good enough.' It sounds very modest, but . . . it is a denial of the faith. You think that you are being humble. But you will never be good enough; nobody has ever been good enough. The essence of the Christian salvation is to say that He is good enough and that I am in Him!

As long as you go on thinking about yourself and saying, 'Ah, yes, I would like to, but I am not good enough; I am a sinner, a great sinner,' you are denying God and you will never be happy. . . . I try to say [this] from the pulpit every Sunday because I think it is the thing that is robbing most people of the joy of the Lord.

Spiritual Depression, pp. 33–4

. . . *all Christians are meant to manifest all of these characteristics*. Not only are they meant for all Christians, but of necessity, therefore, all Christians are meant to manifest all of them. . . . It is not right to say some are meant to be 'poor in spirit' and some are meant to 'mourn', and some are meant to be 'meek', and some are meant to be 'peacemakers', and so on. No; every Christian is meant to be all of them, and to manifest all of them, at the same time. Now I think it is true and right to say that in some Christians some will be more manifest than others; but that is not because it is *meant* to be so. It is just due to the imperfections that remain in us. When Christians are finally perfect, they will all manifest all these characteristics fully; but here in this world, and in time, there is a variation to be seen . . . the character of this detailed description is such that it becomes quite obvious the moment we analyse each Beatitude, that each one of necessity implies the other. For instance, you cannot be 'poor in spirit' without 'mourning' in this sense; and you cannot mourn without 'hungering and thirsting after righteousness'; and you cannot do that without being one who is 'meek' and a 'peacemaker'. Each one of these in a sense demands the others. It is impossible truly to manifest one of these graces, and to conform to the blessing that is pronounced upon it, without at the same time inevitably showing the others also. The Beatitudes are a complete whole and you cannot divide them; so that, whereas one of them may be more manifest perhaps in one person than in another, all of them are there. The relative proportions may vary, but they are all present, and they are all meant to be present at the same time.

Studies in the Sermon on the Mount, i, p. 34

To the first question about the power of God, [Habakkuk] received a positive answer. But this problem of the holiness of God is more difficult. After stating his absolutes and bringing his problem into this context, there is still no clear answer. Now in experience it is often like that. You apply the same method which has worked so well in other cases, but there is no immediate answer. What does one do in such a case? Certainly do not rush to conclusions and say, 'Because I do not understand it therefore I wonder whether God is righteous after all.' No!... We make a mistake when we talk to ourselves and then to other people, and ask, 'Why this? Isn't it strange?' We must do what the prophet did: take the problem to God and leave it with Him.

A Christian may be kept in this position for a week, or months, or years. It has often so happened. But leave it with God! This . . . was the attitude adopted by the Son of God Himself when He was in this world. . . . He knew that His Father could have delivered Him out of the hands, not only of the Jews, but of the Romans also. . . . But if He was to be made sin, and sin was to be punished in His body, it meant that He must be separated from the Father . . . and the Son of God was faced with the greatest perplexity of His human life on earth . . . what did He do? Precisely what the prophet did; He prayed and said, 'O my Father, if it be possible, let this cup pass from me: nevertheless not as I will, but as thou wilt' (Matthew 26:39). 'I do not understand it', He said in effect, 'but if it is Thy way, very well, I am going on.' He took the problem He did not understand to God and left it there . . . confident that God's will is always right, and that a holy God will never command anything that is wrong.

From Fear to Faith, pp. 34–5

['Thy Kingdom come'—the second petition of our Lord's Prayer] . . . there is a logical order in these petitions. They follow one another by a kind of inevitable, divine necessity. We began by asking that the name of God may be hallowed amongst men. But . . . we are reminded of the fact that His name is not hallowed thus. At once the question arises, 'Why do not all men bow before the sacred name?' . . . because of sin, because there is another kingdom . . . the kingdom of darkness. And there, at once, we are reminded of the . . . human predicament. Our desire as Christian people is that God's name shall be glorified. But the moment we start with that we realize that there is this opposition. . . . There is another who is 'the god of this world'; there is a kingdom of darkness . . . and it is opposed to God and His glory and honour. But God . . . is yet going to establish His kingdom in this world of time. . . . He is again going to assert Himself and turn this world and all its kingdoms into His own glorious kingdom . . . running right through the Old Testament, there are the promises and the prophecies concerning the coming of the kingdom of God. . . . And, of course . . . when our Lord Himself was here on earth, this matter was very much in the forefront of men's minds. John the Baptist had been preaching his message, 'Repent ye: for the kingdom of heaven is at hand'. He called the people to be ready for it. And when our Lord began preaching, He said exactly the same thing. . . . At that immediate historical point He was teaching His disciples to pray that this kingdom of God should come increasingly and come quickly, but the prayer is equally true and equally right for us as Christian people in all ages until the end shall come.

Studies in the Sermon on the Mount, ii, pp. 62–3

Look at nothing and nobody but look entirely to Christ and say:

> My hope is built on nothing less
> Than Jesu's blood and righteousness,
> I dare not trust my sweetest frame,
> But wholly lean on Jesu's Name,
> On Christ the solid Rock I stand,
> All other ground is sinking sand.

You must so believe that as to be able to go further and say with holy boldness:

> The terrors of law and of God
> With me can have nothing to do,
> My Saviour's obedience and blood
> Hide all my trangressions from view.

Would you like to be rid of this spiritual depression? The first thing you have to do is to say farewell now once and for ever to your past. Realize that it has been covered and blotted out in Christ. Never look back at your sins again. Say, 'It is finished, it is covered by the Blood of Christ.' This is your first step. Take that and finish with yourself and all this talk about goodness, and look to the Lord Jesus Christ. It is only then that true happiness and joy are possible for you. What you need is not to make resolutions to live a better life, to start fasting and sweating and praying. No! you just begin to say:

> I rest my faith on Him alone
> Who died for my transgressions to atone.

Take that first step and you will find that immediately you will begin to experience a joy and a release that you have never known in your life before. 'Therefore we conclude that a man is justified by faith without the deeds of the Law.' Blessed be the Name of God for such a wondrous salvation for desperate sinners.

Spiritual Depression, p. 35

[Jesus] asks . . . Why do you allow yourself to be worried thus about the future? 'The morrow shall take thought for the things of itself. Sufficient unto the day is the evil thereof.' If the present is bad enough as it is, why go to meet the future? To go on from day to day is enough in and of itself; be content with that. . . . Worry about the future is so utterly futile and useless; it achieves nothing at all . . . worry is never of any value at all. This is seen with particular clarity as you come to face the future. Apart from anything else, it is a pure waste of energy because however much you worry you cannot do anything about it. In any case its threatened catastrophes are imaginary; they are not certain, they may never happen at all.

But above all that, says our Lord, can you not see that . . . you are mortgaging the future by worrying about it in the present? Indeed, the result of worrying about the future is that you are crippling yourself in the present; you are lessening your efficiency with regard to today . . . worry is something that is due to an entire failure to understand the nature of life in this world. . . . Man has to labour and must meet trials and troubles. . . .

The great question is, how are we to face them? According to our Lord, the vital thing is not to spend every day of your life in adding up the grand total of everything that is ever likely to happen to you in the whole of your life in this world. If you do that, it will crush you. That is not the way. Rather, you must think of it like this. There is, as it were, a daily quota of problems and difficulties in life. Every day has its problems; some of them are constant from day to day, some of them vary. But the great thing to do is to realize that every day must be lived in and of itself. . . . Here is the quota for today. Very well; we must face that and meet it; and He has already told us how to do so.

Studies in the Sermon on the Mount, ii, pp. 149–50

Take all the writing, preaching and teaching of the past hundred years. In a sense, human ability and effort have never exerted themselves to such an extent. Philosophy has been glorified and man has claimed that he could solve the riddle of life and of the universe. Never has man been so proud of himself and his achievements and his understanding. But what has been the result of all this? What of life today? Is it not clear that we are precisely in the same position as was the world in the time of Paul? Oh, the tragedy of it all! We have boasted of processes and systems, but they have yielded no results. We have taken pride in our ability to think, but it is the function of thinking to arrive at valid conclusions. Let us be honest. Are we any nearer to the solution of the problems of life and living than the philosophers were who lived and died before Paul? The answer is to be found in the state of the modern world. Our knowledge has grown merely with respect to the externals of life, its amenities and pleasures. Life itself still remains an enigma, and the art of living still seems to be as elusive as ever. The rival systems still fail and cannot satisfy our needs. But the gospel is not a human philosophy. It is not man's idea or the result of man's effort and seeking. It is the revelation of what God thinks and says concerning life.

The Plight of Man and the Power of God, pp. 81–2

A wonderful fashion of teaching He hath,
And wise to salvation He makes us through faith

[People] say, 'I know a person who does not claim to be a Christian, never goes to a place of worship, never reads the Bible, never prays, and frankly tells us he is not interested in these things at all. But, you know, I have a feeling that he is more of a Christian than many people who do go to a place of worship and who do pray. He is always nice and polite, never says a harsh word or expresses an unkind judgement and is always doing good.' . . . That is the kind of confusion that often arises through failure to be clear. . . .

Take this man who by nature appears to be such a fine Christian. If that is really a condition or state which conforms to the Beatitudes, I suggest that it is quite unfair, for it is a matter of natural temperament. . . . Some of us are born aggressive, others are quiet; some are alert and fiery, others are slow. We find ourselves as we are. . . . As people differ in their physical appearance, so they differ in temperament, and if that is what determines whether a man is a Christian or not, I say it is totally unfair.

But, thank God, that is not the position at all. Any one of us, every one of us, whatever we may be by birth and nature, is meant as a Christian to be like this . . . we can be like this. That is the central glory of the gospel. It can take the proudest man by nature and make him a man who is poor in spirit. There have been some wonderful and glorious examples of that. I would suggest there has never been a naturally prouder man than John Wesley; but he became a man who was poor in spirit. No; we are not concerned about natural dispositions or what is purely physical and animal, or what appears to simulate the Christian character. . . . Here are characteristics and dispositions that are the result of grace, the product of the Holy Spirit, and therefore possible for all. They cut right across all natural states and natural dispositions.

Studies in the Sermon on the Mount, i, pp. 35–6

True religion was never meant just to produce some general effect. The Bible is a revelation of God's ways with respect to man. It is meant to give 'understanding'. . . . There are many things that we could do that would make us feel better temporarily. There are many ways of forgetting our troubles for a while. Some go to the cinema, others run to the public-house or to the bottle of whisky which they keep at home. Under its effect and influence they feel much better and happier; their problem does not seem so acute. . . . There are many ways of giving temporary relief, but the question is, Do they give understanding, do they really help us to see through our trouble?

Now that sort of false comfort can be given in the house of God. There are some people who seem to think that the right thing to do in the house of God is just to go on singing choruses and a certain type of hymn until you are almost in a state of intoxication. Indeed, the whole service is with a view to 'conditioning'. You come under some emotional influence and you do feel better. . . .

Let us never forget that the message of the Bible is addressed primarily to the mind, to the understanding. There is nothing about the gospel that is more satisfying than this . . . it enables me to understand life. I have knowledge; I have understanding; I know. I can 'give a reason' for the hope that is in me. . . . Thank God that this man [Psalm 73] when he went into the sanctuary of God found an explanation. It was not merely some temporary relief that he received; it was not some kind of injection that was given to him to assuage the pain just a little for the moment, not a treatment that would leave the problem still there, so that when he got home and the effect had passed he would be back again where he was before. Not at all. Having started to think straight in the Temple of God he went home and continued to think straight. And it ended in the production of this Psalm!

Faith on Trial, pp. 44–5

It is sad and tragic that any Christian should ever be miserable . . . one of the reasons why the Christian Church counts for so little in the modern world is that so many Christians are in this condition. If all Christians simply began to function as the New Testament would have us do, there would be no problem of evangelism confronting the Church. . . . It is because we are failing as Christian people in our daily lives and deportment and witness that so few are attracted to God through our Lord Jesus Christ. So for that most urgent reason alone it behoves us to deal with this question.

. . . there are some Christians in this condition because they have never really understood clearly the great central doctrine of justification by faith. . . . The Protestant Reformation brought peace and happiness and joy into the life of the Church in a way she had not known since the early centuries, and it all happened because the central doctrine of justification by faith was rediscovered. It made Martin Luther rejoice and sing and he in turn was the means of leading others to see this great truth. It produced this great note of joy, and while we might hesitate to say that people who have not clearly understood this matter are not Christians at all, the moment they do understand it, they certainly cease to be miserable Christians and become rejoicing Christians.

Spiritual Depression, p. 37

[The Beatitudes] indicate clearly . . . *the essential, utter difference between the Christian and the non-Christian.* The New Testament regards [this difference] as something absolutely basic and fundamental; and . . . the first need in the Church is a clear understanding of this essential difference. It has become blurred; the world has come into the Church and the Church has become worldly. The line is not as distinct as it was. There were times when the distinction was clear cut, and those have always been the greatest eras in the history of the Church. We know, however, the arguments that have been put forward. We have been told that we have to make the Church attractive to the man outside, and the idea is to become as much like him as we can. There were certain popular padres during the first world war who mixed with their men, and smoked with them, and did this, that, and the other with them, in order to encourage them. Some people thought that, as a result, when the war was over, the ex-servicemen would be crowding into the churches. Yet it did not happen, and it never has happened that way. The glory of the gospel is that when the Church is absolutely different from the world, she invariably attracts it. It is then that the world is made to listen to her message, though it may hate it at first. That is how revival comes. That must also be true of us as individuals. It should not be our ambition to be as much like everybody else as we can, though we happen to be Christian, but rather to be as different from everybody who is not a Christian as we can possibly be. Our ambition should be to be like Christ, the more like Him the better, and the more like Him we become, the more we shall be unlike everybody who is not a Christian.

Studies in the Sermon on the Mount, i, pp. 36–7

We must learn to draw a distinction between being tempted and sinning. You cannot control the thoughts that are put into your mind by the devil. He puts them there. Paul talks of 'the fiery darts of the wicked one'. Now that is what had been happening to the Psalmist. [Psalm 73.] . . . The Lord Jesus Christ Himself was tempted. The devil put thoughts into His mind. But He did not sin, because He rejected them. Thoughts will come to you and the devil may try to press you to think that because thoughts have entered your mind you have sinned. But they are not your thoughts—they are the devil's—he put them there. It was the quaint Cornishman, Billy Bray, who put this in his own original manner when he said, 'You cannot prevent the crow from flying over your head, but you can prevent him from making a nest in your hair!' So I say that we cannot prevent thoughts being insinuated into our mind; but the question is what do we do with them? We talk about thoughts 'passing through' the mind, and so long as they do this, they are not sin. But if we welcome them and agree with them then they become sin. I emphasize this because I have often had to deal with people who are in great distress because unworthy thoughts have come to them. But what I say to them is this, 'Listen to what you are telling me. You say that thought "has come to you". Well, if that is true you are not guilty of sin. You do not say, "I have thought"; you say "the thought came". That is right. The thought came to you, and it came from the devil, and the fact that the thought did come from the devil means that you are not of necessity guilty of sin.' Temptation, in and of itself, is not sin.

Faith on Trial, p. 19.

All our great needs are summed up in [these three petitions]. 'Give us this day our daily bread.' 'Forgive us our debts, as we forgive our debtors.' 'And lead us not into temptation, but deliver us from evil.' Our whole life is found there in those three petitions, and that is what makes this prayer so utterly amazing. In such a small compass our Lord has covered the whole life of the believer in every respect. Our physical needs, our mental needs and, of course, our spiritual needs are included. The body is remembered, the soul is remembered, the spirit is remembered. And that is the whole of man, body, soul and spirit. Think of all the activities going on in the world at this moment, the organizing, the planning, the legislation and all other things; they are for the most part concerned with nothing but the body of man, his life and existence in this world of time. That is the tragedy of the worldly outlook, for there is another realm, the realm of relationships—the soul, the thing whereby man makes contact with his fellow man, the means of communication with one another and all social life and activity. It is all here. And above all, we have the spiritual, that which links man with God, and reminds him that he is something other than dust, and that as Longfellow says, 'Dust thou art, to dust returnest, was not spoken of the soul'. Man has been made this way; he cannot escape it, and our Lord has provided for it. We cannot fail to be impressed by the all-inclusiveness of these petitions. That does not mean that we should never enter into details; we must, we are taught to do so. We are taught to bring our life in detail to God in prayer; but here we have only the great headings. Our Lord gives us these and we fill in the details, but it is important for us to be sure that all our petitions should belong under one or other of the headings.

Studies in the Sermon on the Mount, ii, pp. 67–8

How different are the tests that men apply from what we find [in the gospel]! . . . We tend to forget the man himself in our interest in his various parts, and the various phases of his life and activities. . . . How numerous are the questions that men ask! How wide is their field of investigation, and how conflicting their opinions as to what really is the matter! . . . Some, like the Pharisees of old, are simply concerned about outward appearances. The only test they apply is that of outward morality and respectability. To others the one all-important question is the view which we may happen to hold on the subject of war or peace, or on the subject of alcohol, education, or housing. As long as our views on those questions satisfy them, they are agreed that we are Christians; and it is extraordinary to note the zeal and energy, not to say the fiery, warlike spirit, with which they are prepared to preach and propagate these views. To others, again . . . a Christian is, . . . first and foremost, one who subscribes to a certain number of general philosophical propositions. . . . What an utter travesty of the gospel! How false to its method! . . . the gospel has but one preliminary test. It is not our outward behaviour, our good deeds. Nor is it our intelligence, our view on some particularly pressing social question. It is not our wealth or poverty, our ignorance or our learning. It is just this one thing. How do we stand with God? Apart from all we are, and all we do, what about ourselves? It is the man himself in the depths, and at the centre, that really matters. The motive is more important than the action. The unseen is more important than the visible. . . . The vital thing, the only thing that really matters, is how we stand when we are face to face with God alone.

Truth Unchanged, Unchanging, pp. 84–6

Is not this one of the most wonderful things in the whole of Scripture, that the God who is the Creator and Sustainer of the universe, the God who is forming His eternal kingdom and who will usher it in at the end, the God to whom the nations are but as 'the small dust of the balance'—that such a God should be prepared to consider your little needs and mine even down to the minutest details in this matter of daily bread? But that is the teaching of our Lord everywhere. He tells us that even a sparrow cannot fall to the ground without our Father, and that we are of much greater value than many sparrows. . . . If only we could grasp this fact, that the almighty Lord of the universe is interested in every part and portion of us! . . . the smallest and most trivial details in my little life are known to Him on His everlasting throne. . . . But that is the way of God, 'the high and lofty One that inhabiteth eternity, whose name is Holy'; who nevertheless, as Isaiah tells us, dwells with him also 'that is of a contrite and humble spirit'. That is the whole miracle of redemption; that is the whole meaning of the incarnation which tells us that the Lord Jesus Christ takes hold of us here on earth and links us with the almighty God of glory. The kingdom of God, and my daily bread!

It must be emphasized, of course, that all we pray for must be absolute necessities. We are not told to pray for luxuries or super-abundance, nor are we promised such things. But we are promised that we shall have enough. . . . The promises of God never fail. But they refer to necessities only, and our idea of necessity is not always God's. But we *are* told to pray for necessities.

Studies in the Sermon on the Mount, ii, pp. 70–1

The people who had cast out devils and done many wonderful works in the name of Christ were quite sure of their salvation. They had no vestige of doubt about it. They believed that they were forgiven; they seemed to be at peace and to be enjoying the comforts of religion; they seemed to have spiritual power and were living a better life; they said, 'Lord, Lord'; and they wanted to spend their eternity with Him. Yet He said to them: 'I never knew you; depart from me, ye that work iniquity.' Do you realize that it is possible to have a false sense of forgiveness? Do you realize that it is possible to have a false peace within you? . . . You can have false peace, false comfort, false guidance. The man who never knows what it is to have certain fears about himself, fears which drive him to Christ, is in a highly dangerous condition. The devil can give you remarkable guidance. Telepathy, and all sorts of occult phenomena and various other agencies can do so too. There are powers that can counterfeit almost everything in the Christian life. . . .

According to our Lord's teaching, therefore, the similarities between the true and the false can include such matters and extend even so far as that. Nevertheless our Lord's teaching is that though there are many similarities between [the] two men and the two houses in the parable [Matthew 7:24–7], and in the realm of Christian profession, yet there is a vital difference. It is not obvious on the surface, but if you look for it, it is perfectly clear and unmistakable. . . . I can sum it up in the form of a question: What is your supreme desire? Are you out for the benefits and blessings of the Christian life and salvation, or have you a deeper and profounder desire? Are you out for the fleshly carnal results, or do you long to know God and to become more and more like the Lord Jesus Christ? Are you hungering and thirsting for righteousness?

Studies in the Sermon on the Mount, ii, pp. 303–4

. . . the proof that you and I are forgiven is that we forgive others. If we think that our sins are forgiven by God and we refuse to forgive somebody else, we are making a mistake; we have never been forgiven. The man who knows he has been forgiven, only in and through the shed blood of Christ, is a man who must forgive others. He cannot help himself. If we really know Christ as our Saviour our hearts are broken and cannot be hard, and we cannot refuse forgiveness. If you are refusing forgiveness to anybody I suggest that you have never been forgiven . . . whenever I see myself before God and realize even something of what my blessed Lord has done for me, I am ready to forgive anybody anything. I cannot withhold it, I do not even want to withhold it. . . . Pray to God and say, 'Forgive me O God as I forgive others because of what Thou hast done for me. All I ask is that Thou shouldst forgive me in the same manner; not to the same degree, because all I do is imperfect. In the same way, as it were, as Thou hast forgiven me, I am forgiving others. Forgive me as I forgive them because of what the cross of the Lord Jesus Christ has done in my heart.'

This petition is full of the atonement, it is full of the grace of God. We see how important it is by the fact that our Lord actually repeats it . . . (in [Matthew 6] verses 14 and 15) '. . . if ye forgive not men their trespasses, neither will your Father forgive your trespasses'. The thing is absolute and inevitable. True forgiveness breaks a man, and he must forgive. So that when we offer this prayer for forgiveness we test ourselves in that way. Our prayer is not genuine, it is not true, it is of no avail, unless we find there is forgiveness in our heart. God give us grace to be honest with ourselves.

Studies in the Sermon on the Mount, ii, pp. 75–6

. . . the whole idea of man as an economic unit is based upon . . . fallacy . . . they only see one aspect . . . the trouble with all these theories is that they are looking at only one side, one aspect, and so their solutions are partial and incomplete? What they are forgetting . . . is life itself. They are forgetting the sensibilities, and such factors as emotion . . . 'There are more things in heaven and earth, Horatio, than are dreamt of in your philosophy.' . . . That is how Shakespeare put it. I am not sure that Browning did not say it even better. . . . You remember the interview between the old Bishop and the young journalist who had become dissatisfied with the Christian religion [in *Bishop Bloughram's Apology*]? The young man was going to think life right through. He was going to break with everything he had been taught in the past, he was going to think things through for himself and make a new philosophy. The old Bishop said, in effect: Do you know, I was once a young man and I did exactly the same thing. I thought I had a perfect understanding, I assembled all the component parts, I had a complete scheme and philosophy of life, I thought nothing could upset it, but. . . . Just when we think, to use the modern jargon, we have the whole of life 'taped', just when we think our philosophy is perfect,

> Just when we are safest, there's a sunset-touch,
> A fancy from a flower-bell, some one's death,
> A chorus-ending from Euripides—
> And that's enough for fifty hopes and fears . . .
> The grand Perhaps.

You see what Browning means. With our rational mind we draw up our plan of life and think we can explain everything and that we have catered for everything. But just when we have done so . . . we see a sunset, a glorious, golden sunset that moves us to the very depth of our being, in a manner we cannot explain. . . . There is a mystery about it which we cannot fathom. . . . There is something else after all, beyond, above, behind all we can understand.

Faith on Trial, pp. 47–8

The Christian and the non-Christian are absolutely different in what they admire. The Christian admires the man who is 'poor in spirit', while the Greek philosophers despised such a man, and all who follow Greek philosophy, whether intellectually or practically, still do exactly the same thing. . . . The world believes in self-confidence, self-expression and the mastery of life; the Christian believes in being 'poor in spirit'. Take the newspapers and see the kind of person the world admires. You will never find anything that is further removed from the Beatitudes than that which appeals to the natural man and the man of the world. What calls forth his admiration is the very antithesis of what you find here. . . .

Then, obviously, they must be different in what they seek. 'Blessed are they which do hunger and thirst. . . .' After what? Wealth, money, status, position, publicity? Not at all. 'Righteousness.' . . . Take any man who does not claim to be a Christian. . . . Find out what he is seeking and what he really wants, and you will see it is always different from this.

Then, of course, they are absolutely different in what they do. That follows of necessity. . . . The non-Christian is absolutely consistent. He says he lives for this world. 'This', he says, 'is the only world, and I am going to get all I can out of it.' Now the Christian . . . regards this world as but the way of entry into something vast and eternal and glorious. His whole outlook and ambition is different. He feels, therefore, that he must be living in a different way. As the man of the world is consistent, so the Christian also ought to be consistent. If he is, he will be very different from the other man; he cannot help it. [See 1 Peter 2:11, 12]. . . . Another essential difference . . . is in their belief as to what they *can* do. The man of the world is very confident as to his own capacity. . . . The Christian is a man . . . who is truly aware of his own limitations.

Studies in the Sermon on the Mount, i, pp. 37–8

Once we have taken a problem to God, we should cease to concern ourselves with it. We should turn our backs upon it and centre our gaze upon God.

Is not this precisely where we go astray? We have a perplexity, and we have applied the prophetic method . . . [see December 20].But still we do not find satisfaction, and we do not quite know what to do. . . . Having failed to reach a solution, despite seeking the guidance of the Holy Spirit, there is nothing more to do but to take it to God in prayer. But so frequently . . . the moment we get up from our knees we begin to worry about the problem again.

Now if you do that, you might just as well not have prayed. If you take your problem to God, leave it with God. You have no right to brood over it any longer. . . . Leave it with God, and go on to the watch-tower [Habakkuk 2:1]. . . . We have to extricate ourselves deliberately, to haul ourselves out of it, as it were . . . and then take our stand looking to God—not at the problem. . . . Looking to God means not dealing with a problem yourself, not consulting other people, but depending entirely upon God, and 'waiting' only upon Him. . . .

That is the true basis of spiritual peace. That is exactly what Paul meant in Philippians, 'in nothing be anxious' (Philippians 4:6, 7). . . . You must never have that anxious care that is not only spiritually crippling but also physically debilitating. Never be anxious but 'in everything'—it is all-inclusive—'by prayer and supplication with thanksgiving let your requests be made known unto God'. . . . Get up into your watch-tower, and just keep looking up to God. Look at nothing else, least of all your problem.

From Fear to Faith, pp. 37–9

'Lead us not into temptation, but deliver us from evil.' That is the final request [in our Lord's Prayer] and it means this. We are asking that we should never be led into a situation where we are liable to be tempted by Satan. It does not mean that we are dictating to God what He shall or shall not do. God does test His children, and we must never presume to tell God what He is or is not to do. . . . But though it does not mean that we are to dictate to God, it does mean that we may request of Him that, if it be in accordance with His holy will, He should not lead us into positions where we can be so easily tempted, and where we are liable to fall. . . . This is what our Lord meant when He said to His disciples at the end, 'Watch and pray, that ye enter not into temptation.' There are situations which will be dangerous to you; watch and pray, always be on guard lest you fall into temptation. And coupled with that is this other aspect of the petition, that we pray to be delivered from evil. . . . We need to be delivered from it all. It is a great request, a comprehensive petition.

Why should we ask that we may be kept from evil? For the great and wonderful reason that our fellowship with God may never be broken. . . . Our supreme desire should be to have a right relationship with God, to know Him, to have un-interrupted fellowship and communion with Him. That is why we pray this prayer, that nothing may come between us and the brightness and the radiance and the glory of our Father which is in heaven. 'Lead us not into temptation, but deliver us from evil.'

Studies in the Sermon on the Mount, ii, pp. 76–7

It is the Holy Spirit alone who finally can give us an un-shakable assurance of salvation. . . . There are three main ways in which assurance comes to us. . . . The first is that which is to be obtained by believing and applying to ourselves the bare word of the Scripture as the authoritative word of God. . . . There is God's word; we believe it and rest upon it. . . . We need something further, which is the second ground of assur-ance. The First Epistle of John provides us with . . . certain tests of spiritual life. (i) 'We know that we have passed from death unto life, because we love the brethren.' (ii) . . . because we no longer find the commandments of the Lord to be grievous. They are a delight to us. . . . (iii) We believe in the Lord Jesus Christ. (iv) We are aware of the Spirit working in us. (v) We examine ourselves to see if any of the Spirit's fruit is being manifested in us. If we find these things, we can be assured that we are born again. . . .

There is, yet, however, a further form of assurance. It is the highest and most certain of all. . . . 'The Spirit itself beareth witness with our spirit, that we are the children of God. . . .' [Romans 8:15–17.] This is not a form of assurance that I may deduce from the Scriptures, or from evidences which I find in myself. Here is a direct witness of the Spirit. . . . Here is some-thing that the Spirit Himself alone can give us. It is He alone who can speak with a final authority which gives me certitude with regard to my being a child of God, a certitude as great, or greater indeed, as my certainty with regard to anything else in life . . . the saints throughout the centuries . . . declare that the Holy Spirit made them so certain of the reality and presence of the Lord Jesus Christ and His love for them, that they were more certain of that than of any other fact whatsoever. [See also 2 Corinthians 1:22; Ephesians 1:13, 14.]

Authority, pp. 76–8

*And shall we then for ever live
At this poor dying rate?*

It is difficult to describe this man (Mark 8:24). You cannot say that he is blind any longer. What then—is he or is he not blind? You feel that you have to say at one and the same time that he is blind and that he is not blind. He is neither one thing nor the other.

Now that is precisely the condition with which I am anxious to deal at the moment. I am concerned about those Christians who are disquieted and unhappy and miserable because of this lack of clarity. It is almost impossible to define them. You sometimes talk to this type and you think: 'This man is a Christian.' And then you meet him again and you are thrown into doubt at once and you say: 'Surely he cannot be a Christian if he can say a thing like that or do such a thing as that.' . . . Furthermore, the difficulty is that not only do others feel like this about these people, they feel it about themselves . . . they are unhappy because they are not clear about themselves. Sometimes when they have been in a service they will say: 'Yes, I am a Christian, I believe this.' Then something happens and they say: 'I cannot be a Christian. If I were a Christian I could not have such thoughts. I would not want to do the things I do.' . . . They seem to know enough about Christianity to spoil their enjoyment of the world, and yet they do not know enough to feel happy about themselves. They are 'neither hot nor cold'. They see and yet they do not see. . . . It is a distressing condition, and my whole message, as you may anticipate, is to say that nobody should be in it, and nobody should stay in it.

I go still further—*nobody need stay in that condition.*

Spiritual Depression, pp. 39–40

We must emphasize the fact that there is only 'one Lord'. This was the very essence of apostolic preaching. Peter states it unequivocally and boldly when he and John were arraigned before the authorities. 'There is none other name under heaven given among men, whereby we must be saved' (Acts 4:12). There is no other! There is no second! You cannot put anybody by His side. He is absolutely unique. He is no mere man, teacher, or prophet. He is the Son of God! He is the Lord of glory who has taken to Himself human nature! 'One Lord Jesus Christ'—and there is no other. Paul puts it thus in a memorable statement: 'For though there be that are called gods, whether in heaven or in earth . . . but to us there is but one God, the Father, of whom are all things, and we in him; and one Lord Jesus Christ, by whom are all things, and we by him' (1 Corinthians 8:5, 6). He expresses the same truth again in 1 Timothy 2:5: 'There is one God, and one mediator'—and only one—'between God and men, the man Christ Jesus.'

Now in this matter of Christian unity this is essential. The unity is the unity of those who believe that there is only 'one Lord', and that He is so perfect, and His work so perfect, that He needs no assistance. There is no 'co-redemptrix', such as the Roman Catholics claim the Virgin Mary to be. There is no assistant needed. The Christian does not need the supererogation of the saints, and does not need to pray to them. There is only one Mediator, and He is enough. He is complete in and of Himself, and nothing must be added to Him and His perfect completed work. . . . We look to this unique Lord, and we look at no one but Him. He is the first and the last, the Alpha and the Omega, the beginning and the end; He is the all and in all . . . 'One Lord'!

The Basis of Christian Unity, pp. 28–9

[In verse 19 (of Matthew 6)] our Lord introduces . . . this great question of the Christian living his life in this world in relationship to God as his Father, involved in its affairs and feeling its cares, its strains and its stresses. It is, in fact, the whole problem of what is so often called in the Bible, 'the world'. . . .

Now what do the Scriptures mean by the expression 'the world'? It does not mean the physical universe, or merely a collection of people; it means an outlook and a mentality, it means a way of looking at things, a way of looking at the whole of life. One of the most subtle problems with which the Christian ever has to deal is this problem of his relationship to the world. Our Lord frequently emphasizes that it is not an easy thing to be a Christian. He Himself when He was here in this world was tempted of the devil. He was also confronted by the power and subtlety of the world. The Christian is in precisely the same position. There are attacks which come upon him when he is alone, in private. There are others which come when he goes out into the world. You notice our Lord's order. [Matthew 6:17.] How significant it is. You prepare yourself in the secrecy of your own chamber. You pray and do various other things— fasting and almsgiving and doing your good deeds unobserved. But you also have to live your life in the world. That world will do its best to get you down, it will do its utmost to ruin your spiritual life. So you have to be very wary. It is a fight of faith, and you need the whole armour of God, because if you have not got it, you will be defeated. 'We wrestle not against flesh and blood.' It is a stern battle, it is a mighty conflict.

Studies in the Sermon on the Mount, ii, pp. 78–9

In a sense a depressed Christian is a contradiction in terms, and he is a very poor recommendation for the Gospel. We are living in a pragmatic age. People today are not primarily interested in Truth but they are interested in results. The one question they ask is: Does it work? They are frantically seeking and searching for something that can help them. Now we believe that God extends His Kingdom partly through His people, and we know that He has oftentimes done some of the most notable things in the history of the Church through the simple Christian living of some quite ordinary people. Nothing is more important, therefore, than that we should be delivered from a condition which gives other people, looking at us, the impression that to be a Christian means to be unhappy, to be sad, to be morbid, and that the Christian is one who 'scorns delights and lives laborious days'. There are many indeed who give this as a reason for not being Christian. . . . They say: Look at Christian people. . . . And they are very fond of contrasting us with people out in the world, people who seem to be so thrilled by the things they believe in. . . . They shout at their football matches, they talk about the films they have seen, they are full of excitement and want everybody to know it; but Christian people too often seem to be perpetually in the doldrums and too often give this appearance of unhappiness and of lack of freedom and of absence of joy. . . . It behoves us therefore . . . for the sake of the kingdom of God and the glory of the Christ in whom we believe, to represent Him and His cause, His message and His power in such a way that men and women, far from being antagonized, will be drawn and attracted as they observe us, whatever our circumstances or condition. We must so live that they will be compelled to say: Would to God I could be like that . . . and go through this world as that person does.

Spiritual Depression, pp. 11–12

[The gospel] *works*—it is '*the power* of God unto salvation'. It is not surprising that Paul uses the word 'power' in writing to Rome. That was their great word. And they tended to judge everything in terms of power. . . . power was to Rome what wisdom was to Athens. They would not consider anything unless it worked and had power . . . Paul knew that, and it was because he knew it that he uttered his challenge. Did they test a gospel by its results? Very well, he is ready to meet them. Nay, more; he is ready to challenge them. What had all their learning and culture and their multitude of religions really produced? If they were interested in results—well, let them produce them. . . . What is the point and the value of all the philosophies if they cannot deal with the problems of life? . . . He, Paul himself, had once boasted of the Jewish Law and of his success in keeping it. But he came to see that all of which he had boasted was merely something external; when he came to see the real inner spiritual meaning of the law, he discovered that he was an utter failure. He works out that theme in chapter 7 of [Romans]. All man's efforts to solve the problems of life fail, whether they be along purely intellectual lines, or consist in moral effort and striving, or in painful trudging along the mystic way. But the gospel which he, Paul, now preached, works! It had worked in his own life. It had changed and transformed everything. It had brought peace and rest to his soul and given victory in his life. And it had done the same to countless thousands of others. How did it do so? . . . the gospel alone faces and exposes, and really deals with, the fundamental problem of man and his needs. . . . It alone diagnoses accurately; it alone has the remedy.

The Plight of Man and the Power of God, pp. 84–5

The whole basis of society today . . . [is the assumption] that as long as man is put right in this respect and that, the result must be that ultimately he will be entirely right. That is the rationale of the modern belief in what is called the social application of the gospel. It is the basis also of the innumerable societies which clutter the religious ground like mushrooms. It is the background of the belief that by means of greater knowledge and instruction the ills of mankind can be cured. Never has the world been busier in trying to treat itself than it has been during the past hundred years. . . . But there is no question about the persistence of problems. . . . Leagues and movements against this or that particular sin, organizations to propagate various teachings. . . . Never was the mechanism for making life happy and enjoyable so elaborate and so perfected.

But what of the result? . . . All the effort seems to have resulted in failure, and that for the good reason . . . that the man himself has been forgotten. He can be put right in many respects and still remain miserable and unhappy in himself. Have we not all known men who are clever, cultured, well-mannered, popular, who, as far as one could see, had everything in their favour, and all that could be desired, but who nevertheless knew themselves to be utter failures in life, and were miserable in themselves? They could manage anyone and anything but themselves. A man may be clever. He may hold idealistic views on most subjects. He may perform many beneficent acts. But the question still is: What are his motives? Is he right at the centre?

Truth Unchanged, Unchanging, pp. 87–9

I hunger and I thirst;
Jesus, my manna be:
Ye living waters, burst
Out of the rock for me

What does it mean ['to hunger and thirst']? . . . It means a consciousness of our need, of our deep need . . . a consciousness of our desperate need; it means a deep consciousness of our great need even to the point of pain. It means something that keeps on until it is satisfied. It does not mean just a passing feeling, a passing desire. You remember how Hosea says to the nation of Israel that she is always, as it were, coming forward to the penitent form and then going back to sin. Her righteousness, he says, is as 'a morning cloud'—it is here one minute and gone the next. . . . 'Hunger' and 'thirst', these are not passing feelings. Hunger is something deep and profound that goes on until it is satisfied. It hurts, it is painful, it is like actual, physical hunger and thirst. It is something that goes on increasing and makes one feel desperate. It is something that causes suffering and agony. . . .

To hunger and thirst is to be like a man who wants a position. He is restless, he cannot keep still; he is working and plodding; he thinks about it, and dreams about it; his ambition is the controlling passion of his life. . . . 'Hungering and thirsting.' . . . The Psalmist has summed it up perfectly in a classical phrase: 'As the hart panteth after the water brooks, so panteth my soul after thee, O God . . .' Let me quote some words of the great J. N. Darby which I think put this exceedingly well. He says, 'To be hungry is not enough; I must be really starving to know what is in His heart towards me.' Then comes the perfect statement of the whole thing. He says, 'When the prodigal son was hungry he went to feed upon husks, but when he was starving, he turned to his father.' Now that is the whole position. To hunger and thirst really means to be desperate, to be starving, to feel life is ebbing out, to realize my urgent need of help.

Studies in the Sermon on the Mount, i, 80–1

May 7   　　　*There is a way which seemeth right unto a man,*
　　　　　　but the end thereof are the ways of death
　　　　　　　　　　　　　　　　　　　(Proverbs 14:12)

The importance of 'the end' is something which is constantly emphasized in the Bible.

Our Lord has put it once and for ever in the Sermon on the Mount. 'Enter ye in at the strait gate: for wide is the gate, and broad is the way, that leadeth to destruction, and many there be which go in thereat: because strait is the gate, and narrow is the way, which leadeth unto life, and few there be that find it.' . . . Look at the broad way, how marvellous it seems. You can go in with the crowd, you can do what everybody else is doing, and they are all smiling and joking. Wide and broad are the gate and the way. It all seems so marvellous. And this other seems so miserable—'strait is the gate'. One at a time, a personal decision, fighting self, taking up the cross. . . . And it is because they look only at the beginning that so many people are on the broad way. . . . They do not look at the end. . . .

The end of the one is destruction, of the other, life. The trouble in life today is that people look only at the beginning. Their view of life is what we may call the cinema or film-star view of life. It always attracts, and all those who live that life are apparently having a marvellous time. Alas that so many young people are brought up to think that that is life, and that always to live like that must be supreme happiness . . . people are attracted by the appearance. They look only at the surface; they look only at the beginning. They do not look at this type of life in its end; they give no thought whatsoever to the ultimate outcome. Nevertheless, it is as true today as it has ever been, and the Bible has always said it, that the end of these things is 'destruction'.

Faith on Trial, pp. 50–1

I remember very well the case of a man who was an outstanding surgeon in London and in great prominence. Suddenly to the amazement and astonishment of all who knew him it was announced that he had given it all up and had become a ship's doctor. What had happened to that man was this. He was a great man in his profession and he had legitimate ambitions with respect to certain honours in the profession. But disappointment in that respect suddenly opened his eyes to the whole situation. He arrived at the conclusion that there was no abiding satisfaction in the life he was living. He saw through it all, but he did not become a Christian. He just became cynical and left it all. There have been many other notable examples of men who have given up everything and have gone into some isolated position where they have found a measure of peace and happiness without becoming Christians. That is one possibility.

But they may even go further, they may see the excellences of the Christian life as indicated in the Sermon on the Mount. They say, 'There is no question at all about it, the Christian life is the life, if only everyone lived like that!' They may also have read the lives of the saints, and have recognized that these were men who had something wonderful about them. There was a time when they were not interested, but now they have come to see that the life depicted in the Sermon on the Mount is real life and living, and again, seeing life as portrayed in 1 Corinthians chapter 13, they say, 'If only we all lived like that, the world would be Paradise.' They have come to see that much very clearly.

Spiritual Depression, p. 41

Do you see how essentially different [the Christian] is from the non-Christian? The vital questions which we therefore ask ourselves are these. Do we belong to this kingdom? Are we ruled by Christ? Is He our King and our Lord? Are we manifesting these qualities in our daily lives? Is it our ambition to do so? Do we see that this is what we are meant to be? Are we truly blessed? Are we happy? Have we been filled? Have we got peace? I ask, as we [consider the Beatitudes], what do we find ourselves to be? It is only the man who is like that who is truly happy, the man who is truly blessed. It is a simple question. My immediate reaction to these Beatitudes proclaims exactly what I am. If I feel they are harsh and hard, if I feel that they are against the grain and depict a character and type of life which I dislike, I am afraid it just means I am not a Christian. If I do not want to be like this, I must be 'dead in trespasses and sins'; I can never have received new life. But if I feel that I am unworthy and yet I want to be like that, well, however unworthy I may be, if this is my desire and my ambition, there must be new life in me, I must be a child of God, I must be a citizen of the kingdom of heaven and of God's dear Son.

Let every man examine himself (1 Corinthians 11:28)

Studies in the Sermon on the Mount, i, p. 41

It is also the Holy Spirit alone who can give us true spiritual understanding of the Scriptures, an understanding of the doctrine. John puts this clearly (1 John 2:20). He is dealing with the 'anti-Christs', those people who had been in the Church, but who had gone out of the Church because they were not of it. They had thought that they were converted, and had been accepted as such. But they had now gone out. They had never really been true believers. . . . The question arises as to how we can differentiate. How were these ignorant first Christians, most of whom were slaves, to discriminate in these matters? John says, 'But ye have an unction from the Holy One, and ye know all things.' He repeats it in verse 27, 'But the anointing which ye have received of him abideth in you, and ye need not that any man teach you.'

There is an anointing and an unction given by the Holy Ghost which gives us understanding. And thus it has often come to pass in the long history of the Church that certain ignorant, more or less illiterate people have been able to discriminate between truth and error much better than the great doctors of the Church. They were simple enough to trust to the 'anointing', and thus they were able to distinguish between things that differ. The saintly Samuel Rutherford, that mighty man of God who lived three hundred years ago in Scotland, commented one day, 'If you would be a deep divine, I recommend to you sanctification.' Ultimately the way to understand the Scriptures and all theology is to become holy. It is to be under the authority of the Spirit. It is to be led of the Spirit.

Authority, pp. 78–9

[Jesus] says, 'Lay not up for yourselves treasures upon earth.' What does He mean by this? First of all we must avoid interpreting this only with respect to money. Many have done that, and have regarded this as a statement addressed only to rich people. That, I suggest, is foolish. It is addressed to all others also. He does not say, 'Lay not up for yourselves money', but 'Lay not up for yourselves treasures'. 'Treasures' is a very large term and all-inclusive. It includes money, but it is not money only. It means something much more important. Our Lord is concerned here not so much about our possessions as with our attitude towards our possessions. . . . There is nothing wrong in having wealth in and of itself; what can be very wrong is a man's relationship to his wealth. And the same thing is true about everything that money can buy.

Indeed we go further. It is a question of one's whole attitude towards life in this world. Our Lord is dealing here with people who get their main, or even total satisfaction in this life from things that belong to this world only. What He is warning against here . . . is that a man should confine his ambition, his interests and his hopes to this life . . . it becomes a much bigger subject than the mere possession of money. Poor people need this exhortation . . . quite as much as the rich. We all have treasures in some shape or form. It may not be money. It may be husband, wife or children. . . . To some people their treasure is their house. That whole danger of being house proud, of living for your house and home is dealt with here. No matter what it is . . . if it is everything to you, that is your treasure, that is the thing for which you are living. This is the danger against which our Lord is warning us at this particular point.

Studies in the Sermon on the Mount, ii, pp. 80–1

How can you plan for life and the world and at the same time exclude God who is the Maker and Sustainer and Controller of all things? God has not only made the world, He is actively concerned in it, and constantly intervenes in its affairs. His laws are absolute and cannot be avoided. . . . God has decided and ordered and arranged that a life of forgetfulness of Him, and of antagonism to Him, shall not be successful and happy. . . . That is the whole story of mankind from the very beginning, and it has continued until this day, and it will continue to be so until the end of time. Mankind has refused to recognize this —indeed, has ridiculed it. It has been confident that it could succeed without God. But what of the results? Constant failure. God cannot be thwarted. The facts of life, the story of history, proclaim the wrath of God against all ungodliness and unrighteousness. That is our first problem. We have sinned against God. We are in the wrong relationship to Him. His wrath is upon us. We have made it impossible for Him to bless us. . . . None can keep the law. . . . Is there no hope, therefore? Can nothing be done? God be thanked, the gospel of Christ provides the answer. . . . God has dealt with our sins in Christ. The demands of holiness and justice have been satisfied. . . . God in Christ is prepared to receive us. . . . God in Christ offers us pardon and forgiveness, and instead of cursing, blessing. Without God we cannot be happy, 'for there is no peace, saith my God, to the wicked'. Try as we will, and as mankind has, we cannot succeed. The first step is to have the favour of God, and in Christ it is gloriously possible—indeed, it is offered us.

The Plight of Man and the Power of God, pp. 85–7

. . . [Some] people . . . never fully accept the teaching and the authority of the Scriptures. . . . They do not come to the Bible and submit themselves utterly and absolutely to it. If only we came to the Scriptures as little children and took them at their face value and allowed them to speak to us, this sort of trouble would never arise. These people will not do that. What they do is to mix their own ideas with spiritual truth. Of course they claim that basically they take it from the scriptures, but, and that is the fatal word, they immediately proceed to modify it. They accept certain biblical ideas, but there are other ideas and philosophies which they desire to bring with them from their old life. They mix natural ideas with spiritual ideas. They say that they like the Sermon on the Mount and 1 Corinthians, chapter 13. They claim that they believe in Christ as Saviour, but still they argue that we must not go too far in these matters, and that they believe in moderation. Then they begin to modify the Scriptures. They refuse to accept it authoritatively in every respect, in preaching and living, in doctrine and world outlook. 'Circumstances are changed', they say, 'and life is not what it used to be. We are now living in the twentieth century.' So they modify it here and there to suit their own ideas instead of taking Scriptural doctrine right through from beginning to end, and confessing the irrelevancy of talk about the twentieth century. This is God's Word which is timeless, and because it is God's Word we must submit to it and trust Him to employ His own methods in His own way.

Spiritual Depression, pp. 44–5

There is no entry into the kingdom of heaven . . . [for one] who is not *poor in spirit*. It is the fundamental characteristic of the Christian and of the citizen of the kingdom of heaven, and all the other characteristics are in a sense the result of this one . . . it really means an emptying, while the others are a manifestation of a fullness. We cannot be filled until we are first empty. You cannot fill with new wine a vessel which is partly filled already with old wine, until the old wine has been poured out. . . . There are always these two sides to the gospel; there is a pulling down and a raising up. You remember the words of the ancient Simeon concerning our Lord and Saviour when he held Him as an Infant in his arms. He said, 'this child is set for the fall and rising again of many'. The fall comes before the rising again. It is an essential part of the gospel that conviction must always precede conversion; the gospel of Christ condemns before it releases. Now that is obviously something which is fundamental. If you prefer me to put it in a more theological and doctrinal form, I would say that there is no more perfect statement of the doctrine of justification by faith only than this Beatitude: 'Blessed are the poor in spirit: for theirs (and theirs only) is the kingdom of heaven.' Very well then, this is the foundation of everything else.

Studies in the Sermon on the Mount, i, p. 42

I remember once reading a phrase in an article written by a man about a meeting in which he had listened to two speakers. It was a political, not a religious meeting, but what he said about those two speakers came to me as a conviction from the Holy Spirit. He said that, as he listened to the two men, he felt that this was the main difference between them: the first had spoken brilliantly as an advocate; the second had spoken as a witness. And I asked myself, which am I? Am I an advocate of these things or am I a witness? You can be an advocate of Christianity without being a Christian. You can be an advocate of these things without experiencing them. . . . You can present all the arguments. . . . And it may sound wonderful. But you may be standing outside the true experience of it the whole time. You may be talking about something which you do not really know, about Someone you have never met. You are an advocate, perhaps even a brilliant advocate. But note what the Lord said to the apostles: 'Ye shall be my witnesses.'

. . . What the Holy Ghost does with His authority is to make us *witnesses*. . . . After the resurrection . . . our Lord came to these men who had been with Him for three years and said: 'But ye shall receive power, after that the Holy Ghost is come upon you: and ye shall be witnesses . . .' (Acts 1:8). . . . Here were men who had been with Him for three years. They knew Him intimately, they had listened to His sermons, they had seen His miracles. They had stood there and had watched Him as He died upon the cross. They had seen Him buried. . . . They knew that He had risen from the dead . . . (see Luke 24). If ever men were in a position to testify to the resurrection and to all the facts about the Lord, it was these disciples. And yet what our Lord told them is that they would be quite unable to do it until they had been baptized with the Holy Ghost.

Authority, pp. 82–3

> *A stranger in the world below,*
> *I calmly sojourn here;*
> *Nor can its happiness or woe*
> *Provoke my hope or fear*

The great fact of which we must never lose sight is that in this life we are but pilgrims. We are walking through this world under the eye of God, in the direction of God and towards our everlasting hope. . . . That is the great principle taught in Hebrews 11. Those mighty men, those great heroes of the faith had but one purpose. They walked 'as seeing him who is invisible'. They said they were 'strangers and pilgrims on the earth', they were making for 'a city which hath foundations, whose builder and maker is God'. So when God called out Abraham he responded. He turned to a man like Moses who had amazing prospects in the Egyptian court and commanded him to leave it all and to become a miserable shepherd for forty years, and Moses obeyed. . . . And so with all of them. What made Abraham ready to sacrifice his beloved son Isaac? What made all the other heroes of the faith prepared to do the things they did? It was that they desired 'a better country, that is, an heavenly'.

. . . If we have a right view of ourselves in this world as pilgrims . . . everything falls into its true perspective. We shall immediately take a right view of our gifts and our possessions. We begin to think of ourselves only as stewards who must give an account of them. We are not the permanent holders of these things. . . . The worldly man thinks he himself owns them all. But the Christian starts by saying, 'I am not the possessor of these things; I merely have them on lease. . . . I cannot take my wealth with me, I cannot take my gifts with me. I am but a custodian of these things'. And, at once, the great question that arises is: 'How can I use these things to the glory of God? . . . It is to Him that I shall have to render up an account of my stewardship. . . . Therefore I must be careful how I use these things. I must do all the things He tells me to do in order that I may please Him.'

Studies in the Sermon on the Mount, ii, p. 84

Why is it that man ever chooses to sin? The answer is that man has fallen away from God . . . and his whole nature has become perverted and sinful. Man's whole bias is away from God. . . . He objects to the whole idea of God and the demands which God makes upon him. . . . Furthermore, man likes and covets the things which God prohibits, and dislikes the things and the kind of life to which God calls him. These are no mere dogmatic statements. They are facts. . . . But all who are not Christian face the facts in such a superficial manner that their proposals with respect to them must of necessity fail. . . . [They ignore] the central problem, which is: Why should man ever desire the wrong? . . . Man's very nature is fallen. Man is wrong at the centre of his being, and therefore everything is wrong. . . . What can be done for him? . . . Can man change the whole bias of his life? Give him new clothing, provide him with a new house in new surroundings, entertain him with all that is best and most elevating, educate him and train his mind, enrich his soul with frequent doses of the finest culture ever known, do all and more, but still he will remain the same essential man. . . . Man needs a new nature. Whence can he obtain it? There is but one answer, in Jesus Christ the Son of God. He came from Heaven and took upon Him human nature perfect and whole. He is God and man. In Him alone are the divine and the human united. And He offers to give us His own nature. . . . All who believe on Him, and receive Him, obtain this new nature. . . . Those who hated God now love Him and desire to know more and more about Him. Their supreme desire now is to please Him and to honour and to glorify Him. . . . And this in turn brings them into an entirely new relationship with their fellow men. Loving the Lord their God first, they find themselves loving their neighbours as themselves. . . . A new society is only possible when we have new men; and Christ alone can produce new men.

The Plight of Man and the Power of God, pp. 87–9

There is nothing so hopeless in the world . . . as the bankruptcy of the non-Christian view of life. . . . Charles Darwin . . . confessed at the end of his life that, as a result of concentrating on one aspect only of life, he had lost the power to enjoy poetry and music, and to a large extent even the power to appreciate nature itself. Poor Charles Darwin. . . . The end of H. G. Wells was very similar. He who had claimed so much for the mind and human understanding, and who had ridiculed Christianity with its doctrines of sin and salvation, at the end of his life confessed that he was baffled and bewildered. The very title of his last book—*Mind at the End of its Tether*—bears eloquent testimony to the Bible's teaching about the tragedy of the end of the ungodly. Or take the phrase from the autobiography of a rationalist such as Dr Marrett who was the head of a college in Oxford. . . . 'But to me the war brought to a sudden end the long summer of my life. Henceforth I have nothing to look forward to but chill autumn and still chillier winter, and yet I must somehow try not to lose heart.' The death of the ungodly is a terrible thing. Read their biographies. Their glittering days are at an end. . . . They have nothing to look forward to, and, like the late Lord Simon, try to comfort themselves by reliving their former successes and triumphs. . . .

In the Book of Proverbs we read that 'the way of the wicked is as darkness'. 'But the path of the just is as the shining light, that shineth more and more unto the perfect day' (Proverbs 4: 19, 18). What a glory! . . . then listen to the Apostle Paul (2 Timothy 4:6–8). . . . One of John Wesley's proudest claims for his early Methodists was, 'Our people die well.' . . . The Bible everywhere urges us to consider our 'latter end'. . . . Yield yourself to Him and rely upon Him and His power. . . . And the end will be glorious.

Faith on Trial, pp. 51–3

What then is the cure? What is the right way? It is to be honest and to answer our Lord's question truthfully and honestly. . . . He turned to this man (Matthew 8:22–26) and asked, 'Do you see aught?' And the man said, absolutely honestly, 'I do see, but I am seeing men as if they were trees walking.' What saved this man was his absolute honesty. Now . . . where do we stand? What exactly do we see? Have we got things clearly? Are we happy? Do we really see? We either do or we do not, and we must know exactly where we are. Do we know God? Do we know Jesus Christ? Not only as our Saviour but do we know Him? Are we 'rejoicing with joy unspeakable and full of glory'? That is the New Testament Christian. Do we see? Let us be honest. . . .

What then? Well, the last step is to submit yourself to Him, to submit yourself utterly to Him as this man did. He did not object to further treatment, he rejoiced in it, and I believe that if our Lord had not taken the further step he would have asked Him to do so. And you can do the same. Come to the Word of God. . . . Say 'I want the truth whatever it costs me' . . . plead with Him to give you clear sight, perfect vision, and to make you whole . . . I promise you in His Blessed Name that He will do it. He never leaves anything incomplete. . . . This man was healed and restored and 'saw every man clearly'. The Christian position is a clear position. We are not meant to be left in a state of doubt and misgiving, of uncertainty and unhappiness. . . . He came that we might see clearly, that we might know God. He came to give eternal life and 'This is eternal life, that they may know thee the only true God and Jesus Christ whom thou hast sent.' . . . He is pledged to do it and He will do it, and you will no longer be an uncertain Christian seeing and not seeing. You will be able to say, 'I see, I see in Him all I need and more, and I know that I belong to Him.'

Spiritual Depression, pp. 47–8

. . . [The first Beatitude (Matthew 5:3)] is obviously, therefore, a very searching test for every one of us, not only as we
face ourselves, but especially as we come to face the whole
message of the Sermon on the Mount. You see, it at once
condemns every idea of the Sermon on the Mount which thinks
of it in terms of something that you and I can do ourselves,
something that you and I can carry out. It negatives that at
the very beginning. That is where it is such an obvious condemnation of all those views which . . . think of it as being a
new law, or in terms of bringing in a kingdom amongst men.
We do not hear so much of that talk now, but it still lingers and
it was very popular in the early part of this century. Men talked
about 'bringing in the kingdom', and always used as their text
the Sermon on the Mount. They thought of the Sermon as
something that can be applied. You have to preach it and then
men immediately proceed to put it into practice. But this view
is not only dangerous, it is an utter denial of the Sermon itself,
which starts with this fundamental proposition about being
'poor in spirit'. The Sermon on the Mount, in other words,
comes to us and says, 'There is the mountain that you have to
scale, the heights you have to climb; and the first thing you must
realize, as you look at that mountain which you are told you
must ascend, is that you cannot do it, that you are utterly
incapable in and of yourself, and that any attempt to do it in
your own strength is proof positive that you have not understood it.' It condemns at the very outset the view which regards
it as a programme for man to put into operation immediately,
just as he is.

                    Studies in the Sermon on the Mount, i, p. 43

May 21　　　*In an Early Christian prayer-meeting:*
　　　　　　RHODA: Peter is standing outside!'
　　　　　　THE OTHERS: 'You're crazy!'
　　　　　　What had they been praying for, then?
　　　　　　And why were they 'amazed'? (see Acts 12:5–16)

. . . *we must look for the answer.* 'I will watch to see', says Habakkuk [2:1]. The military watchman's task is to keep his eye on that landscape in front for the slightest indication of movement on the part of the enemy. Habakkuk is looking for the answer. We so often fail because we just pray to God and then forget about it. If we pray to God we must expect answers to our prayers. . . .

God, of course, may answer in a number of different ways. For instance, you can expect God to answer you as you read His Word, for it is the commonest way of all in which He does this. As you are reading Scripture, suddenly a strange and wonderful light is cast upon your problem. . . .

Then God sometimes answers directly in our spirits. . . . God speaks to me by speaking in me. . . . He can impress something upon our spirits in an unmistakable manner. . . . So does God answer at times.

Then again He sometimes answers our prayers by so providentially ordering our circumstances, and the day-to-day happenings of our lives, that it becomes quite plain what God is saying. God never calls us to do any work without opening the door. He may take a long time, but if God wants us to do some special task He will shut other doors and open that particular one. Our whole life will be directed to that end. This is a common experience of the Christian life. . . . God's will is certain. The point is that we must be *looking* for these answers, and ready to recognize them when they come. Having committed my problem to God I must expect God to answer. I should also compare one indication of guidance with another, because if God is always consistent with Himself in His dealings with me, I can expect them all to converge.

From Fear to Faith, pp. 39–40

The so-called rich young ruler . . . was right in many different respects; and yet, when he met our Lord, he became convinced that he had a real need and a lack at the very centre of his life. Was not this also the case with Martin Luther before his conversion? He had spent his time in fasting and prayer and sweating. He was trying to put his life in order . . . and yet, in spite of heroic efforts, he remained centrally miserable and unhappy. But when the glorious doctrine about justification by faith suddenly dawned upon him, and was made plain to him, Luther was put right at the centre and became the mighty reformer whose works we know. John Wesley may serve as another example of the need of a Christ-centre in one's life. There was never a more sincere and honest man. There was never a man who gave such time and energy to the improving of himself. He suffered persecution in Oxford in order that he might preach to the prisoners in the gaols. He eventually gave up his college fellowship and prospects, and crossed the Atlantic to preach to the slaves in Georgia, all in an effort to put himself right. And yet he found that although he had dealt with many aspects and portions of his life, he still remained centrally unhappy and defeated. And then he tells how, quietly, in that meeting in the room in Aldersgate Street in London, he felt his heart suddenly strangely warmed. John Wesley himself had at last been put right in the centre. His soul had come to that direct knowledge of God which is to be found in Jesus Christ. The eye had been made single, and John Wesley was a new man.

Truth Unchanged, Unchanging, pp. 89–90

Do I tell myself every day I live, that this is but another milestone I am passing, never to go back, never to come again? I am pitching my moving tent 'a day's march nearer home'. . . . I am a child of the Father placed here for His purpose, not for myself. I did not choose to come; I have not brought myself here; there is a purpose in it all. God has given me this great privilege of living in this world, and if He has endued me with any gifts, I have to realize that, although in one sense all these things are mine, ultimately, as Paul shows at the end of 1 Corinthians 3, they are God's. Therefore, regarding myself as one who has this great privilege of being a caretaker for God, a custodian and a steward, I do not cling to these things. They do not become the centre of my life and existence, I do not live for them or dwell upon them constantly in my mind; they do not absorb my life. On the contrary, I hold them loosely; I am in a state of blessed detachment from them. I am not governed by them; rather do I govern them; and as I do this I am steadily securing, and safely laying up for myself 'treasures in heaven'. . . .

The Lord Jesus Christ tells us to lay up for ourselves treasures in heaven, and the saints have always done so. They believed in the reality of the glory that awaited them. They hoped to get there and their one desire was to enjoy it in all its perfection and in all its fullness. If we are anxious to 'follow in their train' and to enjoy the same glory we had better listen to our Lord's exhortation, 'Lay not up for yourselves treasures upon earth . . . but lay up for yourselves treasures in heaven.'

Studies in the Sermon on the Mount, ii, p. 85

Let us realize that we can be orthodox but yet dead. Let us realize that we can be highly intellectual and theological and be useless. Let us realize that even our proclamation of this Word in our own strength and power is finally null and void. 'Mighty through God'! Through the power of God! . . . If ever a man could have used his brain, his reason, his logic, and relied upon them it was [Paul]. But he didn't. . . . The power and the authority and the demonstration were to be 'of God'. . . . Listen to him again in 1 Corinthians 4:2: he says '. . . the kingdom of God is not in word, but in power'. It is the mighty power of the Holy Ghost; and apart from this we can do nothing. . . . At the beginning of the eighteenth century certain orthodox men could see the position falling away and they said, what can we do to safeguard the Truth? They decided to set up what are called The Boyle Lectures . . . they were designed to defend the Christian Faith. And a great bishop . . . wrote a book, Bishop Butler's *Analogy*. He was going to defend the Christian Faith. And another man called Paley did much the same thing.

But they were not what saved the situation, good as they were. What saved the situation? . . . It was the Holy Ghost coming upon George Whitefield at his ordination. It was John Wesley's heart being 'strangely warmed' in Aldersgate Street on May 24, 1738. It was the outpouring of the Spirit of God. It was the power! 'Mighty through God'! For here is the very power that had floored and humbled, and convinced the Apostle Paul himself. . . . He had to be knocked down, he had to be humbled, he had to be floored. . . . The same happened to the great St Augustine, the same to Luther, the same to Calvin, the same to Blaise Pascal. It is the same thing with all of them with their giant intellects, and learning and understanding. And it is as true tonight as it has ever been throughout the running centuries.

The Weapons of our Warfare, pp. 22–3

God has . . . revealed Himself in nature, and the Apostle
Paul argues in Romans (1:19ff.) that we are without excuse if
we do not see Him there. . . . God has also revealed Himself in
history. Further, God has revealed Himself to the Old Testament fathers in various ways. But, as evangelical Christians, we
start with the great central fact of the Lord Jesus Christ. The
whole Bible is really about *Him*. The Old Testament looks
forward to Him. It tells us that Someone is coming. The
promise seems vague, nebulous and indefinite at some points,
clearer and more specific at others. But there it is. God is
going to do something, and Someone will come. At last, the
Voice will be heard. An Authority is going to speak. The Old
Testament attitude is one of waiting on tiptoe, as it were. Then,
of course, as soon as we come to the New Testament we find it
is full of Him. . . .

When the Apostle Paul (our great example in this matter of
preaching, teaching and evangelizing) went to Corinth . . . he
determined solemnly . . . 'not to know anything among them,
save Jesus Christ, and him crucified'. . . . Paul decided that he
was not going to waste his time with them in arguing about
presuppositions. He was not going to start with a preliminary
philosophical argument and then gradually lead them on into
the truth. No! He begins by proclaiming authoritatively the
Lord Jesus Christ . . . we must come back to this. . . . We must
become fools for Christ's sake, says Paul . . . (1 Corinthians 3:
18). We assert Him, we proclaim Him, we start with Him,
because He is the ultimate and the final Authority. . . . He is
really at the centre of the whole of our position and the whole
of our case rests upon Him . . . the really big claim which is
made in the whole of the New Testament, is for the supreme
authority of the Lord Jesus Christ.

Authority, pp. 13–15

How complex and how complicated is the modern treatment of the parts of man's life! How futile, too, when the central principle is not right. If the eye is evil the whole body also must be full of darkness, however great the struggle to make the different parts light. If the well is poisoned, the stream issuing from it must constantly contain poison, however great the effort to cleanse bucketfuls. James expresses the idea thus in his Epistle: 'From whence come wars and fightings among you? Come they not hence, even of your lusts that war in your members?' (James 4:1). Or as our Lord reminds us, 'Out of the heart proceed evil thoughts, murders, adulteries, fornications, thefts, false witness, blasphemies (Matthew, 15:19). What needs to be treated therefore is the centre, the heart, the cause of the trouble and not the various manifestations. Either make the tree good and its fruit good, or else make the tree corrupt and its fruit corrupt (Matthew 7:15–20) we are adjured by our Lord. Treatment must start at the centre. It is not what man does, or what he knows, or anything about him which needs to be put right but man himself in his fundamental central relationship to God. It is a poor physician who treats the symptoms and complications only and ignores the disease. And the disease is the soiled and tarnished condition of man's soul as the result of sin. His spiritual eye is beclouded and blinded. The light of God cannot enter it. All the darkness within is due to that and that alone. That alone needs to be treated. How simple and direct is the gospel!

Truth Unchanged, Unchanging, pp. 90–1

May 27   *The world is but a broken toy,*
                            Its pleasure hollow—false its joy,
                            Unreal its loveliest hue (W. S. Gilbert)

Our Lord is saying (Matthew 6:19) that worldly treasures do
not last; that they are transitory, passing, ephemeral. 'Change
and decay in all around I see.' '. . . where moth and rust doth
corrupt'.

How true it is. There is an element of decay in all these
things, whether we like it or not. . . . These things never fully
satisfy. There is always something wrong with them; they
always lack something. There is no person on earth who is
fully satisfied; and though in a sense some may appear to have
everything that they desire, still they want something else. . . .

There is another way of looking at the effect of moth and
rust spiritually. Not only is there an element of decay in these
things; it is also true that we always tend to tire of them. . . .
That is why we are always talking about new things and seeking
them. Fashions change; and though we are very enthusiastic
about certain things for a while, soon they no longer interest
us as they did. . . . The last fact, therefore, about these things
is that they inevitably perish. Your most beautiful flower is
beginning to die immediately you pluck it. You will soon have
to throw it away. That is true of everything in this life and
world. . . . Things develop holes and become useless . . . the most
perfect physique will eventually give way and break down and
die. . . . However wonderful and beautiful and glorious things
may be, they all perish. That is why, perhaps, the saddest of
all failures in life is the failure of the philosopher who believes
in worshipping goodness, beauty and truth; because there is
no such thing as perfect goodness, there is no such thing as
unalloyed beauty; there is an element of wrong and of sin and
a lie in the highest truths. 'Moth and rust doth corrupt.'

Studies in the Sermon on the Mount, ii, pp. 88–9

148

The Bible . . . does not merely record history. It helps us to understand the meaning of history. It teaches certain principles very clearly. The first is that all things, even the evil powers, are under God's hand. . . . Nothing happens apart from God. 'The Lord reigneth.' . . . It is of vital importance that we should grasp the biblical doctrine of Providence. It can be defined as, 'That continued exercise of the divine energy whereby the Creator upholds all His creatures, is operative in all that transpires in the world, and directs all things to their appointed end.' . . . In connexion with this we have to remember God's permissive will. It is beyond our understanding, but it is clearly taught that He permits certain things to happen for His own purposes.

Another thing we see clearly here is that the whole position of the ungodly is precarious and dangerous. They are in 'slippery places'. All they have is but temporary. . . . Age and decay, death and judgement, are certain. The most terrible thing about sin is that it blinds men to the realization of this. They do not see that their pomp and glory is but for a season. . . .

The Psalmist saw this so clearly in the sanctuary of God [Psalm 73] that he not only ceased to be envious of the ungodly, but we get the impression that he even began to feel sorry for them as he realized the truth about their position. Thus, his thinking with respect to the ungodly was put right, and there is perhaps no better test of our own profession of the Christian faith than just this. Do we feel sorry for the ungodly in their blindness? Have we even a sense of compassion for them as we see them as sheep without a shepherd?

Faith on Trial, p. 55

The gospel is not something partial or piecemeal: it takes in the whole of life, the whole of history, the whole world. It tells us about the creation and the final judgement and everything in between. It is a complete, whole view of life, and many are unhappy in the Christian life because they have never realized that this way of life caters for the whole of man's life and covers every eventuality in his experience. There is no aspect of life but that the gospel has something to say about it. The whole of life must come under its influence because it is all-inclusive; the gospel is meant to control and govern everything in our lives. . . . So many, because they . . . only apply their Christianity to certain aspects of their lives, are bound to be in trouble. It is quite inevitable. That is the first thing we see here. We must realize the greatness of the gospel, its vast eternal span. We must dwell more on the riches, and in the riches, of these great doctrinal absolutes. We must not always stay in the Gospels. We start there but we must go on; and then as we see it all worked out and put into its great context we shall realize what a mighty thing the gospel is, and how the whole of our life is meant to be governed by it.

Spiritual Depression, pp. 55–6

. . . I have noticed at times a tendency even to fail to
appreciate what is regarded by the Bible as the greatest virtue
of all, namely, humility. I have heard people on a committee
discuss a certain candidate and say, 'Yes, very good; but he is
rather lacking in personality,' when my opinion of that particular candidate was that he was humble. There is a tendency . . .
to justify a man's making use of himself and his own personality and trying to put it forward, or as the horrible phrase
has it, 'to put it across'. The advertisements that are being
increasingly used in connexion with Christian work proclaim
this tendency very loudly. You read the old records of the
activities of God's greatest workers, the great evangelists and
others, and you observe how self-effacing they were. But today,
we are experiencing something that is almost a complete
reversal of this. . . .

What does it mean? 'We preach not ourselves', says Paul,
'but Christ Jesus the Lord.' When he went to Corinth, he tells
us, he went 'in weakness, and in fear, and in much trembling'.
He did not step on to the platform with confidence and assurance and ease, and give the impression of a great personality.
Rather, the people said of him, 'His appearance is weak and his
speech contemptible'. How far we tend to wander from the
truth and the pattern of the Scriptures. Alas! How the Church
is allowing the world and its methods to influence and control
her outlook and life. To be 'poor in spirit' is not as popular
even in the Church as it once was and always should be.
Christian people must re-think these matters. Let us not take
things on their face value; let us above all avoid being captivated
by this worldly psychology; and let us realize from the outset
that we are in the realm of a kingdom which is unlike everything that belongs to this 'present evil world'.

Studies in the Sermon on the Mount, i, pp. 46–7

We must believe that God is always true to His word, and that His promises never fail. So, having committed myself and my problem to God, I must persist in looking with an eagerness which knows that God is certain to answer. It is dishonouring to Him not to do so. If I believe that God is my Father, and that the very hairs of my head are all numbered, and that God is much more concerned about my welfare and my well-being than I am myself; if I believe that He is much more concerned about the honour of His great and holy name than I am, then it is surely dishonouring to Him not to look for an answer after I have prayed to Him. . . . The men of faith not only prayed, but they expected answers. Sometimes, in a panic, we pray to God; then, after the panic is over, we forget all about it. The test of our faith is whether we expect an answer. [Habakkuk] stood upon his watch, and set him upon the tower. Though he could not understand God's actions, he took the problem to God and then looked for an answer. . . . It is an absolute law in the spiritual realm that if we adopt Habakkuk's method, and behave as he behaved, God will always honour His promises. In effect, God said, 'It is all right, Habakkuk, I have heard your prayer, I understand your perplexity. Here is My answer. The Chaldeans whom I am going to raise up to punish Israel will themselves in turn be routed and destroyed.' The greatness of the Chaldeans was going to be short-lived. . . . God told the prophet to write the prophecy very clearly, so that anyone reading it could at once understand and run to obey and warn others.

From Fear to Faith, pp. 40–2

'Lay up for yourselves treasures in heaven, where neither moth nor rust doth corrupt, and where thieves do not break through nor steal.' This is wonderful and full of glory . . . these heavenly things are imperishable and the thieves cannot break through and steal. Why? Because God Himself is reserving them for us. There is no enemy that can ever rob us of them, or can ever enter in. It is impossible because God Himself is the Guardian. Spiritual pleasures are invulnerable, they are in a place which is impregnable . . . (Romans 8:3f.). Furthermore, there is nothing impure there; naught that corrupts shall enter in. There is no sin there, nor element of decay. It is the realm of eternal life and eternal light . . . Heaven is the realm of life and light and purity, and nothing belonging to death, nothing tainted or polluted can gain admission there. It is perfect; and the treasures of the soul and of the spirit belong to that realm. . . .

It is an appeal to common sense. Do we not know that these things are true? Are they not true of necessity? Do we not see it all as we live in this world? Take up your morning newspaper and look at the death column; look at all that is happening. We know all these things. Why do we not practise them and live accordingly? Why do we lay up treasures on earth when we know what is going to happen to them? And why do we not lay up treasures in heaven where we know that there is purity and joy, holiness and everlasting bliss?

Studies in the Sermon on the Mount, ii, pp. 90–1

. . . we often fail to realize the greatness and the wholeness of the message, we also fail to realize that the whole man must likewise be involved in it and by it—'Ye have obeyed from the heart the form of doctrine delivered unto you'. Man is . . . mind, he is heart and he is will. . . . God has given him a mind, He has given him a heart, He has given him a will whereby he can act. Now one of the greatest glories of the gospel is this, that it takes up the whole man. . . . there is nothing else that does that; it is only this complete gospel, this complete view of life and death and eternity, that is big enough to include the whole man. It is because we fail to realize that, that many of our troubles arise. We are partial in our response to this great gospel. . . . Sometimes . . . you will find people who have one part of their personality engaged only—head only, heart only, will only. We will agree that they must be wrong. Yes, but let us be clear . . . it is equally wrong to have any two only. It is equally wrong to have the head and the heart only without the will, or the head and the will without the heart, or the heart and the will without the head. . . . The Christian position is three-fold; it is the three together, and the three at the same time, and the three always. A great gospel like this takes up the whole man, and if the whole man is not taken up, think again as to where you stand. . . . What a gospel! What a glorious message! It can satisfy man's mind completely, it can move his heart entirely, and it can lead to wholehearted obedience in the realm of the will. That is the gospel. Christ has died that we might be complete men, not merely that parts of us may be saved; not that we might be lop-sided Christians, but that there may be a balanced finality about us.

Spiritual Depression, pp. 56, 60

. . . what is the [meaning] of being 'poor in spirit' . . . ? It is that Isaiah said (57:15): 'For thus saith the high and lofty One that inhabiteth eternity, whose name is Holy; I dwell in the high and holy place, with him also that is of a contrite and humble spirit, to revive the spirit of the humble, and to revive the heart of the contrite ones.' That is the quality of spirit, and you have endless illustrations of it in the Old Testament. It was the spirit of a man like Gideon, for instance, who, when the Lord sent an angel to tell him the great thing he was to do, said, 'No, no, this is impossible; I belong to the lowest tribe and to the lowest family in the tribe.' That was not Uriah Heep, it was a man who really believed what he said and who shrank from the very thought of greatness and honour, and thought it was incredible. It was the spirit of Moses, who felt deeply unworthy of the task that was laid upon him and was conscious of his insufficiency and inadequacy. You find it in David, when he said, 'Lord, who am I that thou shouldst come to me?' The thing was incredible to him; he was astonished by it. You get it in Isaiah in exactly the same way. Having had a vision, he said, 'I am a man of unclean lips'. That is to be 'poor in spirit', and it can be seen right through the Old Testament.

But let us look at it in the New Testament. You see it perfectly, for instance, in a man like the Apostle Peter who was naturally aggressive, self-assertive and self-confident—a typical modern man of the world, brimful of this confidence and believing in himself. But look at him when he truly sees the Lord. He says, 'Depart from me; for I am a sinful man, O Lord.' Look at him afterwards as he pays his tribute to the Apostle Paul, in 2 Peter 3:15, 16. But . . . he never ceases to be a bold man; he does not become nervous and diffident. . . . The essential personality remains; and yet he is 'poor in spirit' at the same time.

Studies in the Sermon on the Mount, i, p. 49–50

It is no part of the gospel to denounce pleasure and enjoyment; in fact, the gospel offers a joy greater than anything else can give. But it is not content with testing by this one standard only. It desires to know the nature of the joys or the pleasures, whether it is good, whether it is true, and whether it is beautiful. . . . Men and women today do not like thought processes and discrimination. Like children, they desire to do what they like. . . . They therefore hate discipline and the facing of difficulty. They object to the inconvenience of having to face the questions of truth, goodness, evil, and beauty. They do what they want to do, pleading the rightness of self-expression. They have but one standard of value, that of pleasure. . . . They are content with the one test only—is it enjoyable? . . . Is not this utterly suicidal, judged by the true standard of human nature? . . . if you desire merely to satisfy the lust and the craving for pleasure, then go in for the modern cult. But if you desire the whole of yourself to be developed and expressed, regard this suggestion as the very suggestion of hell itself. . . .

But . . . let us apply the practical test. Read the Bible. . . . Was David the King of Israel at his best and highest, was he expressing his true self when he applied the single test of pleasure in the matter of Bathsheba, thereby becoming a thief and a murderer? Was St Augustine giving the truer expression to self when he was an immoral philosopher, or rather afterwards, when he became the disciplined saint. . . . Think of all the members of the noble army of saints and martyrs who have denied themselves . . . and obeyed the teaching of the gospel! Compare and contrast them with the sensuous . . . libertines of history. . . . The way to express self truly is the way of discipline and order, the way of reason and prayer. . . . You will have a self that will be worthy of expression, and which will grow from day to day.

Truth Unchanged, Unchanging, pp. 25–8

The Christian should know why he is a Christian. The Christian is not a man who simply says that something marvellous has happened to him . . . he is able and ready 'to give a reason for the hope that is in him'. If he cannot, he had better make sure of his position. The Christian knows why he is what he is, and where he stands. He has had doctrine presented to him, he has received the truth. This 'form of sound teaching' has come to him. It came to his mind, and it must ever start with his mind. Truth comes to the mind and to the understanding enlightened by the Holy Spirit. Then having seen the truth the Christian loves it. It moves his heart. He sees what he was, he sees the life he was living, and he hates it. If you see the truth about yourself as a slave of sin you will hate yourself. Then as you see the glorious truth about the love of Christ you will want it, you will desire it. So the heart is engaged. Truly to see the truth means that you are moved by it and that you love it. You cannot help it. If you see the truth clearly, you must feel it. Then that in turn leads to this, that your greatest desire will be to practise it and to live it.

That is Paul's whole argument. He says: Your talk about continuing in sin is unthinkable. If you only realized your unity with Christ, that you have been planted together in the likeness of His death and have therefore risen with Him, you could never speak like that. You cannot be joined to Christ and be one with Him, and at the same time ask 'shall we continue in sin?' Does this great truth give me licence to go on doing those things which formerly appealed to me? Of course not. It is inconceivable. A man who knows and believes that he is 'risen with Christ' will inevitably desire to walk in newness of life with Him.

Spiritual Depression, pp. 61–2

Here was a man, with great powers, and obviously, as a natural man, fully aware of them. But in reading his Epistles you will find that the fight he had to wage to the end of his life was the fight against pride. That is why he kept on using the word 'boasting'. Any man gifted with powers is generally aware of them; he knows he can do things, and Paul knew this. He has told us in that great third chapter of the Epistle to the Philippians about his confidence in the flesh. If it is a question of competition, he seems to say, he fears no one; and then he gives us a list of the things of which he can boast. But having once seen the risen Lord on the road to Damascus all that became 'loss', and this man, possessed of such tremendous powers, appeared in Corinth . . . 'in weakness and fear and much trembling'. That is the position right through, and, as he goes on with the task of evangelism, he asks, 'Who is sufficient for these things?' If any man had a right to feel 'sufficient' it was Paul. Yet he felt insufficient because he was 'poor in spirit'.

But of course, we see this most of all as we look at the life of our Lord Himself. He became a Man, He took upon Him 'the likeness of sinful flesh'. Though He was equal with God He did not clutch at the prerogatives of His Godhead. He decided that while He was here on earth He would live as a man, though He was still God. And this was the result. He said, 'I can do nothing of myself.' It is the God-Man speaking. 'I can do nothing of myself!' He said also, 'The words that I speak unto you I speak not of myself; but the Father that dwelleth in me, he doeth the works' (John 14:10). 'I can do nothing, I am utterly dependent upon Him.' That is it. And look at His prayer life. It is as you watch Him praying, and realize the hours He spent in prayer, that you see His poverty of spirit and His reliance upon God.

Studies in the Sermon on the Mount, i, p. 50

Sin . . . entered human life from the outside and it attacked even the Son of God. That I am forgiven is glorious, that I have a new nature is wonderful and still better. But still I am left to face this terrible power that is set over against me, and which strives ever to defeat me. . . . It has defeated the mightiest and the strongest. It has not hesitated to match its strength even with God Himself. Its subtlety and suggestions meet me everywhere. Who am I to confront such a foe? What is man at his best against such an antagonist? . . . Man cannot, for all men have failed. . . . Is all hopeless? Must we continue to strive and strive in vain? No! A David has appeared and smitten this Goliath; a Jonathan has routed the Philistines again. The Man has entered the lists and delivered the enemy a mortal wound from which he can never recover. . . .

Jesus of Nazareth, the Son of God, has conquered Satan. Tried and tested to the utmost, He not only emerged unscathed, but hath 'cast out the prince of this world'. . . . He has conquered death and the grave and every power that is inimical to man and his highest interests. The Lion of the tribe of Judah has prevailed—yea, and not only for Himself, but for us. He offers us His own power and promises to clothe us with His own might. Not only need we not be defeated any longer; in Him we can become more than conquerors over any and every power that may raise itself against us.

These are the problems of the world. . . . They are exposed in the gospel and they are solved by it. Christ satisfies every need and He alone does so. He has 'done all things well'. The message of the gospel is about Him and what He has done. It is not theory. It works, it is a fact as the lives of Christians of all ages testify. Ashamed of Jesus? A thousand times no!

The Plight of Man and the Power of God, pp. 89–91

These New Testament people had believed and had become Christian, and yet it was necessary for the Apostles Paul and Peter and John and others to write letters to them because they were in trouble in one way or another. They were unhappy for various reasons, they were not enjoying the Christian life. Some were tempted to look back to the life out of which they had been saved; others were tempted severely, others persecuted cruelly. Thus the very existence of the New Testament Epistles shows us that unhappiness is a condition which does afflict Christian people. There is in this, therefore, a strange kind of comfort which is nevertheless very real. If anyone reading my words is in trouble, let me say this: The fact that you are unhappy or troubled is no indication that you are not a Christian; indeed, I would . . . say that if you have never had any trouble in your Christian life I should very much doubt whether you are a Christian at all. . . . The whole of the New Testament and the history of the Church throughout the centuries bear eloquent testimony to the fact that this is a 'fight of faith'; and not to have any troubles in your soul is, therefore, far from being a good sign. It is, indeed, a serious sign that there is something radically wrong, and there is a very good reason for saying that. For from the moment we become Christians we become the special objects of the attention of the devil. As he besieged and attacked our Lord, so does he besiege and attack all the Lord's people. 'Count it all joy', says James, 'when ye fall into divers temptations' or trials. That is the way your faith is proved, . . . in a sense it is a proof that you have faith. It is because we belong to Him that the devil will do his utmost to disturb and upset us. He cannot rob us of our salvation, thank God, but . . . he can make us miserable.

Spiritual Depression, pp. 65–6

Thou didst not spare Thine only Son,
But gav'st Him for a world undone,
And freely with that blessèd One,
Thou givest all

A farmer one day went happily and with great joy in his heart to report to his wife and family that their best cow had given birth to twin calves, one red and one white. And he said, 'You know I have suddenly had a feeling and impulse that we must dedicate one of these calves to the Lord. We will bring them up together, and when the time comes we will sell one and keep the proceeds, and we will sell the other and give the proceeds to the Lord's work'. His wife asked him which he was going to dedicate to the Lord. 'There is no need to bother about that now,' he replied, 'we will treat them both in the same way, and when the time comes we will do as I say'. . . . In a few months the man entered his kitchen looking very miserable and unhappy. When his wife asked him what was troubling him, he answered, 'I have bad news to give you. The Lord's calf is dead.' 'But', she said, 'you had not decided which was to be the Lord's calf.' 'Oh yes', he said; 'I had always decided it was to be the white one, and it is the white one that has died. The Lord's calf is dead.' We may laugh at that story, but God forbid that we should be laughing at ourselves. It is always the Lord's calf that dies. When money becomes difficult, the first thing we economize on is our contribution to God's work. It is always the first to go. Perhaps we must not say 'always', for that would be unfair; but with so many it is the first thing, and the things we really like are the last to go. . . . These things tend to come between us and God, and our attitude to them ultimately determines our relationship to God. The mere fact that we believe in God, and call Him Lord, Lord, and likewise with Christ, is not proof in and of itself that we are serving Him, that we recognize His totalitarian demand.

Studies in the Sermon on the Mount, ii, pp. 95–6

Men said that Christ and His saints slept
(The English Chronicle c. 1140 AD)

The Psalmist asks, 'Will the Lord cast off for ever? and will he be favourable no more? Is his mercy clean gone for ever? doth his promise fail for evermore? Hath God forgotten to be gracious?' ... some of the greatest saints have sometimes been tempted to ask these questions when things have gone against them. ... Does God care, and if He does care why does He not stop these things? Is it that He cannot? And so doubts about the character of God lead to doubts about His power.

How often people have asked these questions! How often did people say in the last World War: Why does God permit a man like Hitler to live? If He is God and is all-powerful why doesn't He strike him down? ...

Now this man had been assailed by just such questions, and here, now, he finds his answer. At once he is put right by remembering the greatness and the power of God:—'*thou* didst set them in slippery places' [Psalm 73:18]. There is nothing outside the control of God. ... It is, indeed, one of the great themes of the Bible. ... He is eternal in all His powers and in all His attributes. 'He spake, and it was done'. ...

'In the beginning God.' That is a fundamental postulate; the Bible asserts it everywhere. Whatever the explanation may be of all that is happening in the world, it is not that God is not capable of stopping it. ... He is absolute; He is the everlasting, eternal God to whom everything on earth is but as nothing. He owns everything; He governs. He controls everything; all things are under His hands. 'The Lord reigneth.'

Faith on Trial, pp. 56–7

[Satan] persuades a man that by denying God he is being rational; but . . . what is really happening is that he makes him a creature of lust and desire whose mind is blinded and whose eye is no longer single. The greatest faculty of all has become perverted.

If you are not a Christian do not trust your mind; it is the most dangerous thing you can do. But when you become a Christian your mind is put back in the centre and you become a rational being. There is no more pathetic illusion than for a man to think of the Christian faith as sob-stuff, the dope of the people, something purely emotional and irrational. The true view of it is stated perfectly by the Apostle Paul in Romans 6:17. You have 'obeyed from the heart that form of doctrine which was delivered you'. The doctrine was preached to them, and when they came to see it they liked it, believed it, and put it into practice. They received the truth of God first of all with the mind. Truth must be received with the mind, and the Holy Spirit enables the mind to become clear. That is conversion, that is what happens as the result of regeneration. The mind is delivered from this bias of evil and darkness; it sees the truth and loves and desires it above everything else. That is it. There is nothing more tragic than for a man to find at the end of his life that he has been entirely wrong all the time.

Studies in the Sermon on the Mount, ii, pp. 105–6

The trouble with this type of unhappy Christian is that he does not really believe the Scriptures. . . . You say: 'My trouble is that terrible sin which I have committed.' Let me tell you in the Name of God that that is not your trouble. Your trouble is unbelief. You do not believe the Word of God. I am referring to the First Epistle of John and the first chapter where we read this: 'If we confess our sins, He is faithful and just to forgive us our sins and to cleanse us from all unrighteousness.' That is a categorical statement. . . . There is no limit to it. . . . Whatever your sin—it is as wide as that—it does not matter what it is, it does not matter what it was, 'if we confess our sins He is faithful and just to forgive us our sins and to cleanse us from all unrighteousness.' So if you do not believe that word, and if you go on dwelling on your sin, I say that you are not accepting the Word of God, you are not taking God at His word, you do not believe what He tells you and that is your real sin. . . . 'What God hath cleansed, that call thou not common' (Acts 10:15). . . . That is precisely what I would say at this moment to anybody who may have been held in depression by the devil for a number of years over some particular sin. . . . I do not care what it is. . . . 'The blood of Jesus Christ His Son cleanseth us from all sin' and all unrighteousness. Believe the Word of God, my friend. . . . Believe God's Word. Do not ask Him for a message of forgiveness. He has given it to you. Your prayer may well be an expression of unbelief at that point. Believe Him and His Word.

Spiritual Depression, pp. 72–3

. . . am I poor in spirit? How do I really feel about myself as I think of myself in terms of God, and in the presence of God? . . . what are the things I am saying, what are the things I am praying about, what are the things I like to think of with regard to myself? What a poor thing it is, this boasting of the things that are accidental and for which I am not responsible, this boasting of things that are artificial and that will count as nothing at the great day when we stand in the presence of God. This poor self! That hymn of Lavater's puts it perfectly: 'Make this poor self grow less and less', and 'O Jesus Christ, grow Thou in me'.

How does one therefore become 'poor in spirit'? The answer is that you do not look at yourself or begin by trying to do things to yourself. That was the whole error of monasticism. Those poor men . . . said, 'I must go out of society, I must scarify my flesh and suffer hardship, I must mutilate my body.' No, no, the more you do that the more conscious will you be of yourself, and the less 'poor in spirit' . . . look at God. Read this Book about Him, read His law, look at what He expects from us, contemplate standing before Him. It is also to look at the Lord Jesus Christ and to view Him as we see Him in the Gospels. The more we do that the more we shall understand the reaction of the apostles when, looking at Him and something He had just done, they said, 'Lord, increase our faith. . . . We thought we had something because we had cast out devils and preached Thy word, but now we feel we have nothing; increase our faith.' . . . Look at Him, keep looking at Him. Look at the saints, look at the men who have been most filled with the Spirit and used. But above all, look again at Him.

Studies in the Sermon on the Mount, i, pp. 51–2

Things may be going wrong with you. . . . Blow upon blow may be descending upon you. You have been living the Christian life, reading your Bible, working for God, and yet the blows have come. . . . Everything seems to be going wrong. . . . One trouble follows hard after another. . . . Are you able to say in the face of it all, 'God is always good?' . . . Are you able to say, 'All things work together for good' without any hesitation? That is the test. But . . . while the Psalmist says, 'God is always good to Israel', he is careful to add, 'Even to such as are of a clean heart'. . . . if you and I are sinning against God, then God will have to deal with us, and it is going to be painful. But even when God chastises us He is still good to us. It is because He is good to us that He chastises us. . . . But . . . if we want to see this clearly we must be of a clean heart. . . .

I sometimes think that the very essence of the whole Christian position, and the secret of a successful spiritual life, is just to realize two things. They are in these first two verses [of Psalm 73]. . . . I must have complete, absolute confidence in God, and no confidence in myself. As long as you and I are in the position in which we 'worship God in the Spirit, and rejoice in Christ Jesus, and have no confidence in the flesh' all is well with us. That is to be truly Christian. . . . If I take that view of myself, it means that I shall always be looking to God. And in that position I shall never fail.

May God grant us grace to apply some of these simple principles to ourselves and, as we do so, let us remember that we have the greatest and the grandest illustration of it all in our blessed Lord Himself. I see Him in the Garden of Gethsemane, the very Son of God, and I hear Him uttering these words, 'Father, if it be possible. . . .' There was perplexity. . . . But He humbled Himself. . . . He just committed Himself to God saying in effect, 'Thy ways are always right, Thou art always good. . . . Not My will, but Thine, be done'.

Faith on Trial, pp. 20–1

[Habakkuk 2] verse 4 reads 'but the just shall live by his faith.' . . . This important statement is quoted several times in the New Testament. Scholars disagree as to the exact translation of the first part of the verse. Either it can be 'His soul which is lifted up is not upright in him' (AV) or, as quoted in Hebrews 10:38, where it is stated that God has no pleasure in the soul of him that draws back (or withdraws himself). The truth stated is that there are only two possible attitudes to life in this world: that of faith and that of unbelief. Either we view our lives in terms of our belief in God, and the conclusions which we are entitled to draw from that; or our outlook is based upon a rejection of God and the corresponding denials. We may either 'withdraw' ourselves from the way of faith in God, or else we may live by faith in God. The very terms suggest corresponding ways of life. As a man believes so is he. . . . The just, the righteous, shall live by faith; or, in other words, the man who lives by faith is righteous. On the other hand, the man who 'draws back' is unrighteous because he is not living by faith. Here is the great watershed of life, and all of us are on one side of it or the other. Whatever my political or philosophical views may be, they must have this common denominator; either my life is based on faith or it is not. If it is not, it does not much matter what my views may be, or whether I am controlled by political, social, economic, or any other considerations. What matters is whether I am accepting God's rule or not.

From Fear to Faith, p. 50

This . . . marks off the Christian as being quite unlike the man who is not a Christian and who belongs to the world. . . . The one thing the world tries to shun is mourning; its whole organization is based on the supposition that that is something to avoid. The philosophy of the world is, Forget your troubles; turn your back on them, do everything you can not to face them. . . . The whole organization of life, the pleasure mania, the money, energy and enthusiasm that are expended in entertaining people, are all just an expression of the great aim of the world to get away from this idea of mourning and this spirit of mourning. But the gospel says, 'Happy are they that mourn.' Indeed, they are the only ones who are happy! [see also Luke 6]. . . .

This . . . is something which is never found in the world . . . this is something which is not as evident in the Church today as it once was and as it is in the New Testament . . . [an] idea has gained currency that if we as Christians are to attract those who are not Christians we must deliberately affect an appearance of brightness and joviality . . . not something that rises from within, but something which is put on. . . .

I cannot help feeling that the final explanation of the state of the Church today is a defective sense of sin and a defective doctrine of sin. Coupled with that, of course, is a failure to understand the true nature of Christian joy . . . [these things,] working together, of necessity produce a superficial kind of person and a very inadequate kind of Christian life. . . . It is not surprising that the Church is failing in her mission if her dual conception of sin and joy are thus defective and inadequate . . . conviction must of necessity precede conversion, a real sense of sin must come before there can be a true joy of salvation. . . . So many people spend all their lives in trying to find this Christian joy. . . . They want joy apart from the conviction of sin. But that is impossible; it can never be obtained.

Studies in the Sermon on the Mount, i, pp. 53–6

You and I must never look at our past lives; we must never look at any sin in our past life in any way except that which leads us to praise God and to magnify His grace in Christ Jesus. I challenge you to do that. If you look at your past and are depressed by it . . . you must do what Paul did. 'I was a blasphemer', he said, but he did not stop at that. Does he then say, 'I am unworthy to be a preacher of the gospel'? In fact he says the exact opposite: 'I thank Christ Jesus our Lord who hath enabled me, for that he counted me faithful putting me into the ministry.' When Paul looks at the past and sees his sin he does not stay in a corner and say, 'I am not fit to be a Christian, I have done such terrible things'. Not at all. What it does to him, its effect upon him, is to make him praise God. He glories in grace and says, 'And the grace of our Lord was exceeding abundant with faith and love which is in Christ Jesus.'

That is the way to look at your past. So, if you look at your past and are depressed, it means that you are listening to the devil. But if you look at the past and say, 'Unfortunately it is true I was blinded by the god of this world, but thank God His grace was more abundant, He was more than sufficient and His love and mercy came upon me in such a way that it is all forgiven, I am a new man', then all is well. That is the way to look at the past, and if we do not do that, I am almost tempted to say that we deserve to be miserable. Why believe the devil instead of believing God? Rise up and realize the truth about yourself, that all the past has gone, and you are one with Christ, and all your sins have been blotted out once and for ever. O let us remember that it is sin to doubt God's word, it is sin to allow the past, which God has dealt with, to rob us of our joy and our usefulness in the present and in the future.

Spiritual Depression, pp. 75–6

He that spared not His own Son, how shall he not also with him freely give us all things?

[Our Lord's] argument [Matthew 6:25] is a very profound and powerful one; and how prone we are to forget it! He says in effect, 'Take this life of yours about which you are tending to worry and become anxious. How have you got it? Where has it come from?' And the answer, of course, is that it is a gift from God. . . . So the argument which our Lord uses is this. If God has given you the gift of life—the greater gift—do you think He is now suddenly going to deny Himself and His own methods, and not see to it that that life is sustained and enabled to continue? God has His own ways of doing that, but the argument is that I need never become anxious about it. Of course I am to plough and sow and reap and gather into barns. I am to do the things that God has ordained for man and life in this world. I must go to work and earn money and so on. But . . . I need never be concerned or worried or anxious that suddenly there will not be sufficient to keep this life of mine going. That will never happen to me; it is impossible. If God has given me the gift of life, He will see to it that that life is kept going. [Jesus] is not arguing as to *how* this will be done. He is just saying that it will be.

I commend to your study, as a matter of great interest and vital importance, the frequency with which that argument is used in the Scriptures. . . . It is a very common biblical argument, the argument from the greater to the lesser, and we must always be watching for it and applying it. The Giver of the gift of life will see that the sustenance and support of that life will be provided . . . that is exactly what God does with the [birds of the air]. They have to find their food, but it is He who provides it for them; He sees that it is there for them.

Studies in the Sermon on the Mount, ii, pp. 113–14

The disciples received [the power of the Holy Spirit] on the day of Pentecost. . . . Peter began to preach immediately with boldness, authority and power, and three thousand were converted. We read in Acts 4 that the authorities could not dispute the boldness with which Peter and John bore witness to the resurrection and said these things. It was nothing but a manifestation of the Holy Ghost. The same Peter who had been so nervous and so apprehensive (indeed, who had been such a coward that, because he was afraid of losing his life, he had denied his own Lord, his greatest Friend and Benefactor), now stands up with boldness ready to confront the whole world and all the devils in hell, and proclaims this Jesus whom he had so recently denied. . . . What is this? The authority of the Holy Spirit, the Holy Spirit manifesting His authority in an extraordinary manner.

We read later that after these men had been arrested and had become free again, they met together and had a prayer meeting (Acts 4:23–33). 'When they had prayed, the place was shaken where they were assembled together, and they were all filled with the Holy Ghost, and they spake the word of God with boldness'. . . . Again, in Acts 4:33 we find that 'with great power gave the apostles witness of the resurrection of the Lord Jesus. . . .' What was the secret of their power? That they were able to argue scientifically that resurrection is possible? That they were able to reconcile the miraculous with the scientific? No! It was the authority and power of the Holy Ghost turning these men into living witnesses who were irresistible. 'And great grace was upon them all.'

Authority, pp. 83–4

June 20

To appoint unto them that mourn in Zion, to give unto them a garland for ashes, the oil of joy for mourning, the garment of praise for the spirit of heaviness

To 'mourn' is . . . quite inevitable. As I confront God and His holiness, and contemplate the life that I am meant to live, I see myself, my utter helplessness and hopelessness. . . . But it obviously does not stop there. A man who truly faces himself . . . is a man who must of necessity mourn for his sins also . . . if I bemoan these things in myself, I am truly mourning.

Yet the Christian does not stop even at that. The man who is truly Christian . . . mourns also because of the sins of others. . . . He sees that the whole world is in an unhealthy and unhappy condition. He knows that it is all due to sin; and he mourns because of it.

That is why our Lord Himself mourned. . . . He saw this horrid, ugly, foul thing called sin which had come into life . . . and had upset life and made life unhappy. . . .

That is what is meant by mourning in this spiritual sense in the New Testament. . . . It is the very antithesis of the spirit and mind and outlook of the world, which, as our Lord puts it, 'laughs now'. . . . It laughs, and says, 'Don't dwell too much upon these things'. . . . The Christian man's attitude is essentially different. . . .

[But] our Lord in these Beatitudes makes a complete statement and it must be taken as such. 'Blessed are they that mourn', He says, 'for they shall be comforted.' The man who mourns is really happy, says Christ; that is the paradox. In what respect is he happy? . . . The man who truly mourns because of his sinful state and condition is a man who is going to repent; he is, indeed, actually repenting already. . . . If we truly mourn, we shall rejoice, we shall be made happy, we shall be comforted. . . . That is the astounding thing about the Christian life. Your great sorrow leads to joy, and without the sorrow there is no joy.

Studies in the Sermon on the Mount, i, pp. 58–60

172

[The Psalmist] is very sorry for himself. There is nothing wrong with his life. He is a very good man. But he is being very hard pressed, he is being dealt with very unfairly, and even God seems to be unfair to him. That is how he thought about himself while he was outside the sanctuary. But inside the sanctuary all this is changed. '. . . So foolish was I, and ignorant: I was as a beast before thee' [Psalm 73:22]. What a transfiguration! What an entirely different view of himself! And it is all the result of his thinking being put right, and made truly spiritual. . . .

This man . . . not only reveals his honesty and his sincerity, and the truthfulness that was so essentially a part of his make-up, but also—and this is the thing I want to emphasize—he displays an understanding of the nature of the spiritual life.

In these two verses [21–22] we have this man's account of his repentance. We learn what he said to himself about himself and, in particular, about his recent conduct. It is, indeed, a classic example of honest self-examination. I invite you to consider it with me because of its important bearing on Christian discipline. This repentance, this state in which a man pauses and looks at himself and talks to himself about himself, is one of the most essential and vital aspects of what is commonly called the discipline of the Christian life. I do not apologize for emphasizing this again, because it is a matter which is being seriously neglected at the present. How often do we hear about the discipline of the Christian life these days? How often do we talk about it? How often is it really to be found at the heart of our evangelical living? There was a time in the Christian Church when this was at the very centre, and it is, I profoundly believe, because of our neglect of this discipline that the Church is in her present position. Indeed, I see no hope whatsoever of any true revival and reawakening until we return to it.

Faith on Trial, pp. 65–6

Don't cripple your present by thoughts of your past

[Some people] are crippled in the present as the result of looking back into the past . . . to the fact that they spent so much time outside the Kingdom and are so late in coming into it . . . to be miserable in the present because of some failure in the past is a sheer waste of time and energy. . . . The past cannot be recalled and you can do nothing about it . . . The world in its wisdom tells us it is 'no use crying over spilt milk'. Well, quote that to the devil! Why should a Christian be more foolish than anybody else? . . . We must never for a second worry about anything that cannot be affected or changed by us. It is a waste of energy. . . . But let us go further and realize that to dwell on the past simply causes failure in the present. While you are sitting down and bemoaning the past and regretting all the things you have not done, you are crippling yourself and preventing yourself from working in the present. . . . It is always wrong to mortgage the present by the past, it is always wrong to allow the past to act as a brake upon the present. Let the dead past bury its dead. There is nothing that is more reprehensible, judged by common canons of thought, than to allow anything that belongs to the past to cause you to be a failure in the present. . . . The people I am describing are failing in the present. Instead of living in the present and getting on with the Christian life they are sitting down bemoaning the past. They are so sorry about the past that they do nothing in the present. How wrong it is!

Spiritual Depression, p. 80, pp. 82–3

The body is a gift from God, and therefore we can be quite happy and certain in our minds that He will somehow or other provide the means whereby these bodies of ours can be covered and clothed. Here we come to one of His great principles. . . . There is nothing of which this modern generation needs to be reminded so much as just this . . . we have forgotten . . . that the things we enjoy in this life are the gift of God. . . . How often do we thank God for the gift of life itself? We tend to think that with our scientific knowledge we can understand the whole origin and essence of life. So we think of these things in terms of natural causes and inevitable processes. . . . [But] where does life come from? Read your modern scientists on the origin of life and you will find that they cannot explain it. They cannot bridge the gulf from the inorganic to the organic. . . . Where has this principle called life come from? What is its origin? If you say it started with the inorganic somehow becoming organic, I ask where did the inorganic come from? . . . And there is only one satisfactory answer—God is the Giver of life . . . it is God who has given us the gift of life and being and existence. It is a tremendous conception. We are not merely individuals thrown up or thrown out by an evolutionary process. God is concerned about us one by one. We should never have come into this world if God had not willed it. We must take a firm hold and grasp of this great principle. There should never be a day in our lives when we fail to thank God for the gift of life and food and existence, and the marvel and wonder of the body that He has given us. These things are solely and entirely His gift. And, of course, if we fail to realize that, we shall fail everywhere.

Studies in the Sermon on the Mount, ii, pp. 114–15

June 24
　　　　　　　　　　You are here!
　　　　　　　　　　(red arrow-label affixed to London
　　　　　　　　　　Underground maps)

It is not the time of your entry into the Kingdom that matters but the fact that you are in the Kingdom. . . . How foolish it is to mourn the fact that we were not in earlier, and to allow that to rob us of the things we might be enjoying now. It is like a man going to a great exhibition and discovering that there is a long queue. He has come rather late. He arrives at the exhibition but he has to wait a long time, he is about the last to get in. What would you think of such a man if, having got in through the door he simply stands at the door and says, 'What a shame I wasn't the first to get in, what a pity I wasn't in earlier'? You laugh at that, and rightly so, but . . . you are probably laughing at yourself, for that is precisely what you are doing spiritually. 'O that I have left it so late.' My friend, begin to enjoy the pictures, look at the sculpture, enjoy the treasures. What does the time of your entering matter? The fact is that you are in, and the exhibition is there, all spread out before you. . . . Go back to the twentieth of Matthew again. Those men were the last to enter the vineyard, it was the eleventh hour, but they were in. That was the thing that counted. They had been taken hold of, they had been employed, they had been brought in. It is the being in that matters, not when you come in, or how you come in. . . . It is not the mode or manner of conversion that matters, what matters is the fact that you are saved. But people will sit down and worry about how they came, the time, the mode, the manner, the method. It does not matter at all; what matters is that you are in. And if you are in, rejoice in it, and forget you were ever out.

Spiritual Depression, pp. 86–7

It is God Himself who gives us life, and the body in which we live it; and if He has done that we can draw this deduction, that His purpose with respect to us will be fulfilled. God never leaves unfinished any work He has begun. . . . And therefore we come back to this, that there is a plan for every life in the mind of God. We must never regard our lives in this world as accidental. No. 'Are there not twelve hours in the day?' Christ said one day to His timorous and frightened disciples. And we need to say that to ourselves. We can be certain that God has a plan and a purpose for our lives, and it will be carried out. So we must never be anxious about our life and about its sustenance and its support. We must not be anxious if we find ourselves in a storm at sea, or in an aeroplane, and things seem to be going wrong, or if in a railway train we suddenly remember that there was an accident on that line the previous week. That sort of thing is abolished if we really get this right view about life itself and the body as gifts of God. They are from Him and are given by Him. He does not just start a process like that and then allow it to continue anyhow, somehow. No; once He starts it He keeps it going. God who decreed all things at the beginning is carrying them out; and God's purpose for mankind and God's purpose for the individual are certain and always sure.

Studies in the Sermon on the Mount, ii, pp. 115–16

If we only spent more of our time in looking at Him we should soon forget ourselves . . . stop looking at yourself and begin to enjoy Him. What is the difference between a Christian and a non-Christian? Paul in the second Epistle to the Corinthians, chapter 3, says it is this, that the non-Christian is a man who looks at Christ and God with a veil over his eyes and therefore cannot see. What is the Christian? This is his description (v. 18): 'But we all'—every one of us as Christians—'we all with open face (the veil has gone), beholding as in a glass the glory of the Lord, are changed into the same image from glory to glory.' That is the Christian. He spends his time in looking at Christ, in gazing upon Him. He is so enraptured by the sight of Him that he has forgotten himself. If you were to feel more interest in Christ you would be less interested in yourself. Begin to look at Him, gaze upon Him with this open, unveiled face. And then go on to learn that in His Kingdom what matters is not the length of service but your attitude towards Him, your desire to please Him. . . . He does not count service as other people do. He is interested in the heart. We are interested in time, we all clock in and count the time we have spent, the work we have done. Like the first men in the parable (Matthew 20:1–16) we claim to have done all, and boast of the time we have spent in the work. And if we are not among those who went in at the beginning we are concerned because we have not done this and that, and because we have missed all this time. Our Lord is not interested in our work in this way. It is the widow's mite He is interested in. It is not the amount of money, it is the woman's heart. . . . That is also the case that Paul puts here (1 Corinthians 15:8–10). 'Last of all he revealed himself unto me also.' But thank God that does not make any difference . . . He is not interested in time, He is interested in relationship.

Spiritual Depression, pp. 88–9

We cannot do better than remind ourselves again of . . . the faith of God's people throughout the centuries. That is the faith and teaching to be found, for example, in the hymns of Philip Doddridge. A typical example is found in his great hymn:

> O God of Bethel, by whose hand
> Thy people still are fed;
> Who through this weary pilgrimage
> Hast all our fathers led.

That is his great argument, based ultimately upon the sovereignty of God, that God is the Ruler of the Universe, and we are known to Him one by one, and are in a personal relationship to Him. It was the faith of all the great heroes of the faith described in Hebrews 11. That is what kept those men going. Quite frequently they did not understand but they said, 'God knows and God undertakes'. They had this final confidence that He who had brought them into being, and who had a purpose for them, would not leave them nor forsake them. He would surely sustain and lead them all the journey through, until their purpose in this world has been completed, and He would receive them into their heavenly habitation where they would spend their eternity in His glorious presence. 'Be not anxious about your life, what ye shall eat, or what ye shall drink; nor about your body, wherewithal it shall be clothed. Is not the life more than meat, and the body than raiment?' Argue it out, start with first principles and draw the inevitable deduction. The moment you do so, care and worry and anxiety will vanish, and as a child of your heavenly Father you will walk with peace and serenity in the direction of your everlasting home.

Studies in the Sermon on the Mount, ii, p. 116

Here is a man [Psalm 73] suddenly tempted, tempted to say something, or . . . to do something. The force of the temptation is so great that he is almost thrown off his balance. He is on the point of falling to the temptation, and he tells us what it was that saved him. Here it is: 'If I say'—he was on the point of saying something—'If I say, I will speak thus; behold, I should offend. . . .' What does he do? What is his method?

The first thing he does is to take himself in hand. . . . He just kept himself from saying what was on the tip of his tongue. It was there, but he did not say it. Now this is tremendously important. The Psalmist realized the importance of never speaking hurriedly, of never speaking on an impulse. . . . It is a perfectly good point for a man to make who is not a Christian at all . . . there are things which we have to do in connexion with this spiritual discipline that at first sight do not seem to be particularly Christian. But if they hold you, use them.

There are many people who are so anxious to be always on the mountain top in a spiritual sense that for that very reason they often find themselves falling down into the valley. They disregard these ordinary methods. They do not avoid doing what the man who wrote Psalm 116 had done. . . . He makes a very honest confession. He says, 'I said in my haste, All men are liars.' He said that in his haste, and that was the mistake. This man in Psalm 73 had discovered, even when he was on the point of falling, the importance of not saying anything in haste. It is wrong for a Christian to say or do anything in haste . . . [see James 1:19] . . . is it not obvious that if only we all implemented this particular principle then life would be much more harmonious? . . . What a lot of pinpricks and irritations, what a lot of quarrelling and backbiting and unhappiness would be avoided in every realm of life, if only we all heeded this injunction! . . . Stop and think. If you can do nothing else, stop!

Faith on Trial, pp. 24–5

... this is how [Paul] speaks: 'Last of all He was seen of me also'.... He was the last of the apostles to see the risen Lord.... They had all seen Him in different ways together. Paul was not with them then; he was a blasphemer and a persecutor at that time. So 'last of all' means the last of the apostles. But not only was he the last of the apostles, he was literally the last person of all persons to see the risen Lord. No one has ever seen the risen Lord with his naked eyes since the Apostle Paul saw Him on the road to Damascus ... he was the very last of all.... He was not like the others. The others had listened to the Lord's teaching, they had been with Him all along.... They were with Him from the beginning and right through to the end. But Paul on the contrary had had a kind of unnatural, an ultimately spiritual birth; he has come, in some odd, strange way and—last of all.

That is what he says about himself. And of course he could only think of that with regret. He should have been in at the beginning, he had had the facilities, he had had the opportunities; but he had hated the gospel. He 'verily' thought ... that [he] should do many things contrary to the Name of Jesus. ...' He regarded Him as a blasphemer. ... There he was outside, but all the others were in. But—'last of all' and in this strange way, he came in. How easy it would have been for him to have spent the rest of his life in vain regrets about the past! ... He did not spend the rest of his life sitting in a corner and saying: 'I am the last to come in. Why did I do that? How could I have rejected Him?' That is what the people suffering from spiritual depression do. But Paul did not. What struck him was the amazing grace that brought him in at all. And so he entered into the new life with tremendous zeal, and though 'last of all' yet, in a sense, he became the first.

Spiritual Depression, pp. 84–5

God is our Father, and if our Father takes [such] great care of the birds to whom He is related only in His general providence, how much greater, of necessity, must be His care for us. An earthly father may be kind, for instance, to the birds or to animals; but it is inconceivable that a man should provide sustenance for mere creatures and neglect his own children. If this is true of an earthly father, how much more is it true of our heavenly Father. . . .

You see our Lord's method of reasoning and arguing; every word is important and must be noted carefully and closely. Observe the subtle transition from God caring providentially for the birds of the air, to 'your heavenly Father' . . . we notice and observe these facts of nature. . . . But because we are Christians we must look at them with a deeper understanding and say to ourselves, 'No; things do not just happen in nature. They have not just come into being anyhow, somehow, fortuitously, as so many modern scientists would have us believe. Not at all. God is the Creator, and God is the sustainer of all things that are. He provides even for the birds, and the birds know instinctively that it is there, and He sees to it that it is there. Very well then; but what about myself? I now remind myself that I am a child of God, that He is my heavenly Father. God is not to me merely a Creator. He is the Creator, but He is more than that; He is my God and Father in and through the Lord Jesus Christ.' We should reason thus with ourselves, according to our Lord; and the moment we do that, care and anxiety and worry are quite impossible. . . . God is our heavenly Father if we are truly Christian. We must add that, because all that we are considering applies only to Christians . . . it is only the man who is a Christian who knows God to be his Father.

Studies in the Sermon on the Mount, ii, pp. 119–20

Remember what is perhaps one of the most comforting and wonderful things that is found anywhere in Scripture. It was spoken to the prophet Joel as he was given that great vision and understanding of the coming of Christ, the Christ that was to come. This was the word he was given to utter: 'I will restore to you the years that the locust hath eaten' (Joel 2:25). He has promised to do it; He can do it. The wasted years, the barren years, the years that the locusts and the canker-worms and the caterpillars and all these other things have devoured, until there was nothing apparently left, of them He says: 'I will restore to you the years that the locust hath eaten.' If you think of it in terms of what you can do with your strength and power, then time is of the essence of the contract. But we are in a realm in which that does not matter. He comes in and He can give us a crop in one year that will make up for ten—'I will restore to you the years that the locust hath eaten.' That is the character of our Master, that is our Saviour, that is our God. I say, therefore, in the light of this: Never look back again; never waste your time in the present; never waste your energy; forget the past and rejoice in the fact that you are what you are by the grace of God, and that in the Divine alchemy of His marvellous grace you may yet have the greatest surprise of your life and existence and find that even in your case it will come to pass that the last shall be first. Praise God for the fact that you are what you are, and that you are in the Kingdom.

Spiritual Depression, pp. 89–90

[The Christian] finds himself guilty of sin, and at first it casts him down and makes him mourn. But that in turn drives him back to Christ; and the moment he goes back to Christ, his peace and happiness return and he is comforted. . . . The man who mourns truly is comforted and is happy; and thus the Christian life is spent in this way, mourning and joy, sorrow and happiness, and the one should lead to the other immediately.

But . . . there is another comfort, that which we may call 'the blessed hope', elaborated by the Apostle Paul in Romans 8. . . . He says that at the present moment even we who 'have the firstfruits of the Spirit, even we ourselves groan within ourselves, waiting for the adoption, to wit, the redemption of our body'. 'For we are saved by hope', he continues, and we are confident that 'the sufferings of this present time are not worthy to be compared with the glory which shall be revealed' . . . as the Christian looks at the world, and even as he looks at himself, he is unhappy. He groans in spirit; he knows something of the burden of sin as seen in the world which was felt by the apostles and by the Lord Himself. But he is immediately comforted. He knows there is a glory coming; he knows that a day will dawn when Christ will return, and sin will be banished from the earth. There will be 'new heavens and a new earth, wherein dwelleth righteousness'. O blessed hope! 'Blessed are they that mourn: for they shall be comforted.'

Studies in the Sermon on the Mount, i, pp. 60–1

[The Gospel] works *for everyone, for anyone, for all.* . . . No type or kind of person is excluded from its all-embracing scope and span . . . All the things about which others boasted, and in which they gloried, were sectional and partisan in their appeal and limited in the number of their adherents. They all lacked universality . . . and what satisfied one was rejected by another. . . . The world was divided and discord prevailed. . . .

But the gospel of Christ is different. It is for anyone, for everyone. Its secret is that it postulates nothing in man except failure and sin and weakness. . . . The gospel is not concerned about our natural differences. It centres on that which we share in common—sin and rebellion against God, failure in our lives, and a sense of shame. It demolishes all distinctions by placing us all together before God. And it does so, further, by postulating our weakness and helplessness, and relying for its efficacy upon the power of God Himself.

It matters not therefore who we are nor what we are. None can be too high or too low for this. There is no such thing as wise and unwise, great and small, learned and ignorant, wealthy or poor. There is no longer Jew and Gentile, Barbarian or Scythian, male or female, bond or free. God sees us as souls lost and desperate, helpless and forlorn. And He offers us the same salvation.

The Plight of Man and the Power of God, pp. 91–2

Look at the . . . lilies of the field, the natural wild flowers, the grass. The authorities again spend many pages in trying to decide exactly what a 'lily' means. But surely He is referring to some common flowers which were growing in the fields of Palestine, and with which they were all perfectly familiar. And He says, Look at these things—consider; these do not toil, neither do they spin, and yet look at them. Look at the marvel, look at the beauty, look at the perfection. Why, even Solomon in all his glory was not arrayed like one of these. The glory of Solomon was proverbial amongst the Jews. You can read of his magnificence in the Old Testament, the marvellous clothing and all the wonderful vestures of the king and his court, his palaces of cedarwood with their furniture overlaid with gold and encrusted with precious stones. And yet, says our Lord, all that pales into insignificance when compared with one of these. There is an essential quality in the flowers, in the form, in the design, in the texture and substance, and in the colouring that man, with all his ingenuity can never truly imitate.

> To me the meanest flower that blows can give
> Thoughts that do often lie too deep for tears.

That is what *He* sees. He sees the hand of God; He sees the perfect creation; He sees the glory of the Almighty. The little flower that is never perhaps seen during the whole of its brief existence in this world, and which seemingly 'wastes its sweetness on the desert air', is nevertheless perfectly clothed by God. That is a fact, is it not? If so, draw the deduction from it. 'If God so clothe the grass of the field . . . shall he not much more clothe you, O ye of little faith?'

Studies in the Sermon on the Mount, ii, pp. 123–4

(*continued on September 18*)

We must learn to . . . deal with ourselves faithfully. It is a vital matter in the Christian life. . . .

First and foremost we must really confess what we have done. . . . We must not spare ourselves. . . . We must not shield ourselves in any way; we must not attempt to slide over our sin. . . . We must hold the facts before ourselves deliberately and say, 'This is what I did; this is what I thought and what I said.'

But not only that. I must analyse this thing . . . and consider all that it involves and implies. . . . We shall never really abhor ourselves unless we do that . . . we have to particularize and to descend to details. I know this is very painful . . . it is not enough just to come to God and say, 'God, I am a sinner' . . . the essence of this matter is to get right down to details, to particularize . . . to put every detail down before yourself, to analyse yourself. . . . That is what the masters in the spiritual life have always done. Read their manuals, read the journals of the most saintly people who have adorned the life of the Church, and you will find that they have always done that. . . . John Fletcher not only asked twelve questions of himself before he went to sleep each night but he got his congregation to do the same. He did not content himself with a cursory general examination; he examined himself in detail, with such questions as: Do I lose my temper? Have I lost my temper? Have I made life more difficult for somebody else? Did I listen to that insinuation that the devil put into my mind, that unclean idea? Did I cling to it or immediately reject it? You go through the day and you put it all before yourself and face it. That is true self-examination. Then we must view it all in the sight of God— 'before thee'.

Faith on Trial, pp. 69–71

[In Matthew, chapter 7] Jesus is enforcing again the all-importance of our remembering that we are walking under the Father's eye. The particular subject He handles is one which is mainly concerned with our relationship with other people; but still the important thing to realize is that our relationship to God is the fundamental matter . . . we are reminded all along that our life here is a journey and a pilgrimage, and that it is leading on to a final judgement, an ultimate assessment, and the determination and proclamation of our final and eternal destiny.

. . . Half our troubles are due to the fact that we live on the assumption that this is the only life and the only world. . . . If we were questioned and asked whether we believe that we go on living after death, and that we shall have to face God in judgement, we would undoubtedly say 'yes'. But as we live from hour to hour are we mindful of that? . . . the thing that really differentiates God's people from all others is that they have always been people who walk in the consciousness of their eternal destiny. The natural man does not care about his eternal future; to him this is the only world. It is the only world he thinks about; he lives for it and it controls him. But the Christian . . . should walk through this life as conscious that it is but transient and passing, a kind of preparatory school. He should always know that he is walking in the presence of God, and that he is going on to meet God; and that thought should determine and control the whole of his life. . . . We are undergoing a process of judgement the whole time, because we are being prepared for the final judgement . . . we shall have to render an account.

Studies in the Sermon on the Mount, ii, pp. 159–60

. . . there is only one answer to the question. It is the great essential New Testament message concerning 'justifying faith'. That was the very nerve and centre of apostolic preaching. . . . 'The just shall live by faith' (Romans 1:16). This was the kernel of apostolic preaching—that it is by faith a man is justified, not by the deeds of the law, or any righteousness of his own.

We have a classic statement of it in Romans 3. . . . 'Being justified freely by his grace through the redemption that is in Christ Jesus; whom God hath set forth to be a propitiation through faith in his blood, . . . that he might be just, and the justifier of him which believeth in Jesus . . .' (vv. 24–26).

That is the great central message of the gospel. It is through this faith in the Lord Jesus Christ and His work that we are justified. That is the meaning of this 'one faith'. It is, of course, the whole argument of the Epistle to the Galatians. 'This is the gospel, and there is no other gospel', says the apostle. And the gospel is that 'God justifieth the ungodly who believe in Jesus'. This 'one faith' is something that is set over against every other teaching with regard to the way of salvation. It is this 'one faith' over against . . . all notions that we can justify ourselves by works or actions, our own, or those of others. It is the teaching that it is Christ alone who saves, and that we become participants in this salvation through faith. So we have 'one Lord, one faith'.

The Basis of Christian Unity, pp. 30–1

The spirit we receive of wisdom, grace and power;
And always sorrowful we live, rejoicing evermore
(Charles Wesley)

Let us, then, try to define this man who mourns. What sort of a man is he? He is a sorrowful man, but he is not morose. He is a sorrowful man, but he is not a miserable man. He is a serious man, but he is not a solemn man. He is a sober-minded man, but he is not a sullen man. He is a grave man, but he is never cold or prohibitive. There is with his gravity a warmth and attraction. This man, in other words, is always serious; but he does not have to affect the seriousness. The true Christian is never a man who has to put on an appearance of either sadness or joviality. No, no; he is a man who looks at life seriously; he contemplates it spiritually, and he sees in it sin and its effects. He is a serious, sober-minded man. His outlook is always serious, but because of these views which he has, and his understanding of truth, he also has 'a joy unspeakable and full of glory'. So he is like the Apostle Paul, 'groaning within himself', and yet happy because of his experience of Christ and the glory that is to come. The Christian is not superficial in any sense, but is fundamentally serious and fundamentally happy. You see, the joy of the Christian is a holy joy, the happiness of the Christian is a serious happiness . . . it is a solemn joy, it is a holy joy. . . .

That is the man who mourns; that is the Christian. . . . A deep doctrine of sin, a high doctrine of joy, and the two together produce this blessed, happy man who mourns, and who at the same time is comforted. The way to experience that, obviously, is to read the Scriptures, to study and meditate upon them, to pray to God for His Spirit to reveal sin in us to ourselves, and then to reveal to us the Lord Jesus Christ in all His fullness. 'Blessed are they that mourn, for they shall be comforted.'

Studies in the Sermon on the Mount, i, p. 62

Men who have been the hopeless slaves and victims of sin, and who have reduced their families and homes to conditions of abject poverty, once they have been converted and brought to Christ have proceeded to transform their whole surroundings and conditions. In regenerating a man, the gospel changes even his personal appearance. He begins to pay new attention to his clothing and that of his wife and children; the very furniture of his home is altered, and the aspect of his premises improved. Once the man himself is put right, he proceeds to put everything else right. The great movement for popular education in the eighteenth and nineteenth centuries came as a direct result of the awakening of men, under the influence of the gospel, to the realization of the fact that they had minds and brains. They showed a desire to read the Bible, to familiarize themselves with culture, and to understand life. The number of changes that followed the great spiritual awakening is almost endless. We can illustrate again in terms of a picture. If the source is made pure, the stream is likely to be pure. If the disease itself is treated and cured, the symptoms are likely to disappear. . . . nothing else . . . ever can produce truly improved social conditions except the gospel . . . to educate men and give them better houses, does not necessarily guarantee new men or better living. . . . All the problems start at the centre, in the eye, in the soul of man that has become beclouded.

Truth Unchanged, Unchanging, pp. 93–4

What matters first of all if you are a Christian is not what you once were, but what you are. Does that sound ridiculous? It is so perfectly obvious. . . . Yes, how obvious when I put it like this, but how difficult to see it sometimes when the devil attacks us. The Apostle said that he was 'not worthy to be called an apostle because [he] persecuted the Church of God', but he goes on to add: 'But by the grace of God I am what I am.' What does it matter what I was? 'I am what I am.' Put your emphasis there. Do not be for ever thinking about what you were. The essence of the Christian position is that you should remind yourself of what you are. Certainly there is the past with all its sins. But say this to yourself:

> Ransomed, healed, restored, forgiven,
> Who like [me] His praise should sing?

'I am what I am'—whatever the past may have been. It is what I am that matters. What am I? I am forgiven, I am reconciled to God by the Blood of His Son upon the Cross. I am a child of God. I am adopted into God's family, and I am an heir with Christ, a joint-heir with Him. I am going to glory. That is what matters, not what I was, nor what I have been. Do what the Apostle did, therefore, if the enemy is attacking you along this line. Turn to him and say: 'What you are saying is perfectly true. I was all you say. But what I am interested in is not what I was but what I am, and "I am what I am by the grace of God". '

Spiritual Depression, p. 85–6

This Beatitude [Blessed are the meek], this particular description of the Christian, causes real surprise because it is so completely and entirely opposed to everything which the natural man thinks. 'Blessed are the meek; for they shall inherit the earth.' World conquest—possession of the whole universe—given to the meek, of all people! The world thinks in terms of strength and power, of ability, self-assurance and aggressiveness. That is the world's idea of conquest and possession. The more you assert yourself and express yourself, the more you organize and manifest your powers and ability, the more likely you are to succeed and get on. But here comes this astounding statement, 'Blessed are the meek: for they shall inherit the earth'—and they alone. Once more, then, we are reminded . . . that the Christian is altogether different from the world. It is a difference in quality, an essential difference. He is a new man, a new creation; he belongs to an entirely different kingdom. And not only is the world unlike him; it cannot possibly understand him. He is an enigma to the world. And if you and I are not, in this primary sense, problems and enigmas to the non-Christians around us, then this tells us a great deal about our profession of the Christian faith.

Studies in the Sermon on the Mount, i, p. 63

We are going to consider the case of those who . . . are afraid of the future . . . a very common condition and it really is most extraordinary to notice the way in which the enemy often produces the self-same fundamental condition in the same people by these apparently diametrically opposed methods. When you have put them right about the past, they immediately begin to talk about the future, with the result that they are always depressed in the present. You have satisfied them about forgiveness of sin, yes, even that particular sin which was so exceptional. . . . And then they say, 'Ah, yes, but . . .', and they begin to talk about fears concerning the future and what lies ahead. . . . Now it is right that we should think about the future. . . . But what we are always warned against in Scripture is about being worried about the future. 'Take no thought for the morrow', means 'Do not be guilty of anxious care about the morrow.' It does not mean that you do not take any thought at all, otherwise the farmer would not plough and harrow and sow. He is looking to the future, but he does not spend the whole of his time wondering and worrying about the end results of his work. No, he takes reasonable thought and then he leaves it . . . although it is very right to think about the future, it is very wrong to be controlled by it. . . . To take thought is right, but to be controlled by the future is all wrong. Now that is a fundamental proposition and the world has discovered it. It has told us not to cross our bridges until we get to them. Put that into your Christian teaching, for the world is right there . . . many Scriptural statements to the same effect have become proverbial—'take no thought for the morrow', 'Sufficient unto the day is the evil thereof.' . . . That is sound common sense. . . . 'One step enough for me' . . . do not let your future mortgage your present any more than you should let your past mortgage your present.

Spiritual Depression, p. 94, pp. 98–9

What then is this condition which is described by our Lord as being 'little faith'? . . . We can say . . . in general that it is one which is confined to one sphere of life only. It is faith that is confined solely to the question of the salvation of our souls, and it does not go beyond that. It does not extend to the whole of life and to everything in life. This is a common complaint among us as Christian people. On the question of the salvation of our souls we are perfectly clear. . . . We have seen . . . that the only way of deliverance is in the Lord Jesus Christ. . . . And we believe on Him, and have that saving faith with regard to the present and to all eternity. That is saving faith, the thing that makes us Christians, and without which we are not Christian at all. Yes; but Christian people often stop at that, and they seem to think that faith is something that applies only to that question of salvation. The result is, of course, that in their daily lives they are often defeated; in their ordinary lives there is very little difference to be seen between them and people who are not Christian. They become worried and anxious, and they comform to the world in so many respects. Their faith is something that is reserved only for their ultimate salvation, and they do not seem to have any faith with regard to the every-day affairs of life and living in this world. Our Lord is concerned about that very thing. These people have come to know God as their heavenly Father, and yet they are worried about food and drink and clothing. Their faith is confined; it is a little faith in that way; its scope is so curtailed and limited.

Studies in the Sermon on the Mount, ii, p. 127

Timothy at the moment was guilty of the spirit of fear, he was gripped by it; so Paul reprimands him—'God hath not given us the spirit of fear but of power and of love and of a sound mind' (2 Timothy 1:7) . . . our essential trouble, if we suffer from this particular manifestation of spiritual depression, is our failure to realize what God has given us, and is giving us, in giving us the gift of the Holy Ghost. . . . It is a failure to realize what God has done for us, and what God is still doing in us. . . . The Apostle has to tell Timothy to stir up the gift of God.

Our fears are due to our failure to stir up—failure to think, failure to take ourselves in hand. You find yourself looking to the future and then you begin to imagine things and you say: 'I wonder what is going to happen?' And then your imagination runs away with you. You are gripped by the thing; you do not stop to remind yourself of who you are and what you are, this thing overwhelms you and down you go. Now the first thing you have to do is to take a firm grip of yourself, to pull yourself up, to stir up yourself, to take yourself in hand and to speak to yourself . . . the big thing that Paul is saying in effect to Timothy is: 'Timothy, you seem to be thinking about yourself and about life and all you have to do as if you were still an ordinary person. But, Timothy, you are not an ordinary person! You are a Christian, you are born again, the Spirit of God is in you. But you are facing all these things as if you are still what you once were, an ordinary person!'

Spiritual Depression, pp. 99–100

. . . these Beatitudes as they proceed become increasingly difficult . . . what we are now considering is more searching, more difficult, more humbling and even more humiliating. . . . The first Beatitude asks us to realize our own weakness and our own inability . . . it makes us feel we have nothing. . . . But here, I say, is something which is still more searching—'Blessed are the meek.'

Now why is this? Because here we are reaching a point at which we begin to be concerned about other people. Let me put it like this, I can see my own utter nothingness and helplessness face to face with the demands of the gospel and the law of God. I am aware, when I am honest with myself, of the sin and the evil that are within me, and that drag me down. And I am ready to face both these things. But how much more difficult it is to allow other people to say things like that about me! I instinctively resent it. We all of us prefer to condemn ourselves than to allow somebody else to condemn us. I say of myself that I am a sinner, but instinctively I do not like anybody else to say that I am a sinner. . . . So far, I myself have been looking at myself. Now, other people are looking at me, and I am in a relationship to them, and they are doing certain things to me. How do I react to that? That is the matter which is dealt with at this point. I think you will agree that this is more humbling and more humiliating than everything that has gone before. It is to allow other people to put the searchlight upon me instead of my doing it myself.

Studies in the Sermon on the Mount, i, pp. 64–5

'God hath not given us the spirit of fear.' What, then, is the spirit He has given us? . . . '. . . *but of power.*' . . . We have a task, we know our own weakness. Yes, but here is a power even for weaklings, and it means power in the most comprehensive sense conceivable. Are you afraid that you will not be able to live the Christian life? The answer is: 'Work out your own salvation with fear and trembling, for it is God that worketh in you both to will and to do.' The fear and the trembling remain . . . but you are enabled to work by the power 'that worketh in you both to will and to do' . . . it means also power to endure, power to go on whatever the condition, whatever the circumstances, power to hold on and to hold out . . . it means that the most timorous person can be given power in all things, even to die. You see it in the apostles, you see it in a man like Peter who was afraid of death, afraid to die. He even denied his Lord because of that fear. . . . But look at him afterwards. . . . The spirit of power had entered into him and now he is ready to die. He will face the authorities, he will face anybody. . . . I never tire of telling Christians to read the stories of the martyrs and the Confessors and the Protestant Fathers, of the Puritans and the Covenanters. Read their stories, and you will find not only strong, courageous men, you will find weak women and girls and even little children dying gloriously for Christ's sake. They could not in and of themselves, but they were given the spirit of power . . . [Paul] says to Timothy . . . 'God has given you the spirit of power. Go forward. He will be with you. You won't know yourself; you will be amazed at yourself. And even though it may mean facing death, you will rejoice that you have been accounted worthy to suffer shame and even death for His glorious Name's sake.' Power! It is given.

Spiritual Depression, pp. 101–2

Faith does not work automatically . . . you have to apply it. Faith does not grow automatically either; we must learn to talk to our faith and to ourselves. . . . Do you remember how the Psalmist puts it in Psalm 42? Look at him turning to himself and saying, 'Why art thou cast down, O my soul? and why art thou disquieted within me?' That is the way to make faith grow. You must talk to yourself about your faith. You must question yourself as to what is the matter with your faith. You must ask your soul why it is cast down, and wake it up! . . . Your faith does not grow mechanically, you have to attend to it. To use our Lord's analogy, you have to dig round and about it, and pay attention to it. Then you will find it will grow.

. . . a large part of faith . . . consists of just refusing anxious thoughts . . . refusing to think about worrying things, refusing to think of the future in that wrong sense. The devil and all adverse circumstances will do their utmost to make me do so, but having faith means that I shall say: 'No; I refuse to be worried. I have done my reasonable service; I have done what I believed to be right and legitimate, and beyond that I will not think at all.' That is faith, and it is particularly true with regard to the future. When the devil comes with his insinuations, injecting them into you—all the fiery darts of the evil one—say, 'No; I am not interested. The God whom I am trusting for today, I will trust for tomorrow. I refuse to listen; I will not think your thoughts.' Faith is refusing to be burdened because we have cast our burden upon the Lord. May He, in His infinite grace, give us wisdom and grace to implement these simple principles and thereby rejoice in Him day by day.

Studies in the Sermon on the Mount, ii, pp. 156–7

The next thing [Paul] mentions [in 2 Timothy 1:7] is 'love'. Now I find this most interesting and fascinating. I wonder how many of you would have put love at this point on our list? Why, do you think, does he put it here? What does he mean by it? 'God hath not given us the spirit of fear but of power. . . .' Yes, I understand that I need power. But love—why love? . . . Here is a superb bit of psychology, for what after all, is the main cause of this spirit of fear? The answer is 'self'—self-love, self-concern, self-protection . . . how can I do this, what if I fail? 'I'—they are constantly turning in upon themselves, looking at themselves and concerned about themselves. And it is just here that the spirit of love comes in, for there is only one way to get rid of yourself. . . . You will never deal with self yourself. That was the fatal fallacy of those poor men who became monks and anchorites. They could get away from the world and from other people, but they could not get away from themselves. . . . There is only one way to get rid of self, and that is that you should become so absorbed in someone or something else that you have no time to think about yourself. Thank God, the Spirit of God makes that possible. He is not only 'the spirit of power', but He is also 'the spirit of love'. What does that mean? It means love to God, love to the great God who made us, love to the great God who has made the way of redemption for us. . . . He has 'loved us with an ever-lasting love'. Think of that, says Paul to Timothy, and as you become absorbed in the love of God you will forget all about yourself. 'The spirit of love!' It will deliver you from self-interest, self-concern, and from depression about self. . . . It gets rid of self at all points. So talk to yourself about this eternal, amazing love of God.

Spiritual Depression, pp. 102–3

Look at the portrait of that great gentleman—in many ways, I think, the greatest gentleman in the Old Testament—Abraham, and as you look at him you see a great and wonderful portrait of meekness. It is the great characteristic of his life. You remember his behaviour with respect to Lot, and how he allows the younger man to assert himself and take the first choice and does it without a murmur and without a complaint —that is meekness. You see it again in Moses, who is actually described as the most meek man on the face of the earth. Examine his character and you see the same thing, this lowly conception of himself, this readiness not to assert himself but rather to humble and to abase himself—meekness. There were wonderful possibilities ahead of him, all the possibility of the court of Egypt and his position as the son of Pharaoh's daughter. But how truly he evaluated it all, saw it as it was, and humbled himself completely to God and His will.

The same is true of David, especially in his relations with Saul. David knew he was to be king. He had been informed, he had been anointed; and yet how he suffered Saul and Saul's unjust and unkind treatment of him! Read the story of David again and you will see meekness exemplified in a most extra-ordinary manner. Again, take Jeremiah and the unpopular message that was given to him. He was called upon to speak the truth to the people—not the thing he wanted to do—while the other prophets were saying smooth and easy things. He was isolated. He was an individualist—non-co-operative they would call him today—because he did not say what everybody else was saying. He felt it all bitterly. But read his story. See how he suffered it all and allowed the unkind things to be said about him behind his back, and how he went on delivering his message. It is a wonderful example of meekness.

Studies in the Sermon on the Mount, i, pp. 65–6

Every time we take a step in the direction of God [James 4:8] . . . God will take a step in our direction. . . . If we approach Him truly, if we approach Him honestly, we can always be certain that God will meet us. He is the God of salvation. That is a very good reason for drawing near to Him. He has every blessing that we need. There is nothing we can ever stand in need of but God has it. . . . He is the Giver of 'every good gift and every perfect gift'. He has put them all in Christ, and He has given us Christ. 'All things are yours', says Paul to the Corinthians. Why? Because 'ye are Christ's'. It is an inevitable piece of logic. . . . It is only when I am near to God in Christ that I know my sins are forgiven. I feel His love, I know I am His child and I enjoy the priceless blessings of peace with God and peace within and peace with others. I am aware of His love and I am given a joy that the world can neither give nor take away.

Anyone who has ever tasted of these things must say that there is nothing comparable to being near to God. Look back across your life. Pick out the most glorious moments in your experience, the moments of supreme peace and joy. Have they not been the times when you have been nearest to God? There is nothing to equal the happiness and joy and peace which result from being near to God. There you are lifted up above your circumstances. . . . You are made independent of circumstances and accident and chance, independent of all things. It is good to be near to God because it is the place of salvation, because it is the place where you experience all the blessings. It means that you are immersed in the ocean of God's love and are staying there. Let us adopt this man's resolve to keep near to God.

Faith on Trial, pp. 122–3

How are we to deal with this problem of 'feelings'? [My first suggestion] is a very practical one—it is just this. If you are at all depressed at this moment you should make certain that there is no obvious cause for the absence of joyous feelings. For instance, if you are guilty of sin, you are going to be miserable. 'The way of the transgressor is hard.' If you break God's laws and violate His rules you will not be happy. If you think that you can be a Christian and exert your own will and follow your own likes and dislikes, your Christian life is going to be a miserable one. There is no need to argue about it, it follows as the night the day, that if you are harbouring some favourite sin, if you are holding on to something that the Holy Spirit is condemning through your conscience, you will not be happy. And there is only one thing to do, confess it, acknowledge it, repent, go to God at once and confess your sin, open your heart, bare your soul, tell Him all about it, hold nothing back and then believe that because you have done so, He forgives you. 'If we confess our sins, He is faithful and just to forgive us our sins and to cleanse us from all unrighteousness.' If unconfessed sin is the cause of your unhappiness I should be wasting my time and yours by going on with my list of other causes. How many are trapped at this point. Let us be perfectly clear about it; let your conscience speak to you; listen to the voice of God as He speaks through the Spirit that is within you, and if He is placing His finger upon something, get rid of it. You cannot hope to solve this problem while you are harbouring some sin.

Spiritual Depression, pp. 113–14

The trouble with us Christian people is that we do not realize what we are as children of God, we do not see God's gracious purposes with respect to us. . . . He contrasted us as children with the grass of the field. The grass is here today in the field, but tomorrow it will be thrown as fuel into the oven to bake bread. But God's children are destined for glory. All the purposes and the promises of God are meant for us and designed with respect to us, and the one thing we have to do . . . is just to realize what God has told us about ourselves as His children. The moment we grasp that, worry becomes impossible. A man then begins to apply the logic which argues: 'If, when we were enemies, we were reconciled to God by the death of his Son, much more, being reconciled, we shall be saved by his life' (Romans 5:10). That is it. Whatever happens to us, 'He that spared not his own Son, but delivered him up for us all, how shall he not with him also freely give us all things?' The mighty argument continues in Romans 8 . . . We may have to face problems and distresses and sorrow, but 'in all these things we are more than conquerors through him that loved us'. The vital thing is to see ourselves as His children. The argument follows of necessity. If God so clothe the grass how much more shall He clothe you? Your heavenly Father, who sees the birds, feedeth them. Are ye not much better than they? We have to realize what we are as God's children.

Studies in the Sermon on the Mount, ii, pp. 131–2

Christ! I am Christ's! and let the name suffice you,
Paul has no honour and no friend but Christ

Look at this Colossus of a man, Paul, who had one of the greatest minds the world has ever known.... And yet Paul tells us that when he went to Corinth he was 'in weakness, and in fear, and in much trembling'. He did not bounce on to a platform radiating self-confidence and self-assurance and authority. And he did not let off a few jokes to put himself right with the congregation. He was not perfectly at ease, a 'master of assemblies'. 'Weakness, fear and much trembling.' Why? Because Paul knew his own limitations. He knew what he could not do, and he was terrified, indeed he trembled, lest in any way he or his personality might come between those souls and this tremendous message which had been committed unto him. He did not put on things which he knew would appeal to them. He did the exact opposite. He determined 'not to know anything among you, save Jesus Christ, and him crucified'. Moreover, he says, 'My speech and my preaching was not with enticing words of man's wisdom, but in demonstration of the Spirit and of power: that your faith should not stand in the wisdom of men, but in the power of God.' Both with regard to his matter and manner he would not pander to the popular taste. And the result was that when he spoke, though some might say that 'his speech was contemptible', there was power, and men and women were convicted and converted, became Christians and were established in the Church. What was the secret? It was 'the demonstration of the Spirit and of power'. It was this Holy Ghost authority.

Authority, p. 85

Look at the portrait of Stephen and you will see this text [Matthew 5:5] illustrated. Look at it in the case of Paul, that mighty man of God. Consider what he suffered at the hands of these different churches and at the hands of his own country-men and various other people. As you read his letters you will see this quality of meekness coming out, and especially as he writes to the members of the church at Corinth who had been saying such unkind and disparaging things about him. It is again a wonderful example of meekness. But of course we must come to the supreme example, and stand and look at our Lord Himself. 'Come unto me', He said, 'all ye that labour . . . and I will give you rest . . . I am meek and lowly in heart.' You see it in the whole of His life. You see it in His reaction to other people, you see it especially in the way He suffered persecution and scorn, sarcasm and derision. Rightly was it said of Him, 'A bruised reed shall he not break, and smoking flax shall he not quench'. His attitude towards His enemies, but perhaps still more His utter submission to His Father, show His meek-ness. He said, 'The words that I speak unto you, I speak not of myself', and 'the Father that dwelleth in me, he doeth the works'. Look at Him in the Garden of Gethsemane. Look at the portrait of Him which we find in Philippians 2 where Paul tells us that He did not regard His equality with God as a prerogative at which to clutch or something to hold on to at all costs. No, He decided to live as a Man, and He did. He humbled Himself, became as a servant and even went to the death on the cross. That is meekness; that is lowliness; that is true humility; that is the quality which He himself is teaching at this point.

Studies in the Sermon on the Mount, i, pp. 66–7

When the mood comes upon us, we allow it to dominate us
and we are defeated and depressed. We say that we would like
to be delivered, and yet we do nothing about it . . . we must
away with 'dull sloth and melancholy' . . . there is a sense in
which what the Scriptures do is to teach us how to speak to
ourselves. . . . You must talk to yourself and say: 'I am not
going to be dominated by you, these moods shall not control
me. I am going out, I am breaking through'. So get up and
walk, and do something. 'Stir up the gift.' . . . If you allow these
moods to control you, you will remain miserable, but you must
not allow it. Shake them off. Do not recognize them. Say again,
'Away dull sloth'.

But how do you do that? In this way—your business and
mine is not to stir up our feelings, it is to believe. We are never
told anywhere in Scripture that we are saved by our feelings;
we are told that we are saved by believing. . . . Never once are
feelings put into the primary position. Now this is something
we can do. I cannot make myself happy, but I can remind
myself of my belief. I can exhort myself to believe, I can address
my soul as the Psalmist did in Psalm 42: 'Why art thou cast
down O my soul, and why art thou disquieted within me? Hope
thou' . . . believe thou, trust thou. That is the way. And then
our feelings will look after themselves. Do not worry about
them. Talk to yourself, and though the devil will suggest that
because you do not feel, you are not a Christian, say: 'No, I do
not feel anything, but whether I feel or not, I believe the
Scriptures. I believe God's Word is true, and I will stay my soul
on it, I will believe in it come what may.' . . . Yes, J. C. Philpot
was right . . . the child of the light is sometimes found walking
in darkness but he goes on walking. . . . He does not see the face
of the Lord at this point, but he knows that He is there; so he
goes on.

Spiritual Depression, pp. 116–17

The children of God have their names written in the Lamb's Book of Life before the foundation of the world. There is nothing contingent about this. It was 'before the foundation of the world' that we were elected. His purposes are immutable and changeless, and they envisage our eternal destiny and nothing less. This is constantly expressed in various ways in the Scriptures. . . . When people believe things like that they are able to face life in this world in a very different way. That was the secret . . . of the heroes of the faith in Hebrews 11. They understood something of the immutable purposes of God, and, therefore, whether it was Abraham or Joseph or Moses, they all smiled at calamities. They just went on because God had told them to do so, because they knew that His purposes must surely come to pass. Abraham was put to the supreme test of being asked to sacrifice Isaac. He could not understand it but he said: I will do it because I know God's purposes are sure, and though I have to slay Isaac, I know that God can raise him from the dead. The immutable purposes of God! . . .

Then think of His great love. The tragedy of our position is that we do not know the love of God as we should. . . . In a sense the whole of the First Epistle of John was written in order that we might know that. If only we knew the love of God to us and rested in it (1 John 4:16) our whole lives would be different. How easy it is to prove the greatness of that love in the light of what He has already done in Christ. [Remember] those mighty arguments from the Epistle to the Romans. If while we were yet enemies He has done the greatest thing, how much more, we say it with reverence, is He bound to do the lesser things. *The love of God to us!*

Studies in the Sermon on the Mount, ii, 132–3

Let us . . . consider what this man discovered about himself in detail. [Psalm 73:21–2]. The first thing . . . was that he had very largely been producing his own troubles and his own unhappiness . . . his trouble was not really the ungodly at all; it was himself. He found that he had . . . 'worked himself up' into this condition . . . What he is saying [in v. 21] is that he has done something to himself. He is saying, 'I have soured my heart . . . I was preparing for myself a piercing pain'. He had been doing it himself. He had been stimulating his own heart, he had been exacerbating his own trouble, he had been souring his own feelings. He himself had really been producing his own troubles and giving rise to this piercing pain which he had been enduring until he went into the sanctuary of God.

This is clearly a very important and vital principle. The fact is . . . that we tend to produce and exacerbate our own troubles. We, of course, tend to say . . . that it is that thing outside us that produced all the trouble. But it is not that thing at all; it is ourselves . . . [what matters is] you and I and the way we face it, the way we react, our behaviour with respect to it. . . . You may see two persons living exactly the same sort of life, facing precisely the same conditions. And yet they are very different. One is bitter and sour and grumbling and complaining; the other is calm and quiet, happy and composed. Where is the difference? It is not in the conditions; it is not in what is happening to them. It is something in *them*; the difference is in the two persons themselves . . .

> Two men looked out from prison bars.
> The one saw mud, the other stars.

One, you see, looked down; the other looked up. It is not life, it is not the circumstances, it is not the ungodly . . . it is us.

Faith on Trial, pp. 76–7

. . . we worry about things. If only we realized God's loving concern for us, that He knows everything about us, and is concerned about the smallest detail of our lives! The man who believes that can no longer worry.

Then think about His power and ability. 'Our God', 'my God'. Who is my God who takes such a personal interest in me? He is the Creator of the heavens and the earth. He is the Sustainer of everything that is. Read again Psalm 46 to remind yourself of this: 'He maketh wars to cease unto the end of the earth; he breaketh the bow, and cutteth the spear in sunder'. He controls everything. He can smash the heathen and every enemy; His power is illimitable. And as we contemplate all that, we must agree with the deduction of the Psalmist when, addressing the heathen, he said, 'Be still, and know that I am God'. ['Be still'] means, 'Give up (or 'Give in') and admit that I am God'. God is addressing people who are opposed to Him and He says: This is My power; therefore give up and give in, keep silent and know that I am God.

We must remember that this power is working for us. We have seen it in Paul's prayer for the Ephesians: 'The exceeding greatness of his power' (1:19). He 'that is able to do exceeding abundantly above all that we ask or think, according to the power that worketh in us' (3:20). In the light of such statements is not worry ridiculous? Is it not utterly foolish? It just means that we do not think; we do not read our Scriptures, or, if we do, we do so in a perfunctory manner, or are so controlled by prejudices that we do not take them at their face value. We must face these things and draw out our mighty conclusions.

Studies in the Sermon on the Mount, ii, pp. 133–4

The Scripture makes it very plain and clear that there is no part of this Christian life which is without its dangers. Nothing is so false to the teaching of the New Testament as to give the impression that the moment you believe and are converted, all your troubles are at an end and you will never have another problem. Alas, that is not true, and it is not true because we have an enemy, the Adversary of our souls. But not only do we have to contend with the enemy, there is still the old nature within, and these two make it certain that we shall have troubles and difficulties. . . . It is our business to anticipate these things in the light of Scripture . . . and we have before us always that mighty Scripture which teaches: 'Take unto you, therefore, the whole armour of God'. . . .

While it is of vital and supreme importance to start correctly, it is not enough. We must continue in the same way, for, if we do not, we shall soon find ourselves unhappy . . . though the gospel has been presented to us and we have been converted, though we have started correctly and are in the Christian life, though we have heeded the warnings about the initial difficulties—yet if we do not continue, if we do not maintain our course in the same way, we shall soon get into trouble. There is a great illustration of this in the Gospel according to St. John, the eighth chapter, verses 30ff. Our Lord was preaching . . . and we are told that, 'As He spake . . . many believed on him'. Then our Lord looked at them and said: 'If ye continue in my word, then are ye my disciples indeed; and ye shall know the truth, and the truth shall make you free.' They seemed to be starting well but they must continue if they were to be truly free . . . the importance of *continuing* is a very vital principle.

Spiritual Depression, pp. 121–2

[Meekness] is not a natural quality. It is not a matter of a natural disposition, because all Christians are meant to be like this. It is not only some Christians. Every Christian, whatever his natural temperament or psychology may be, is meant to be like this. Now we can prove that very easily. Take these various characters whom I have mentioned, apart from our Lord Himself, and I think you will find that in every case we have a man who was not like this by nature. Think of the powerful, extraordinary nature of a man like David, and yet observe his meekness. Jeremiah similarly lets us into the secret. He says he was almost like a boiling cauldron, and yet he was still meek. Look at a man like the Apostle Paul, a master mind, an extraordinary personality, a strong character; yet consider his utter humility and meekness. No, it is not a matter of natural disposition; it is something that is produced by the Spirit of God. . . .

Meekness does not mean indolence. There are people who appear to be meek in a natural sense; but they are not meek at all, they are indolent. That is not the quality of which the Bible is speaking. Nor does it mean flabbiness. . . . There are people who are easy-going, and you tend to say how meek they are. But it is not meekness; it is flabbiness. Nor does it mean niceness. There are people who seem to be born naturally nice. . . . Nor does it mean weakness in personality or character. Still less does it mean a spirit of compromise or 'peace at any price'. . . . Meekness is compatible with great strength . . . with great authority and power . . . God forbid that we should ever confuse this noble quality . . . with something merely animal or physical or natural.

. . . meekness is not merely a matter of outward manner, but . . . of inward spirit. . . . You cannot spend time with a verse like this [Matthew 5:5] without its humbling you. It is true Christianity; it is the thing for which we are called and for which we are meant.

Studies in the Sermon on the Mount, i, pp. 67–8

Thou shalt be turned into another man
(1 Samuel 10:6)

What a miserable thing self is, what an ugly thing, what a foul thing. We are all guilty of this, every one of us, in some shape or form.... Self needs to be exposed for what it is. Sin in its ugliness and foulness needs to be unmasked. . . . It is the greatest enemy of the soul, and it leads to misery and un-happiness. . . .

That brings me to the cure. What is the treatment? It is to understand the controlling principle of the Kingdom of God . . . in the Kingdom of God everything is essentially different from everything in every other kingdom . . . the Kingdom of God is not like that which you have always known, it is some-thing quite new and different. The first thing we have to realize is that 'if any man be in Christ he is a new creature, old things are passed away, behold all things are become new'. If only we realized as we should, that here we are in a realm in which everything is different! The whole foundation is different, it has nothing to do with the principle of the old life.... We must say to ourselves every day of our lives, 'Now I am a Christian, and because I am a Christian I am in the Kingdom of God and all my thinking has got to be different. Everything here is different. I must not bring with me those old ideas, those old moods and concepts of thought.' We tend to confine salvation to one thing, namely to forgiveness, but we have to apply the principle throughout the Christian life.

Spiritual Depression, pp. 128–9

Faith means taking the bare Word of God and acting upon it because it is the Word of God. It means believing what God says simply and solely because He has said it. Those heroes of the faith in Hebrews 11 believed the Word of God simply because God had spoken. They had no other reasons for believing it. Why, for example, did Abraham take Isaac and go with him up that mountain? Why was he on the point of sacrificing his son? Simply because God had told him to do so.

But living by faith means even more than that. It means basing the whole of our life upon faith in God. The secret of all those Old Testament characters was that they lived 'as seeing him who is invisible'. . . . These men staked all on God's Word. They were prepared to suffer for it, and if necessary endure the loss of all things. The same prospect faced many of the early Christians. . . . 'If you do not say Caesar is Lord', said the authorities, 'you will be thrown to the lions in the arena!' Still they refused to say it. On what grounds? On the grounds of the bare Word of God! . . . They risked all. They died by faith and in faith.

This is our position as Christians today. The choice is being forced upon us more and more. Is there anyone still foolish enough to bank on this world and what it has to offer? What is the controlling principle in our lives? Is it calculation? Is it worldly wisdom . . . ? Or is it the Word of God, warning us that this life and this world are only transient, and that both are merely a preparation for the world to come? It does not tell us to turn our backs entirely upon the world, but it does insist that we have the right view of the world. . . . We must ask ourselves as in the presence of God, the simple questions: Is my life based upon the faith principle? Am I submitting myself to the fact that what I read in the Bible is the word of God and is true? And am I willing to stake everything, my life included, upon this fact?

From Fear to Faith, pp. 52–3

Do not think in terms of bargains and rights in the Kingdom of God. That is absolutely fatal. There is nothing so wrong as the spirit which argues that because I do this, or because I have done that, I have a right to expect something else in return. . . . I know very good evangelical Christian people, who seem to be thinking like that. 'Now', they say, 'if we pray for certain things, we are bound to have them . . . if we pray all night for revival we must have revival.' I have sometimes described this as the 'penny in the slot' idea of Christianity. . . . But that surely is to deny the whole principle which our Lord is teaching. . . . What would the position be if we could command these things at will? But we cannot. Let us get rid of this bargaining spirit. . . . The Holy Spirit is Lord, and He is a Sovereign Lord. He sends these things in His own time and in His own way . . . we must realize that we have no right to anything at all. 'But', says someone, 'does not Paul teach about judgement and rewards in the Second Epistle to the Corinthians, in the fifth chapter?' Certainly he does, and he does so likewise in 1 Corinthians 3, and our Lord Himself in the twelfth chapter of Luke talks about those who are beaten with many stripes and those who receive few stripes and so on. Well, what of that? The reply is that even the rewards are of grace. He need not give them, and if you think you can determine and predict how they are to come you will be quite wrong. Everything is of grace in the Christian life from the very beginning to the very end. To think in terms of bargains and to murmur at results, implies a distrust of Him, and we need to watch our own spirits lest we harbour the thought that He is not dealing with us justly and fairly.

Spiritual Depression, pp. 129–30

[Some apparently Christian people] are worried about food and drink; they are always talking about wealth and position and their various possessions. These things really control them. They are made happy or unhappy by them; they are put out by them or pleased by them; and they are always thinking and talking about them. That is to be like the heathen, says Christ; for the Christian should not be controlled by these things. Whatever may be his position with respect to them, he is not finally to be controlled by them . . . because that is the typical condition of the heathen, who is dominated by them in his whole outlook upon life and in his living in this world.

This is a very good way, therefore, of increasing our faith and of introducing ourselves to the biblical conception of the life of faith. God's people, God's children in this world, are meant to live the life of faith; they are meant to live in the light of that faith which they profess. I suggest therefore, that there are certain questions which we should always be putting to ourselves. Here are some of them. Do I face the things that happen to me in this world as the Gentiles do? When these things happen to me, when there seem to be difficulties about food, or drink, or clothing, or difficulties in some relationship in life, how do I face them? How do I react? Is my reaction just that of the heathen, and of people who do not pretend to be Christian? How do I react during a war? How do I react to illness and pestilence and loss? It is a very good question to ask.

Studies in the Sermon on the Mount, ii, p. 139

. . . there is but one treatment which can heal that diseased eye. We need waste none of our time in trying anything else. We need spend no further money on that which is not bread. We can cease to travel round to the various spiritual spas in our search for health and wholeness. The world has done its utmost to clear its own spiritual eye. Patent after patent has been brought out. Lenses and spectacles of all colours, shapes, and sizes have been offered to us, and have been loudly recommended by great and well-known leaders. . . . But still mankind cannot see, and continues in sin and in misery. The strain is too deep. The nebulae and the mists are not outside the eye but actually within the organ itself. All our own efforts and all our best remedies leave us precisely where we were. Indeed, we find . . . that the experts themselves cannot see, and often end their lives, as did the German philosopher Goethe upon his deathbed, with the cry, 'More light!' . . . Is there no cure? Are we all doomed therefore to perpetual blindness and darkness? There is but one hope. There is but one answer. There is but one cure. According to the gospel, Jesus of Nazareth . . . came down to earth because of the blindness of mankind. . . . He came and brought that treatment which alone can avail. . . . He has given new life and power to our diseased and paralysed spiritual optic nerves. He enables us to see God, to behold our Father's face. And, looking at Him, the light of the eternal countenance irradiates our whole being. . . . He said that He was 'the light of the world' (John 8:12) and that anyone who followed Him need no longer walk in darkness, but have the 'light of life' (John 8:12). . . . The message of the gospel therefore to this modern distracted world is that in simplicity it has but to offer this prayer:

> Holy Spirit, truth divine,
> Dawn upon this soul of mine,
> Word of God and inward light,
> Wake my spirit, clear my sight.

Truth Unchanged, Unchanging, pp. 95–7

'. . . *since Jesus came into my heart . . .*'
Is my life different?

Does my Christian faith affect my view of life and control it in all matters? I claim to be Christian, and hold the Christian faith; the question I now ask myself is, 'Does that Christian faith of mine affect my whole detailed view of life? Is it always determining my reaction and my response to the particular things that happen?' Or, we can put it like this. 'Is it clear and obvious to myself and to everybody else that my whole approach to life, my essential view of life in general and in particular, is altogether different from that of the non-Christian?' It should be. The Sermon on the Mount begins with the Beatitudes. They describe people who are altogether different from all others, as different as light from darkness, as different as salt from putrefaction. If, then, we are different essentially, we must be different in our view of, and in our reaction to, everything. I know of no better question that a man can ask himself in every circumstance in life than that. When something happens to upset you, do you ask, 'Is my reaction essentially different from what it would be if I were not a Christian?' Let us remind ourselves of the teaching . . . at the end of the fifth chapter of [Matthew's] Gospel. You remember that our Lord put it like this: 'If ye salute your brethren only, what do ye more than others?' That is it. The Christian is a man who does 'more than others'. He is a man who is absolutely different. And if in every detail of his life this Christianity of his does not come in, he is a very poor Christian, he is a man 'of little faith'.

Studies in the Sermon on the Mount, ii, pp. 139–40

Sometimes God has been gracious on a Sunday and I have been conscious of exceptional liberty, and I have been foolish enough to listen to the devil when he says, 'Now, then, you wait until next Sunday, it is going to be marvellous, there will be even larger congregations'. And I go into the pulpit the next Sunday and I see a smaller congregation. But then on another occasion I stand in this pulpit labouring, as it were left to myself, preaching badly and utterly weak, and the devil has come and said, 'There will be nobody there at all next Sunday'. But, thank God, I have found on the following Sunday a larger congregation. That is God's method of accountancy. You never know. I enter the pulpit in weakness and I end with power. I enter with self-confidence and I am made to feel a fool. It is God's accountancy. . . . He is always giving us surprises. His book-keeping is the most romantic thing I know of in the whole world.

Our Lord spoke of it again in the third parable in the twenty-fifth chapter of the Gospel according to St Matthew. You remember His description of the people who will come at the end of the world expecting a reward but to whom He will give nothing, and then the others to whom He will say, 'Come ye blessed of My Father, inherit the Kingdom prepared for you'. And they will say, 'We have done nothing. When have we seen you naked, when have we seen you hungry or thirsty and given you drink?' And He will say, 'Because you have done it unto the least of my brethren you have done it unto me'. What a surprise that will be. This life is full of romance. Our ledgers are out of date; they are of no value. We are in the Kingdom of God and it is God's accountancy. It is all of grace.

Spiritual Depression, pp. 131–2

The gospel of Jesus Christ confronts and challenges the modern world with the statement that it alone has the answer to all man's questions and the solution to all his problems. In a world that is seeking a way out of its tragedy and its troubles, the gospel announces that the solution is already available. . . . It denounces the fatal habit of pinning our hopes to something that is going to happen, and announces that all that is needed by men, individually and collectively, has been at the disposal of mankind for nearly two thousand years. For the central message of the gospel is to tell men that everything necessary for their salvation is to be found in the person of Jesus Christ of Nazareth, the only begotten Son of God. He, it proclaims, is the full and final revelation of God. It is in Him, His life and His teaching, that we see what man is meant to be, and the kind of life that man is meant to live. It is in His death upon the Cross that we see the sin of the world finally exposed and condemned. It is through His death that we see the only way whereby man can be reconciled to God. It is from Him alone we can derive new life, and obtain a new beginning. It is only as we receive power from Him that we can live the life that God intended us to live. Indeed, it goes further, and assures us that He is seated at the right hand of God, reigning in power. . . . The gospel proclaims that the time is coming when 'at the name of Jesus every knee shall bow, of things in heaven, and things in earth, and things under the earth' (Philippians 2:10). Thus the gospel of Jesus Christ confronts man, and urges him to turn back, to look back at this unique Person who was here on earth nearly two thousand years ago, and in whom alone salvation is to be found.

Truth Unchanged, Unchanging, pp. 98–9

There He was (Luke 8:22–5), weary and tired, so tired, in fact, that He fell asleep.... Look at Him. There is no doubt about His humanity. He is fatigued, He is tired and weary, so much so that He just falls asleep, and, though the storm has arisen, He still goes on sleeping. He is subject to infirmity, He is a man in the body and flesh like all the rest of us. Ah, yes, but wait a minute. They came to Him and awoke Him saying, 'Master, carest Thou not that we perish?' Then He arose and rebuked the wind and the raging of the sea, and they ceased and there was a calm ... it is not surprising that the disciples, seeing all this, wondered and said one to another, 'What manner of man is this! for he commandeth even the winds and water, and they obey him'. Man, and yet obviously God. He could command the elements, He could silence the wind and stop the raging of the sea. He is the Lord of nature and of creation, He is the Lord of the universe. This is the mystery and the marvel of Jesus Christ—God and Man, two natures in One Person, two natures unmixed yet resident in the same Person....

If you do not believe in the unique deity of the Lord Jesus Christ, you are not a Christian, whatever else you may be. We are not looking at a good Man only, we are not interested merely in the greatest Teacher the world has ever seen; we are face to face with the fact that God, the Eternal Son, has been in this world and that He took upon Him human nature and dwelt amongst us, a Man amongst men—God-Man. We are face to face with the mystery and the marvel of the Incarnation and of the Virgin Birth. It is all here, and it shines out in all the fullness of its amazing glory. 'What manner of man is this?' He is more than Man. That is the answer—He is also God.

Spiritual Depression, p. 136

What, then, is meekness? I think we can sum it up in this way. Meekness is essentially a true view of oneself, expressing itself in attitude and conduct with respect to others. It is therefore two things. It is my attitude towards myself; and it is an expression of that in my relationship to others. You see how inevitably it follows being 'poor in spirit' and 'mourning'. A man can never be meek unless he is poor in spirit. A man can never be meek unless he has seen himself as a vile sinner. These other things must come first. But when I have that true view of myself in terms of poverty of spirit, and mourning because of my sinfulness, I am led on to see that there must be an absence of pride. The meek man is not proud of himself, he does not in any sense glory in himself. He feels that there is nothing in himself of which he can boast. It also means that he does not assert himself. You see, it is a negation of the popular psychology of the day which says 'assert yourself', 'express your personality'. The man who is meek does not want to do so; he is so ashamed of it. The meek man likewise does not demand anything for himself. He does not take all his rights as claims. He does not make demands for his position, his privileges, his possessions, his status in life. No, he is like the man depicted by Paul in Philippians 2. 'Let this mind be in you, which was also in Christ Jesus.' Christ did not assert that right to equality with God; He deliberately did not. And that is the point to which you and I have to come.

Studies in the Sermon on the Mount, i, pp. 68–9

Scripture is full of this idea of the trial of one's faith. Take the eleventh chapter of the Epistle to the Hebrews. . . . Every one of those men was tried. They had been given great promises and they had accepted them, and then everything seemed to go wrong. . . . Think of the trial of a man like Noah . . . of . . . Abraham, the trials that men like Jacob and especially Moses had to endure. God gives the gift of faith and then the faith is tried. . . . That is the theme of all the scriptures. You find it in the history of the Patriarchs and of all the Old Testament saints, you find it running through the New Testament. . . .

We must start by understanding that we may well find ourselves in a position in which our faith is going to be tried. Storms and trials are allowed by God. If we are living the Christian life, or trying to . . . on the assumption that it means just come to Christ and you will never have any more worry in the whole of your life, we are harbouring a terrible fallacy. . . . Our faith will be tried, and James goes so far as to say, 'Count it all joy when ye fall into divers temptations (trials)' (James 1:2). God permits storms, He permits difficulties, He permits the wind to blow and the billows to roll, and everything may seem to be going wrong and we ourselves to be in jeopardy. We must learn and realize that God does not take His people and lead them into some kind of Elysium in which they are protected from all 'the slings and arrows of outrageous fortune'. Not at all, we are living in the same world as everybody else. Indeed, the Apostle Paul seems to go further than that. He tells the Philippians, '. . . unto you it is given in the behalf of Christ, not only to believe on him, but also to suffer for his sake' (Philippians 1:29). 'In the world', says our Lord, 'ye shall have tribulation: but be of good cheer; I have overcome the world' (John 16:33). 'Be of good cheer'—yes, but remember that you will have the tribulation.

Spiritual Depression, pp. 139–40

. . . that blessed condition which is described in Philippians 4:11–13 . . . 'For I have learned, in whatsoever state I am, therewith to be content. . . .' In other words, he has arrived at a condition in which he is no longer hyper-sensitive. He is in a condition in which it does not matter very much what happens to him; it is not going to disturb him. 'I have learned, in whatsoever state I am, therewith to be content.' That is the position in which all of us who are Christians should be. The man who is not a Christian is not there, and cannot possibly be there. He is like a barrel of gunpowder; you never know when there is going to be an explosion. The slightest pin-prick causes great trouble; he is hyper-sensitive because of self. But the Apostle Paul had remembered what our Lord puts first to His disciples, namely, 'If any man will come after me, let him deny himself'. Self must be put out first. Then let him 'take up his cross, and follow me'. Because self is dethroned and put into the background, the disciple is not hyper-sensitive, and these things do not cause troubles and alarms and explosions. He is balanced because self is put out and he is living for Christ.

Let us examine ourselves in the light of this. Let us think of all our grievances; think of all our hardships, all the slights and insults and all the rest of the things we think have been heaped upon us, and all the misunderstandings. . . . There is nothing there really; we have just been making a mountain out of a molehill. If we could but make a list of the things that have upset us, how ashamed we should be. How small, how petty we can be!

Faith on Trial, p. 79

If we have a magical conception of the Christian life, we are certain to find ourselves in trouble, because, when difficulties come, we shall be tempted to ask, 'Why is this allowed?' And we should never ask such a question. . . . Our Lord goes to sleep and allows the storm to come. The position may indeed become quite desperate and we may appear to be in danger of our lives . . . yet—a Christian poet has said it for us:

> When all things seem against us
> To drive us to despair . . .

But it does not drive him to despair because he goes on to say:

> We know one gate is open
> One ear will hear our prayer.

But things may be desperate: 'All things seem against us, to drive us to despair.' Let us then be prepared for that. Yes, but we must go further. While all this is happening to us, our Lord appears to be utterly unconcerned about us. That is where the real trial of faith comes in. The wind and the billows were bad enough and the water coming into the ship. That was terrible, but the thing that to them was most terrible of all was His apparent unconcern. Still sleeping and not apparently caring. . . . Just imagine the feelings of these men. They had followed Him and listened to His teaching . . . they had seen His miracles and were expecting marvellous things to happen; and now it looked as if everything was going to come to an end in shipwreck and drowning. . . . We must be very young indeed in the Christian life if we do not know something about this. . . . The fact that God permits these things and that He often appears to be quite unconcerned about it all really constitutes what I am describing as the trial of faith. These are the conditions in which our faith is tried and tested, and God allows it all, God permits it all.

Spiritual Depression, pp. 140–1

Do I always place everything in my life, and everything that happens to me, in the context of my Christian faith, and then look at it in the light of that context? The heathen cannot do that. . . . He does not believe in God, or know anything about Him; he has not this revelation of God as his Father and himself as His child. . . . But what really proves that we are Christians is that, when these things come to us, or happen to us, we do not see them just as they are; as Christians we take them and put them immediately into the context of the whole of our faith and then look at them again. . . .

Our Lord asked His disciples, 'Where is your faith? Why are you not applying it?' . . . Something happens to us that tends to upset us. The heathen in the natural man makes him lose his temper, or become hurt and sensitive. But the Christian stops and says, 'Wait a minute. I am going to take this thing and put it into the context of everything I know and believe about God and my relationship to Him'. Then he looks at it again. Then he begins to understand what the author of the Epistle to the Hebrews means when he says, 'whom the Lord loveth he chasteneth'. Because the Christian knows that, he is able to enjoy it, in a sense, even while it is happening, because he puts it into the context of his faith. . . . Is my conduct and my behaviour in life such that it shows I am a Christian? Do I show plainly and clearly that I belong to a higher realm, and that I can raise everything about me to that realm? . . . Realize what you are; remember who you are and live accordingly. Rise to the level of your faith; be worthy of your high calling in Christ Jesus. Christian people, watch your lips, watch your tongues. We betray ourselves in our conversation . . . in the things that come out in our unguarded moments . . . the Christian exercises discipline and control because he sees everything in the context of God and of eternity.

Studies in the Sermon on the Mount, ii, pp. 140–1

Heaven and earth shall pass away, but **my**
               words shall not pass away

How careful [Jesus] was always to speak of 'my Father and
your Father'. He does not say 'our Father'. He says '*my* Father'.
He teaches His disciples to pray, 'Our Father', but He never
includes Himself with them. He always takes pains to emphasize this difference, that He is the Son of man. He is man and
yet He is not only man . . . [see Matthew 11:27; John 14:6].
. . . He deliberately sets Himself up as the authoritative
Teacher. . . . 'Ye have heard that it was said by them of old
time. . . . But *I* say unto you . . .' He declares '*I*', with authority
. . . it is this characteristic, personal emphasis which brings
Him into contrast with the prophets. . . . They were great
personalities. . . . But there is not one of them who ever used
this 'I'. They all say, 'Thus saith the Lord'. But the Lord Jesus
Christ . . . says, '*I* say unto you'. At once He is differentiating
between Himself and all others. 'Now is the time for final
authority', He seems to be saying. He emphasizes this fact
constantly in the Sermon on the Mount. . . . When He concludes
that great sermon, He does so by uttering one of the most
staggering and astounding things that He ever said. 'Therefore
whosoever heareth these sayings of mine, and doeth them, I
will liken him unto a wise man, which built his house upon a
rock. . . .' There, you see, His whole emphasis is upon 'these
sayings of *mine*'. Here is His claim to final authority. And if it
is possible to add to such a statement, He did so when He said,
'Heaven and earth shall pass away, but *my* words shall not pass
away'. There is nothing beyond that.

Authority, pp. 18–19

. . . the man who is meek is not even sensitive about himself. He is not always watching himself and his own interests. He is not always on the defensive. We all know about this, do we not? Is it not one of the greatest curses in life as a result of the fall—this sensitivity about self? We spend the whole of our lives watching ourselves. But when a man becomes meek he has finished with all that; he no longer worries about himself and what other people say. To be truly meek means we no longer protect ourselves, because we see there is nothing worth defending. So we are not on the defensive; all that is gone. The man who is truly meek never pities himself, he is never sorry for himself. He never talks to himself and says, 'You are having a hard time, how unkind these people are not to understand you'. He never thinks, 'How wonderful I really am, if only other people gave me a chance'. Self-pity! What hours and years we waste in this! But the man who has become meek has finished with all that. To be meek, in other words, means that you have finished with yourself altogether, and you come to see you have no rights or deserts at all. You come to realize that nobody can harm you. John Bunyan puts it perfectly. 'He that is down need fear no fall.' When a man truly sees himself, he knows nobody can say anything about him that is too bad. You need not worry about what men may say or do; you know you deserve it all and more. Once again, therefore, I would define meekness like this. The man who is truly meek is the one who is amazed that God and man can think of him as well as they do and treat him as well as they do.

Studies in the Sermon on the Mount, **i**, p. 69

Browning . . . defined faith. . . . 'With me, faith means perpetual unbelief kept quiet, like the snake 'neath Michael's foot'. Here is Michael and there is the snake beneath his foot and he just keeps it quiet under the pressure of his foot. . . . Faith is unbelief kept quiet, kept down. That is what these men (Luke 8:22–5) did not do, they allowed this situation to grip them, they became panicky. Faith, however, is a refusal to allow that. It says: 'I am not going to be controlled by these circumstances —I am in control.' So you take charge of yourself, and pull yourself up. . . . You do not let go, you assert yourself. . . .

That is the first thing, but. . . . That is not enough, because that may be nothing but resignation. That is not the whole of faith. Having taken that first step, having pulled yourself up, you then remind yourself of what you believe and what you know. . . . If only they had stopped a moment and said: 'Now then what about it? Is it possible that we are going to drown with Him in the boat? Is there anything He cannot do? We have seen His miracles, He turned the water into wine, He can heal the blind and the lame, He can even raise the dead, is it likely that He is going to allow us and Himself to be drowned in this way? Impossible! In any case He loves us, He cares for us, He has told us that the very hairs of our head are all numbered!' That is the way in which faith reasons. It says: 'All right, I see the waves and the billows but'—it always puts up this 'but'. That is faith, it holds on to truth and reasons from what it knows to be fact.

Spiritual Depression, pp. 143–4

[Our Lord] says: You are concerned about these other things, and you are putting them first. But you must not. What you have to put first is the kingdom of God and His righteousness. He . . . said that, in the model prayer which He taught these people to pray. . . . You come to God. Of course you are interested in life and in this world; but you do not start by saying, 'Give us this day our daily bread'. You start like this: 'Our Father which art in heaven, Hallowed be thy name. Thy kingdom come. Thy will be done in earth, as it is in heaven.' And then, and only then, 'Give us this day our daily bread'. 'Seek ye first'—not 'your daily bread', but, 'the kingdom of God and his righteousness'. In other words, you must bring yourself to that position in mind and heart and desires. It must take absolute priority over everything else.

. . . our Lord . . . is telling [His hearers] how to behave because they are Christian. They are in the kingdom of God, and because they are in it they are to seek it more and more. They are, as Peter puts it, to 'make their calling and election sure' . . . as children of our heavenly Father, we should be seeking to know Him better. Now the author of the Epistle to the Hebrews puts that perfectly when he says in 11:6, 'He that cometh to God must believe that he is, and that he is a rewarder of them that diligently seek him'. Put your emphasis on the 'diligently'. Many Christian people miss so many blessings in this life because they do not seek God diligently. They do not spend much time in seeking His face. . . . The Christian is meant to be seeking the face of the Lord daily, constantly. He takes and makes time to do so.

Studies in the Sermon on the Mount, ii, p. 143

Over and above all other facts is the most glorious fact of all, the fact of Jesus Christ Himself. We are given the details of His earthly life in the Gospels so that we may have consolation in times of trouble. Above all remember that the Son of God Himself has been through this world. He knows all about the contradiction of sinners against Himself. Though He was the Son of God He knew what it was to be tired, to be weary, to be faint in His body, to sweat drops of blood in agony. He knew what it was to face the whole world and all the power of Satan and hell massed against Himself. 'We have not an high priest which cannot be touched with the feeling of our infirmities; but was in all points tempted like as we are, yet without sin' (Hebrews 4:15). He knows all about our weakness and our frailty. The incarnation is not a mere idea but a fact: 'The Word was made flesh.' And in our agony and weakness we can always turn to Him with confidence knowing that He understands, He knows, and He can succour. The Son of God became man in order that He might be our perfect High Priest and be able to lead us to God.

> My hope is built on nothing less
> Than Jesu's blood and righteousness . . .
> When darkness seems to veil His face
> I rest on His unchanging grace;
> In every high and stormy gale
> My anchor holds within the veil . . .
>   On Christ the solid Rock I stand,
>   All other ground is sinking sand.

So, come what may, 'I will rejoice in the Lord, I will joy in the God of my salvation'.

From Fear to Faith, pp. 77–8

'O Lord, I have heard thy speech, and was afraid' [Habakkuk 3:2]. 'Was afraid' does not mean that Habakkuk was afraid of the things that were going to happen as revealed to him by God. . . . The expression suggests awe in the presence of such a great God, worshipful adoration and wonder at God, and His ways. God had told him something about His historical plan, and the prophet, meditating upon the fact that God is in His holy temple and the world beneath His feet, stood in amazement and reverential awe. . . . What is described in the Epistle to the Hebrews as an attitude of 'reverence and godly fear' is an attitude strangely lacking among us. . . . There is far too much easy familiarity with the Most High. Thank God, we can come into His presence with holy boldness through the blood of Christ. But that should never lessen our reverence and godly fear. God's ancient people . . . were so conscious of the holiness and the greatness of God that they trembled even to use His name. The sanctity and the holiness and the almightiness of God was something which made them almost speechless—'I was afraid'. We should approach Him 'with reverence and godly fear, for our God is a consuming fire'.

This is essential for an understanding of the times in which we live. We must learn to see God in His holy temple above the flux of history, and above the changing scenes of time. In God's presence the one thing that stands out is the holy nature of God and our own sin. We humble ourselves and with reverence adore Him.

From Fear to Faith, pp. 62–3

When we are converted and saved and become Christian our temperaments do not change; they remain exactly what they were. You do not become somebody else, you are still yourself . . . You are always yourself, and, though you become Christian, you are still yourself. You have your own peculiar temperament, your own peculiar characteristics, and the result is that we all have our special problems. There are certain problems that are fundamental and common to us all, and even our particular problem comes under the general category of sin and the results of the Fall, but it comes to us in different ways. . . . All members of the Church are not the same, all members of any group, however small, are not the same; we all have certain things about which we have to be particularly and exceptionally careful. Other people are not troubled by these things at all. Ah, yes, but they have other things about which they have to be careful. The hot-tempered person has to watch that temper very closely, and equally the phlegmatic and lethargic person has to be careful, because he is so flabby in his whole mentality that he tends not to stand when he should stand. In other words, we all have our particular difficulties and they generally arise from our own peculiar temperament which God has given us. I can indeed go further in this context and say that probably the thing we have to watch most of all is our strength, our strong point. We all tend to fail ultimately at our strongest point.

Spiritual Depression, p. 151

Paul is ready to preach to all—the Emperor on his throne, the counsellors and captains, but also the soldiers and the slaves, the outcast and despised. He has a message for all, and it is the same message for all. Ashamed of it? Why, it is the one thing which is worthy of our boasting and our exultation, for it alone is big enough and wide enough to deal with the whole world, and to include the praise of all.

How small and petty do the various things seem in which men make their boast, by the side of Jesus Christ and His gospel!

. . . There is but one message that can include the whole world, in spite of all divisions and distinctions. There is but one power that can bring all men together and unite them and bring them to true brotherhood. . . . It is 'the gospel of Christ which is the power of God unto salvation to everyone that believeth'.

All who have ever believed it, and have proved its truth and power, have joined Paul in saying and singing, 'God forbid that I should glory save in the cross of our Lord Jesus Christ'. The chorus is already loud, but it will be louder. For John tells us in his vision that, 'I beheld, and I heard the voice of many angels round about the throne, and the beasts, and the elders: and the number of them was ten thousand times ten thousand, and thousands of thousands; saying with a loud voice, Worthy is the Lamb that was slain to receive power, and riches, and wisdom, and strength, and honour, and glory, and blessing. And every creature which is in heaven, and on the earth, and under the earth, and such as are in the sea, and all that are in them, heard I saying, Blessing, and honour, and glory, and power, be unto him that sitteth upon the throne, and unto the Lamb for ever and ever.' God grant that we may find ourselves among the blessed throng!

The Plight of Man and the Power of God, pp. 93–4

What are the characteristics of this great faith? The first is this—it is a knowledge of the Lord Jesus Christ and His power, with a steady trust and confidence in that. Now Peter . . . starts off well and that is of the essence of true faith. Here was a man with the other disciples in the boat and with the storm raging round them. The sea and the wind were contrary and the boat was being tossed by the waves, and the position was becoming rather desperate. But suddenly our Lord appeared and when they saw Him they said, 'Is that a man walking on the water? It is impossible—it must be some kind of a ghost, it is a spirit'. They cried out for fear, and straightway Jesus spoke and said, 'It is I, be not afraid'. And then we have this magnificent exhibition of the essence of true faith by Peter. Peter answered Him, and said, 'Lord, if it be thou, bid me come unto thee on the water'. Now that is an indication of true faith for you see what it means; it means that Peter was saying in effect to our Lord, 'If you really are the Lord, well, then, I know there is nothing impossible to you. Give proof of it by commanding me to step out of this boat in this raging sea and enabling me to walk on it'. He believed in the Lord, in His power, in His person, in His ability. And he did not believe in it merely theoretically. He tried it! We are told here, 'And when Peter was come down out of the ship, he walked on the water'. Now that is the essence of faith—'Lord, if it be thou. . . .' That is what faith says: 'If it is indeed You, well then I know You can do this: command me to do it.' And he did it. . . . The Christian faith begins and ends with a knowledge of the Lord . . . a knowledge of this Blessed Person.

Spiritual Depression, p. 155

[Meekness] must then go on and express itself in our whole demeanour and in our behaviour with respect to others. . . . A person who is of the type that I have been describing must of necessity be mild . . . think again of the Lord Jesus Christ. Mild, gentle, lowly—those are the terms. Quiet, of a quiet spirit . . . 'meek and lowly' . . . the most approachable Person this world has ever seen was the Lord Jesus Christ. But it also means that there will be a complete absence of the spirit of retaliation, having our own back or seeing that the other person pays for it. It also means, therefore, that we shall be patient and long-suffering, especially when we suffer unjustly [1 Peter 2:19–23]. . . . There is no credit, Peter argues in that chapter, if, when we are buffeted for our faults, we take it patiently; but if we do well and suffer for it and take it patiently, then that is the thing that is praiseworthy in the sight of God. That is meekness. But it also means that we are ready to listen and to learn; that we have such a poor idea of ourselves and our own capabilities that we are ready to listen to others. Above all we must be ready to be taught by the Spirit, and led by the Lord Jesus Christ Himself. Meekness always implies a teachable spirit. It is what we see again in the case of our Lord Himself. Though He was the Second Person in the blessed Holy Trinity, He became man, He deliberately humbled Himself to the extent that He was dependent entirely upon what God gave Him, what God taught Him and what God told Him to do. He humbled Himself to that, and that is what is meant by being meek. We must be ready to learn and listen and especially must we surrender ourselves to the Spirit.

Studies in the Sermon on the Mount, i, pp. 69–70

Surely this is the greatest need at the present time? Go back and read the history of the great revivals in the Church, and you will find that this power of the Holy Ghost and authority is always present. Two hundred years ago a great evangelical awakening was witnessed in England, in America, in Scotland and in Wales. One of the leaders in Wales was a man called Howell Harris. As you read his journals you find that he keeps on saying something like this: 'Arrived at such and such a place; preached. Felt the old authority.' Then another time he says that when he preached in a certain place, 'No authority'. It grieved him and he was unhappy. He fell down before God, searched his heart and confessed his sin and sought 'the authority' again. He was never happy unless he was aware of 'the authority'. . . . He knew that preaching . . . was vain apart from 'the authority'.

One cannot read the journals of Whitefield and of Wesley without finding exactly the same thing. I remember reading in the journals of Whitefield. . . . 'The Lord came down amongst us'. The authority! . . . And John Wesley constantly expresses the same thought. That was the essence of his experience in the meeting at Aldersgate in London when he felt his heart 'strangely warmed'. It was from that moment that he had this authority, with the result that his ministry was entirely transformed. Jonathan Edwards experienced exactly the same thing. Dwight L. Moody is also a special instance of this matter. It was after that experience while he was walking down Wall Street in New York City, when the Holy Ghost came upon him, that Moody received his authority. He preached the sermons he preached before, but they were transformed. Why? He *now* had the authority of the Spirit.

Authority, pp. 86–7

The man who knows himself to be a child of God and an heir of eternity has a very different view of things in this life and world . . . and the greater that faith and knowledge, the smaller will these other things become. Moreover he has a definite specific promise. Let us lay hold on this promise and grasp it firmly. The promise is that, if we do truly seek these things first and foremost, and almost exclusively, these other things shall be added unto us, they will be 'thrown into the bargain'. The heathen does nothing but think about these things. . . . The man of God prays about and seeks the kingdom of God, and these other things are added unto him. It is a specific promise of God.

You have a perfect illustration of this in the story about Solomon. Solomon did not pray for riches and length of days; he prayed for wisdom. And God said . . . Because you have not prayed for these other things I will give you wisdom; and I will give you these other things as well. I will give you riches and length of days into the bargain (see 1 Kings 3). . . . It is not an accident that the Puritans of the seventeenth century, especially the Quakers, became wealthy people. It was not because they hoarded wealth, it was not because they worshipped mammon. It was just because they were living for God and His righteousness and the result was that they did not throw away their money on worthless things. In a sense, therefore, they could not help becoming wealthy. They held on to the promises of God and incidentally became rich!

Put God, His glory and the coming of His kingdom, and your relationship to Him, your nearness to Him and your holiness in the central position, and you have the pledged word of God Himself through the lips of His Son, that all these other things, as they are necessary for your well-being in this life and world, shall be added unto you.

Studies in the Sermon on the Mount, ii, p. 145

. . . The next characteristic of faith is that it persists steadily in looking to Him and at Him. . . . Faith says, 'What He has begun to do He can continue to do. The beginning of the work was a miracle, so if He can initiate a miraculous work He can keep it going; what He has already begun He can continue'. . . . Yes, says Toplady,

> The work which His goodness began
> The arm of His strength will complete.

That is an unanswerable argument.

Secondly, you and I can never doubt while we look at Him and are clear about Him. Without Him we are utterly hopeless. It does not matter how long you have been in the Christian life, you are dependent upon Him for every step. Without Him we can do nothing. We can only conquer our doubts by looking steadily at Him and by not looking at them. The way to answer them is to look at Him. The more you know Him and His glory the more ridiculous they will become. So keep steadily looking at Him. You cannot live on an initial faith—that is what Peter seems to have been trying to do. . . . Do not try to live on your conversion. You will be done before you know where you are . . . you must keep on looking to Him every day. 'We walk by faith' and you live by faith in the Lord Jesus Christ. You need Him as much on your deathbed as you did on the night you were converted; you need Him all the time. . . . One of the most perfect illustrations is the way the Children of Israel had to collect the manna each day but the sabbath. That is the Lord's method. He does not give us enough for a month. We need a fresh supply every day, so start your day with Him and keep in touch with Him. That was Peter's fatal error (Matthew 14:22–33); he looked away from Him. It is 'the fight of faith', you are walking on turbulent waves and the only way to keep walking is to keep looking at Him.

Spiritual Depression, pp. 158–9

Penniless, we own the world!
2 Corinthians 6:10 (N.E.B.)

We are to leave everything—ourselves, our rights, our cause, our whole future—in the hands of God, and especially so if we feel we are suffering unjustly. . . . We leave ourselves and our cause and our rights and everything with God, with a quietness in spirit and in mind and heart. . . .

Now notice what happens to the man who is like this. 'Blessed are the meek; *for they shall inherit the earth.*' What does that mean? We can summarize it very briefly. The meek already inherit the earth in this life, in this way. A man who is truly meek is a man who is always satisfied, he is a man who is already content. Goldsmith expresses it well when he says, 'Having nothing yet hath all'. The Apostle Paul has put it still better, for he says, 'as having nothing, and yet possessing all things'. Again, in writing to the Philippians, he says in effect, 'Thank you for sending your present. I like it, not because I wanted anything, but I like the spirit that made you send it. Yet as for myself, I have all things and abound.' He has already said to them, 'I know both how to be abased, and I know how to abound' and, 'I can do all things through Christ which strengtheneth me.' Notice, too, the striking way in which he expresses the same thought in 1 Corinthians 3. After telling his readers that they need not be jealous or concerned about these things, he says, 'All things are yours', everything; 'whether Paul, or Apollos, or Cephas, or the world, or life or death, or things present, or things to come; all are yours; and ye are Christ's; and Christ is God's'. All things are yours if you are meek and truly Christian; you have already inherited the earth.

Studies in the Sermon on the Mount, i, pp. 70–1

   ... as I confront this mighty, glorious task of denying myself and taking up the cross and following the Lord Jesus Christ I realize that I am to walk through this world as He walked. As I realize that I have been born again and fashioned by God according to the image of His dear Son, and as I begin to ask, 'Who am I ever to live so? How can I ever hope to do that?'— here is the answer, the doctrine of the Holy Spirit, the truth that the Holy Spirit dwells within us. What does it teach? It first of all reminds me of the power of the Holy Spirit that is within me. The Apostle has already said that in verse 13 [of Romans 8]. . . . 'If ye live after the flesh ye shall die: but if ye through the Spirit do mortify the deeds of the body, ye shall live'. Here he comes back to that same teaching. 'For God hath not given us the spirit of fear.' 'You must realize that you are not living by yourselves,' he says in effect to these Romans. 'You have been thinking of this task of yours as if you alone, by yourself, had to live the great Christian life. You realize that you are forgiven, and you can thank God that your sins are blotted out and washed away, but you seem to think that that is all and that you are left to live the Christian life on your own. If you think like that', says Paul, 'it is not surprising that you are in a spirit of fear and bondage, for the whole thing is entirely hopeless. It means that you just have a new law which is infinitely more difficult than the old law. But that is not the position, for the Holy Spirit dwells within you.'

Spiritual Depression, pp. 169–70

The heirs of salvation, I know from His word,
                  Through much tribulation must follow their Lord

This man [Psalm 73] had been taking the blessings and the joys for granted. We all seem to assume that we have the right to these things and that we should have them always. Therefore the moment they are denied us we begin to question and to query. Now the Psalmist should have said to himself, 'I am a godly man, I believe in God. I am living a godly life and I know certain things about the character of God. . . . Now certain painful things are happening to me. . . . But, of course, there must be some very good reason for this.' Then he should have begun to seek for reasons, and to look for an explanation. Had he done so he would undoubtedly have concluded that God had some purpose in all this. . . . He would have to come to the conclusion that even though he might not understand it, God must have a reason, because God never does anything irrational. He would have said, 'I am certain of that, and, therefore, whatever the explanation is, it is not what I thought at first'. He would have thought it out.

But how slow we are to do that. We seem to think that, as Christian people, we should never have any trouble. Nothing should ever go wrong with us, and the sun should always be shining about us, while all who are not Christians, on the other hand, should know constant trouble and difficulty. But the Bible has never promised us that. It has rather promised 'that we must through much tribulation enter into the kingdom of God'. It says also, 'Unto you it is given in the behalf of Christ, not only to believe on him, but also to suffer for his sake' (Philippians 1:29). So the moment we begin to think, we see that the idea that came to us instinctively is utterly false to the teaching of the Bible.

Faith on Trial, pp. 81–2

August 30   *Our Father . . .*
                    (speak those words several times—slowly,
                    reverently, with silences in between)

The presence of the Holy Spirit in us reminds us of our relationship to God. This is a wonderful thing [Romans 8:15]. . . . The presence of the Holy Spirit within us reminds us of our sonship, yes, our adult sonship. We are not infants. . . . We are sons in the fullest sense and in the possession of all our faculties. The clear realization of this gets rid of the spirit of bondage again to fear. It does not do away with 'reverence and godly fear', but it does away with the fear that the spirit of bondage brings. . . .

. . . it enables us to see that our object in living the Christian life is not simply to attain a certain standard, but is rather to please God because He is our Father—'the spirit of adoption whereby we cry, Abba, Father'. The slave was not allowed to say 'Abba' and that slave spirit does not regard God as Father. He has not realized that He is Father, he regards Him still as a Judge who condemns. But that is wrong. As Christian people we must learn to appropriate by faith the fact that God is our Father. Christ taught us to pray 'Our Father'. This eternal everlasting God has become our Father and the moment we realize that, everything tends to change. He is our Father and He is always caring for us, He loves us with an everlasting love, He so loved us that He sent His only begotten Son into the world and to the Cross to die for our sins. That is our relationship to God and the moment we realize it, it transforms everything. Henceforth my desire is not to keep the law but to please my Father. We know something about that by nature. Filial love, filial reverence, filial fear is so different from that old servile fear. . . . Our Christian living is not a matter of rules and regulations any longer, but rather our desire to show Him our gratitude for all He has ever done for us.

Spiritual Depression, p. 172

The kingdom of God really means the reign of God; it means the law and the rule of God. . . . In one sense the kingdom has already come. It came when the Lord Jesus Christ was here. He said, 'If I with the finger of God cast out devils, no doubt the kingdom of God is come upon you'. He said in effect, 'The kingdom of God is here now; I am exercising this power, this sovereignty, this majesty, this dominion; this is the kingdom of God'. . . . The kingdom of God is also here at this moment in the hearts and lives of all who submit to Him, in all who believe in Him. The kingdom of God is present in the Church, in the heart of all those who are truly Christian. Christ reigns in such people. But the day is yet to come when His kingdom shall have been established here upon the earth . . . That day is coming. The whole message of the Bible looks forward to that. Christ came down from heaven to earth to found, to establish, and to bring in this kingdom. He is still engaged upon that task and will be until the end, when it shall have been completed. Then He will, according to Paul, hand it back to God the Father, 'that God may be all in all'.

So our petition really amounts to this. We should have a great longing and desire that the kingdom of God and of Christ may come in the hearts of men . . . that this kingdom should be extended in our own hearts. . . . We should also be anxious to see this kingdom extending in the lives and hearts of other men and women. So that when we pray, 'Thy kingdom come', we are praying for the success of the gospel, its sway and power; we are praying for the conversion of men and women; we are praying that the kingdom of God may come . . . everywhere in the world. But it goes even further than that. . . . It means that we should be anticipating the day when all sin and evil and wrong and everything that is opposed to God shall finally have been routed . . . that the name of God may be glorified and magnified over all.

Studies in the Sermon on the Mount, ii, pp. 63–4

We begin to realize this, that we are now sons of God, children of God. We have this new dignity, this new standing, this new status, this glorious position in which we find ourselves. Go back again to that High Priestly prayer (John 17) and notice how our Lord says that we are to glorify Him in this world exactly as He glorified His Father. Have you realized that? That is the Christian life, that is the reason for living the Christian life; it is to realize that I belong to God and that I must glorify Him. - . . . What a wonderful position! And the Spirit is in me and is enabling me to do it. He transforms my outlook and I lose the spirit of bondage again to fear. . . .

I realize that the Holy Spirit is dwelling within me. . . . The Holy Spirit within us reminds us of our destiny. 'If children, then heirs; heirs of God and joint heirs with Christ.' . . . The Christian is absolutely certain of his destiny. . . . It is not a question of . . . striving to do something; it is a question of getting ready for the place to which you are going. The way to get rid of the spirit of bondage and fear is to know that, if you are a child of God, you are destined for heaven and for glory, and that all the things you see inside yourself and outside yourself cannot prevent that plan from being carried out. . . . 'This is the victory that overcometh the world, even our faith.' Faith in what? Faith in my ultimate destiny. . . . There is nothing that is so calculated to promote holiness as the realization that we are heirs of God and joint heirs with Christ, that our destiny is certain and secure, that nothing can prevent it. . . . That is the way to live the Christian life! Do not turn it into a law, but realize that you have received the Holy Spirit. Then work out this theme. . . . You belong to Christ, you are His brother . . . Do not worry about what you feel. The truth about you is glorious. If you are in Christ, rise to it 'o'er sin and fear and care'. Take your full salvation and triumph and prevail.

Spiritual Depression, pp. 173–5

. . . it is all to be found in those words of our Lord in Luke 14:11: 'Whosoever exalteth himself shall be abased; and he that humbleth himself shall be exalted.'

There, then, is what is meant by being meek. Need I emphasize again that this is obviously something that is quite impossible to the natural man? We shall never make ourselves meek. . . . It cannot be done. Nothing but the Holy Spirit can humble us, nothing but the Holy Spirit can make us poor in spirit and make us mourn because of our sinfulness and produce in us this true, right view of self and give us this very mind of Christ Himself. But this is a serious matter. Those of us who claim to be Christian claim of necessity that we have already received the Holy Spirit. Therefore we have no excuse for not being meek. The man who is outside has an excuse, for it is impossible to him. But if we truly claim that we have received the Holy Spirit, and this is the claim of every true Christian, we have no excuse if we are not meek. It is not something that you do and I do. It is a character that is produced in us by the Spirit. It is the direct fruit of the Spirit. It is offered to us and it is possible for us all. What have we to do? We must face this Sermon on the Mount; we must meditate upon this statement about being meek; we must look at the examples; above all we must look at the Lord Himself. Then we must humble ourselves and confess with shame, not only the smallness of our stature, but our utter imperfection. Then we must finish with that self which is the cause of all our troubles, so that He who has bought us at such a price may come in and possess us wholly.

Studies in the Sermon on the Mount, i, pp. 71–2

Frequently there comes a point at which development and advance seem to have come to an end and we are in some kind of doldrums when it is difficult to know whether the work is moving at all, either backwards or forwards. All seems to be at a standstill and nothing seems to be taking place . . . some of these Galatian Christians had arrived at that particular point . . . the false teaching, the heresies and so on, undoubtedly had something to do with this . . . we are considering people who are not so much tired of the work as tired in it. . . . What shall we say about it and what shall we do about it? Let me say at the outset that there is no aspect of this great problem of depression in which negatives are more important than they are on this particular occasion. Whenever we are found in this position of weariness, before we begin to do anything positive, there are certain negatives that are absolutely all-important.

The first is this: Whatever you may feel about it do not consider the suggestion that comes to you from all directions— not so much from people, but from within yourself, the voices that seem to be speaking around and about you—do not listen to them when they suggest that you should give up, or give way, or give in. That is a great temptation that comes at this point. You say, 'I am weary and tired, the thing is too much for me.' And there is nothing to say at that point but this negative—do not listen. You always have to start with these 'don'ts' on the very lowest level; and that is the lowest level. You must say to yourself, 'Whatever happens I am going on.' You do not give in or give way.

Spiritual Depression, pp. 193–4

Do not carry yesterday or tomorrow with you; live for today
and for the twelve hours you are in. It is very interesting to
notice as you read biographies how many men have failed in
life because they have not done that. Most men who have been
successful in life have been characterized by this wonderful
capacity for forgetting the past. They have made mistakes.
'Well,' they say, 'I have made them and I cannot undo them.
If I meditated upon them for the rest of my life, it would make
no difference. . . . I will let the dead past bury its dead.' The
result is that when they make a decision they do not spend the
night worrying about it afterwards. On the other hand, the man
who cannot help referring back keeps himself awake saying,
'Why did I do that?' And so he saps his nervous energy. . . . As
a consequence he makes more mistakes, completing the vicious
circle of worry by saying, 'If I am making these mistakes now,
what about next week?' The poor man is already down and
defeated.

Here is our Lord's answer to all that. Do not be foolish, do
not waste your energy, do not spend your time thus in worrying
over what has passed, or about the future; here is today, live to
the maximum today . . . the God who helps us today will be
the same God tomorrow, and will help us tomorrow. . . .

Some people fail very grievously in this matter because they
are always trying to anticipate God; they are always sitting
down, as it were, and asking themselves, 'Now I wonder what
God is going to ask me to do tomorrow or in a week's time or
in a year? What is God going to ask of me then?' That is utterly
wrong . . . Live day by day; live a life of obedience to God every
day; do what God asks you to do every day. . . . You must
learn to trust God day by day for every particular occasion,
and never try to go ahead of Him.

Studies in the Sermon on the Mount, ii, pp. 150–1

*In wonder lost, with trembling joy
We take the pardon of our God.*

I have no doubt that up to a point [the Prodigal Son] thought he had been hardly dealt with. He left home for the far country. He was going to assert himself, but things went wrong. . . . Then he came to himself and he went home and said, 'Father, I have sinned against heaven, and in thy sight, and I am no more worthy to be called thy son'. That is just another way of saying the same thing [as Psalm 73:22]. Nothing to recommend us, no excuses; we have just been unutterably stupid, like beasts. We have failed to think and to reason; we have failed to apply these Scriptures. It is this horrible self that has been in control, and . . . nothing and no one is right but ourselves. Let us face it; let us unmask it; let us analyse and face ourselves with it. Let us look at it honestly until we are heartily ashamed of ourselves. Then let us go to that gracious loving God and acknowledge that . . . we have no claim upon Him at all, and no right to His forgiveness. Let us tell Him that we do not wish to be healed quickly, that we feel we do not deserve to be healed at all.

 . . . the trouble with many of us is that we heal ourselves too quickly. We feel we have a right to be forgiven. But the teaching of the Scripture and the example of the lives of the saints is that, like the Prodigal Son, they deserved nothing but damnation, that they had been like beasts in their stupidity, and that they had no claim at all on God. Indeed, they were filled with amazement that God could forgive them. Let us examine ourselves in the light of that. Do we rush back to God feeling we have a right to forgiveness? Or do we feel we have no right to ask for forgiveness? This is how this man felt. . . . Paul, after years of preaching, looked back across the past and said he was the 'chief' of sinners. He was still amazed that God could ever have forgiven him . . . he was still amazed at the wondrous cross and the love of God in Jesus Christ our Lord.

Faith on Trial, pp. 84–5

While there are people who hand in their resignations and say, 'I am quitting', that is not so with the majority. The danger of the majority at this point is just to resign themselves to it and to lose heart and to lose hope. They will go on, but they go on in this hopeless, dragging condition. . . . The danger at this point is to say something like this: 'Well, I have lost that something which I had, and obviously I shall not get it back again. But I am going on, and out of loyalty I will go on, as a sheer duty. I have lost the enjoyment I once had, that is gone and it is undoubtedly gone for ever. I just have to put up with it, I will resign myself to my fate, I won't be a quitter, I won't turn my back on it, I will go on, though I go on feeling rather hopeless about it all, just shuffling down the road, not walking with hope as I once did, but keeping on as best I can'. That is the spirit of of resignation, Stoicism if you like, putting up with it.

Now that is the greatest danger of all . . . it is something which is dangerous not only on the spiritual level, about which we are most concerned, but also on every level in life. We can work like that in our profession, we can live our lives like that . . . We are really saying to ourselves: 'The golden hours have gone, the great days belong to the past. I may never know that again but I will just keep on'. There is something, of course, which seems wonderful about this, something that seems heroic about it. But . . . it is a temptation of the devil. If he can get God's people to lose hope, he will be content indeed. And . . . this is perhaps the greatest danger of all confronting the Christian Church, the danger of doing a thing in a formal spirit and as a matter of duty. Going on, it is true, but wearily trudging along instead of walking as we ought to walk.

Spiritual Depression, pp. 194–5

September 7 *If thou wilt go with me, then I will go: but*
if thou wilt not go with me, I will not go
(Judges 4:8)

There was an old preacher in Wales about one hundred and
fifty years ago who was invited to preach at a preaching con-
vention held in a little town. The people had already assembled,
but the preacher had not come. So the local minister and other
leaders sent a maid back to the house where the preacher was
staying to tell him that they were waiting for him and that
everything was ready. The girl went and when she came back
she said, 'I did not like to disturb him. He was talking to somebody'. 'Oh,' said they, 'that is rather strange, because everybody is here. Go back and tell him that it is after time and that
he *must* come.' So the girl went back again, and again she
returned and reported, 'He *is* talking to somebody.' 'How do
you know that?' they asked. She answered: 'I heard him saying
to this other person who is with him, "I will not go and preach
to those people if you will not come with me".' 'Oh, it is all
right,' replied the ministers. 'We had better wait.'

The old preacher knew that there was little purpose in his
going to preach unless he knew of a certainty that the Holy
Ghost was going with him and giving him authority and power.
He was wise enough, and had sufficient spiritual discernment,
to refuse to preach until he knew that he had his authority, and
that the Holy Ghost was going with him and would speak
through him. You and I, however, often preach* without Him,
and all our cleverness and learning, and all our science and all
our apologetics lead to nothing because we lack the authority
of the Holy Ghost.

Authority, p. 88

---

*This address was originally given to students. But every Christian
preaches in everything that he is and does, all the time! (Ed.)

There is a sense in which we commit ourselves to God once and for ever; there is another sense in which we have to do it every day. There is a sense in which God has given us everything in grace once and for ever. Yes; but He gives grace to us also in parts and portions day by day. We must start the day and say to ourselves, 'Here is a day which is going to bring me certain problems and difficulties; very well, I shall need God's grace to help me. I know God will make all grace to abound, He will be with me according to my need—"as thy days, so shall thy strength be" ' . . . we must learn to leave the future entirely in God's hands.

Take, for instance, that great statement of it in Hebrews 13:8. The Hebrew Christians were passing through troubles and trials, and the author of that Epistle tells them not to worry, and for this reason—'Jesus Christ the same yesterday, and today, and for ever' . . . what He was yesterday, He is today, and He will be tomorrow. You need not anticipate life; the Christ who takes you through today will be the same Christ tomorrow. He is changeless, everlasting, always the same; so you must not think about tomorrow; think instead about the changeless Christ. . . . There will be no trial that will come to you but that God will always provide that way of escape [1 Corinthians 10:13]. . . .

As we learn in wisdom to take our days one by one as they come, forgetting yesterday and tomorrow, so we must learn this vital importance of walking with God day by day, of relying upon Him day by day, and applying to Him for the particular needs of each day. . . . Leave it with Him; leave it entirely with Him, confident and assured that He will always be going before you. . . . He will be there before you to meet the problem. Turn to Him and you will find that He is there, that He knows all about it, and knows all about you.

Studies in the Sermon on the Mount, ii, pp. 151–2

Here we are, weary in well-doing, but what can we do? The first thing must be self-examination. . . . Sit down and say to yourself, 'Well, now, why am I weary?' . . .

There are many possible answers to the question. You may be in that condition simply because you are working too hard physically. You can be tired in the work and not tired of the work. . . . If you go on working too hard or under strain you are bound to suffer. And of course if that is the cause of the trouble the remedy you need is medical treatment. . . . You remember that when Elijah had that attack of spiritual depression after his heroic effort on Mount Carmel, he sat down under a juniper tree and felt sorry for himself. But the real thing he needed was sleep and food; and God gave him both! He gave him food and rest before He gave him spiritual help.

But. . . . Something else may be the cause of the trouble, and very frequently it is that we may have been living the Christian life, or doing Christian work, by means of carnal energy. We may have been doing it all in our own strength instead of working in the power of the Spirit. . . . We may have been trying to do God's work ourselves; and of course if we try to do that there will be only one result, it will ultimately crush us because it is such high work. And so we must examine ourselves and see if there is something wrong with the way in which we are doing this work. It is possible for a man to preach with carnal energy, and if he does he will soon be suffering from this spiritual exhaustion and depression.

Spiritual Depression, pp. 196–7

Just when we have reached our limit, when we are most hopeless and when we are about to give way to final despair . . . suddenly God intervenes . . . and brings us back. He restores us to the fellowship—fellowship with Himself most particularly, but also to the fellowship of His people, and gives us back the joy we had lost. He lifts us up out of 'the horrible pit, out of the miry clay' and sets our feet upon a rock and establishes our goings.

David, king of Israel, knew something about this . . . (2 Samuel 12). . . . God's restoring grace. He brings the soul back again, according to His own wondrous love and His amazing kindness. . . . Is there anything more consoling, more wonderful, than to know that we are in the hands of God? He controls everything. He is the Lord God Almighty, the Lord of the universe, who works everything according to the counsel of His own eternal will. He has set His love upon you; therefore nothing can harm you. 'The very hairs of your head are all numbered.' He will not let you go. You may fall deeply into sin, and go very far astray, but you will not be utterly cast down; He will hold you from that final fall. He will always bring you back. 'He restoreth my soul', says the Psalmist. And after He restores He will lead you into 'green pastures' and by 'the still waters'. And He will deal with you in such a marvellous way that you will find it difficult to believe that you have ever done what you have done. God's restoring grace!

Faith on Trial, p. 94

There are phases in the Christian life as in the whole of life. The New Testament talks about being babes in Christ, it talks about growing. John writes his first epistle to little children and young men and old men. It is a fact, it is Scriptural. The Christian life is not always the same, there is a beginning and a continuing and there is an end. And, because of these phases there are many variations. Feelings, perhaps, are the most variable. You would expect to have most feeling at the beginning, and this is what usually happens. Very often Christian people become weary because certain feelings have gone. They do not realize that what has happened is that they have grown older. Because they are not as they once were they think that they are all wrong. But as we grow and develop spiritually, changes must take place and all these things obviously make a difference in our experience. . . . I happened to see, the other day, a little child, about four years old I should think, coming out of her house with her mother, and I could not help being attracted by the way she came out of that house. She did not walk, she jumped out, she skipped out, she gambolled out like a lamb; but I noticed that the mother walked out . . . there is something like that in the spiritual life. The child is abounding in energy and has not yet learned how to control it. The mother actually had a great deal more energy than the child, although . . . it would seem that she had much less because she walked out quietly. But we know that that is not so. The energy is actually much greater in the adult though it appears to be greater in the child; and it is because they have misunderstood this experience of slowing down, that so many people think they have lost something vital and so become weary and depressed. Let us recognize that there are phases . . . there are stages of development in the Christian life.

Spiritual Depression, pp. 198–9

In [Matthew 5:6] we have one of the most notable statements of the Christian gospel and everything that it has to give us. Let me describe it as the great charter for every seeking soul, the outstanding declaration of the Christian gospel to all who are unhappy about themselves and their spiritual state, and who long for an order and quality of life that they have not hitherto enjoyed.... It is very doctrinal; it emphasizes one of the most fundamental doctrines of the gospel, namely, that our salvation is entirely of grace or by grace, that it is entirely the free gift of God....

It is one of those texts that divides itself for us, and all we have to do is to look at the meaning of the various terms which are used. Obviously, therefore, the one to start with is the term 'righteousness'. 'Blessed—or happy—are they which do hunger and thirst after righteousness.' They are the only truly happy people. Now the whole world is seeking for happiness.... Everybody wants to be happy. That is the great motive behind every act and ambition, behind all work and all striving and effort. Everything is designed for happiness. But the great tragedy of the world is that, though it gives itself to seek for happiness, it never seems to be able to find it. The present state of the world reminds us of that very forcibly. What is the matter? I think the answer is that we have never understood this text as we should have done.... What does it mean? Let me put it negatively like this. We are not to hunger and thirst after blessedness; we are not to hunger and thirst after happiness. But that is what most people are doing. We put happiness and blessedness as the one thing that we desire, and thus we always miss it; it always eludes us. According to the Scriptures happiness is never something that should be sought directly; it is always something that results from seeking something else.

Studies in the Sermon on the Mount, i, pp. 74–5

'Ah,' we say, 'the same old thing week after week.' That is our attitude towards our life, and . . . we become weary. . . . If you regard the Christian life as a dreary task you are insulting God. . . . If you and I come to regard any aspect of this Christian life merely as a task and a duty, and if we have to goad ourselves and to set our teeth in order to get through with it, I say we are insulting God and we have forgotten the very essence of Christianity. The Christian life is not a task. The Christian life alone is worthy of the name life. This alone is righteous and holy and pure and good. It is the kind of life the Son of God Himself lived. It is to be like God Himself in His own holiness. That is why I should live it. I do not just decide to make a great effort to carry on somehow. . . . How have I got into this life—this life that I am grumbling and complaining about, and finding it hard and difficult? . . . there is only one answer . . . because the only begotten Son of God left heaven and came down to earth for our salvation; He divested Himself of all the insignia of His eternal glory and humbled Himself to be born as a babe and to be placed in a manger. He endured the life of this world for thirty-three years: He was spat upon and reviled. He had thorns thrust into his head and was nailed to a cross, to bear the punishment of my sin. That is how I have come to . . . this.

. . . 'Be not weary in well-doing.' My friend, if you think of your Christian life . . . with this sense of grudge, or as a wearisome task or duty, I tell you to go back to the beginning of your life, retrace your steps to the wicket gate through which you passed. Look at the world in its evil and sin, look at the hell to which it was leading you, and then look forward and realize that you are set in the midst of the most glorious campaign into which a man could ever enter, and that you are on the noblest road that the world has ever known.

Spiritual Depression, pp. 199–200

I once heard a man use a phrase which affected me very deeply at the time, and still does. I am not sure that it is not one of the most searching statements I have ever heard. He said that the trouble with many of us Christians is that we believe in the Lord Jesus Christ, but that we do not believe Him. He meant that we believe on Him for the salvation of our souls, but we do not believe Him when He says a thing like this to us, that God is going to look after our food and drink, and even our clothing. He makes such statements as 'Come unto me, all ye that labour and are heavy laden, and I will give you rest', and yet we keep our problems and worries to ourselves, and we are borne down by them and defeated by them, and get anxious about things. He has told us to come to Him when we are like that; He has told us that if we are thirsting in any respect we can go to Him, and He has assured us that whosoever comes to Him will never thirst, and that he that eats of the bread that He shall give shall never hunger. He has promised to give us 'a well of water springing up into everlasting life' so that we shall never thirst. But we do not believe Him. Take all these statements He made when He was here on earth, the words He addressed to the people around Him; they are all meant for us. They are meant for us today as definitely as when He first uttered them, and so also are all the astounding statements in the Epistles. The trouble is that we do not believe Him. That is the ultimate trouble. 'Little faith' does not really take the Scripture as it is and believe it and live by it and apply it.

Studies in the Sermon on the Mount, ii, pp. 128–9

This life of ours on earth is but a preparatory one. . . . You are tired and weary and you feel at times it is too much for you? Go back and look at your life and put it into the context of eternity. Stop and ask yourself what it all means. It is nothing but a preparatory school. This life is but the antechamber of eternity and all we do in this world is but anticipatory of that. Our greatest joys are but the first fruits and the foretaste of the eternal joy that is coming. . . . It is the sheer grind of daily life that gets us down. . . . But the answer is to look at it all and to put it all into its great context and to say, 'We are going on to eternity and this is but the preparatory school'. What a difference that makes. . . .

'The world is too much with us,' that is our trouble. We are too immersed in our problems. We need to look ahead, to anticipate, to look forward to the eternal glories gleaming afar. The Christian life is a tasting of the firstfruits of that great harvest which is to come. 'Eye hath not seen, nor ear heard, neither have entered into the heart of man the things which God hath prepared for them that love Him'. . . . Realize something in mind and heart of the glory of the place to which you are going. That is the antidote, that is the cure. The harvest we shall reap is certain, it is sure. 'Therefore,' says Paul to the Corinthians, 'be ye steadfast, unmovable, always abounding in the work of the Lord forasmuch as ye know that your labour is not in vain in the Lord'. Go on with your task whatever your feelings; keep on with your work. God will give the increase, He will send the rain of His gracious mercies as we need it. There will be an abundant harvest. Look forward to it. 'Ye shall reap.'

Spiritual Depression, pp. 200–1

Think of a man who is suffering from some painful disease. Generally the one desire of such a patient is to be relieved of his pain, and one can understand that very well. No one likes suffering pain. The one idea of this patient, therefore, is to do anything which will relieve him of it. Yes; but if the doctor who is attending this patient is also only concerned about relieving this man's pain he is a very bad doctor. His primary duty is to discover the cause of the pain and to treat that. Pain is a wonderful symptom which is provided by nature to call attention to disease, and the ultimate treatment for pain is to treat the disease, not the pain. So if a doctor merely treats the pain without discovering the cause of the pain, he is not only acting contrary to nature, he is doing something that is extremely dangerous to the life of the patient. The patient may be out of pain, and seems to be well; but the cause of the trouble is still there. Now that is the folly of which the world is guilty. It says, 'I want to get rid of my pain, so I will run to the pictures, or drink, or do anything to help me forget my pain'. But the question is, What is the cause of the pain and the unhappiness and the wretchedness? They are not happy who hunger after happiness and blessedness. No. 'Blessed are they which do hunger and thirst after righteousness; for they shall be filled.'

Studies in the Sermon on the Mount, i, pp. 75–6

And above all let us consider the Master for whom we work. Let us remember how He endured and how patient He was.... How humdrum His life was; most of His time was spent with ordinary petty people who misunderstood Him. But He went steadfastly on and did not complain. How did He do it? 'For the joy that was set before him he endured even the cross, despising the shame.' That is how He did it. It was the joy that was set before Him, He knew about the crowning day that was coming. He saw the harvest that He was going to reap, and, seeing that, He was able not to see these other things but to go through them gloriously and triumphantly. And you and I have the privilege of being like Him. 'If any man would be my disciple, let him deny himself, take up his cross'—that is it—'and follow me.' We may even have the honour of suffering for His Name. Paul says a most extraordinary thing in writing to the Colossians (chapter 1, verse 24). He says that he is privileged to make up in his own body what remains of the suffering of Christ. What if you and I as Christians are having the same privilege without knowing it? Well, remind yourself of your blessed Master and look to Him and ask Him to forgive you for ever having allowed yourself to be weary. Look at your life again in this way, and as certainly as you do so, you will find that you are filled with a new hope, a new strength, a new power. You will not need your artificial stimulants or anything else, for you will find that you are again thrilled with the privilege and joy of it all, and you will hate yourself for having grumbled and complained, and you will go forward still more gloriously, until eventually you will hear Him saying, 'Well done, thou good and faithful servant, enter thou into the joy of thy Lord.' 'Come, ye blessed of my Father, inherit the kingdom prepared for you from the foundation of the world.'

Spiritual Depression, pp. 201–2

'If God so clothe the grass of the field . . . shall he not much more clothe you, O ye of little faith?' If God does that for the flowers of the field, how much more for you?

. . . Here is the argument. . . . What a mighty argument [it] is. The grass of the field is transient and passing. In ancient times they used to cut it and use it as fuel. It was the old way of baking bread. You first of all cut the grass and dried it, and then put it in the oven and set it on fire, and it generated great heat. Then you raked it out and put in the bread which you had prepared for baking. That was a common practice, and it was so in our Lord's day. So you see the powerful argument. The lilies and the grass are transient; they do not last very long. How well aware of this we are. We cannot make our flowers last; the moment we cut them they are beginning to die. They are here today with their exquisite beauty and all their perfection, but it is all gone by tomorrow. These beautiful things come and go, and that is the end of them. You, however, are immortal; you are not only a creature of time, you belong to eternity. It is not true to say that you are here today and gone tomorrow in a real sense. God hath 'set eternity' in the heart of man; man is not meant to die. 'Dust thou art, to dust returnest, was not spoken of the soul.' You go on, and on, and on. You not only have natural dignity and greatness, but you also have an eternal existence beyond death and the grave. When you realize that truth about yourself, can you believe that God who has made you and destined you for that, is going to neglect your body while you are in this life and world? Of course not. 'If God so clothe the grass of the field . . . ?'

Studies in the Sermon on the Mount, ii, p. 124

We desire to read the Bible, we want to study it, we want to read a commentary; but we do not feel like it at the moment, we think it is a bad thing to try to do these things when we do not feel at our best, and we had better put it off until we feel better, there will be a more appropriate opportunity later on. Or we have not the time, or we lack the opportunity. . . . It is beyond dispute that most of us are living lives which are seriously lacking in discipline and in order and in arrangement. . . . There are so many things that distract us. You start with your morning newspaper . . . and then in a few hours comes your evening paper . . . I need not waste time in detailing all those things, the wireless, the television and the things we have to do, meetings to attend, incidents here and there. . . . The fact is that every one of us is fighting for his life at the present time, fighting to possess and master and live our own life. . . .

Now the simple answer to that is, that it is sheer lack of discipline, it is a sheer failure to order our life. It is no use complaining about circumstances. . . . we all have time! If we have time to do these other things, we do have the time, and the whole secret of success . . . is to take that time and insist that it is given to this matter of the soul instead of to these other things. . . .

What is the treatment prescribed by the apostle for this condition? . . . First and foremost he emphasizes 'all diligence'. [2 Peter 1:5.] 'Make every effort'—according to another translation. That is it—'make every effort' . . . give all diligence, or as it is translated in the tenth verse, be more zealous than ever before to do these things. Here is the treatment then, the exercise of discipline and of diligence.

Spiritual Depression, pp. 209–10

Are we familiar with this [doctrine]? There has been no doctrine brought to light by the Protestant Reformation which has given more joy and comfort and consolation to God's people. . . . It explains some of the greatest exploits in the annals of the Christian Church. You do not begin to understand people like the Covenanters of Scotland and the Puritans —men who gave up their lives and did so with a sense of joy and glory—except in the light of this doctrine . . . it is the only way of understanding some of the German Christians who could face a Hitler and defy him.

Now the Psalmist gives us a remarkable statement of that doctrine. . . . What he is saying is, 'You are doing this now, and you will go on doing this; and then "afterwards"—glory'.

The man is not expressing a pious hope; he is absolutely certain. . . .

This is a doctrine which is found throughout the Bible. . . . It is the whole explanation of the heroes of the faith mentioned in Hebrews 11 from Abel onward. . . . There is a magnificent statement of the doctrine in Hebrews 11:13–16 [which] is a perfect summary of the way in which the Old Testament saints lived. . . . It is a declaration of the doctrine of the final perseverance of the saints. In the New Testament it is, as we should expect, very much clearer. And it is clearer for this good reason, that the Son of God has now been on earth and done His work, and therefore we should have a greater assurance than the Old Testament saints had. They had assurance, but we should be doubly sure. The Son of God has come down on earth and returned to heaven. He has been felt and touched and handled. We have all this evidence, and not only that, the Holy Spirit has been given in a way that was not experienced before Christ came. The effect of all this should be to make us doubly sure of this glorious and astounding doctrine of the final perseverance of the saints.

Faith on Trial, pp. 97–9

Our Lord . . . [leads] up to the great climax in that striking picture of the two houses. These represent two men listening to these things; one puts them into practice and the other does not. Once more we are reminded of the greatness of this Sermon on the Mount, its searching character, the profundity of its teaching, indeed its truly alarming character. There never has been such a Sermon as this. It finds us all somehow, somewhere. There is no possibility of escape; it searches us out in all our hiding-places and brings us out into the light of God. There is nothing . . . which is so unintelligent and fatuous as the statement of those who are fond of telling us that what they really like in the New Testament is the Sermon on the Mount. They dislike the theology of Paul and all this talk about doctrine. They say, 'Give me the Sermon on the Mount, something practical, something a man can do himself.' Well, here it is! There is nothing that so utterly condemns us as the Sermon on the Mount; there is nothing so utterly impossible, so terrifying, and so full of doctrine. Indeed, I do not hesitate to say that, were it not that I knew of the doctrine of justification by faith only, I would never look at the Sermon on the Mount, because it is a Sermon before which we all stand completely naked and altogether without hope. Far from being something practical that we can take up and put into practice, it is of all teaching the most impossible if we are left to ourselves. This great Sermon is full of doctrine and leads to doctrine; it is a kind of prologue to all the doctrine of the New Testament.

Studies in the Sermon on the Mount, ii, p. 160

'Add to your faith', says this authorized version (2 Peter 1:5); 'supplement it', says another; 'furnish it out', says another . . . this word 'furnish' is a Greek word that was used in connexion with the performance of a drama. It means the providing of a kind of orchestra or chorus, so that it may be complete. It was something that rounded off the performance . . . That is the meaning of the word, add to it, furnish it, supplement it, make the thing complete, let it be a full-orbed faith.

What do you add to faith? The Apostle gives us this list. . . . The first thing he says is, 'Add to your faith virtue'. . . . Here again is a word the meaning of which has changed since this authorized version was produced. It does not mean virtue in the sense in which we commonly use it. . . . Its meaning here is energy, moral energy, it means power, it means vigour. . . . The condition that the Apostle is dealing with is this languid undisciplined, slack kind of Christian life, and he begins by reminding them that, 'Now you have faith, you believe the truth . . . you have like precious faith with us'. Well, what more need they do about it? He tells them that . . . they must cease to be languid. In other words, add to your faith moral energy, pull yourself together, don't shuffle through your Christian life, walk through it as you should do with vigour, add to it that kind of strength and of power. Do not be a languid Christian, who always gives the impression that he or she is on the point of swooning and fainting and might fail at any moment. Do not be languid, says the Apostle, furnish your faith with manliness and power—virtue.

Spiritual Depression, pp. 212–13

[The desire for righteousness] means a desire to be free from sin, because sin separates us from God. Therefore, positively, it means a desire to be right with God. . . . All the trouble in the world today is due to the fact that man is not right with God, for it is because he is not right with God that he has gone wrong everywhere else. . . . The man who hungers and thirsts after righteousness is the man who sees that sin and rebellion have separated him from the face of God, and longs to get back into that old relationship. . . .

But it also means of necessity a desire to be free from the power of sin. . . . The man we have been looking at . . . is a man who has come to see that the world in which he lives is controlled by sin and Satan. . . . He sees that 'the god of this world' has been blinding him. . . . He wants to get away from this power that drags him down in spite of himself [see Romans 7]. He wants to be free from the power and the tyranny and thraldom of sin. . . .

But it goes further still. It means a desire to be free from the very desire for sin, because we find that the man who truly examines himself in the light of the Scriptures not only discovers that he is in the bondage of sin; still more horrible is the fact that he likes it, that he wants it. Even after he has seen it is wrong, he still wants it. But now the man who hungers and thirsts after righteousness is a man who wants to get rid of that desire for sin, not only outside, but inside as well. . . . Sin is something that pollutes the very essence of our being and of our nature. The Christian is one who desires to be free from all that. . . . To hunger and thirst after righteousness is to desire to be free from self in all its horrible manifestations, in all its forms . . . the man who hungers and thirsts after righteousness . . . wants to be emancipated from self-concern in every shape and form.

Studies in the Sermon on the Mount, i, pp. 77–9

'For so,' he says (2 Peter 1:11) 'an entrance shall be ministered unto you abundantly into the everlasting kingdom of our Lord Jesus Christ.' He is not talking about salvation here because these people are already saved; he is talking about the ultimate entrance into glory . . . 'if you do these things', says Peter, 'if you discipline your life, if you order your life and furnish out your faith in this way and with these various other qualities', he says, 'you will never fall' in the present, you will have great joy and happiness resulting from your assurance, and when the end comes you will go out of this life into the next with your sails filled with the glorious breezes of Heaven. There will be no hesitation about it, it will not be an entrance with torn sails; rather an 'abundant entrance' will be ministered unto you. . . . For it will not be a putting out into some unknown sea, but rather an ending of the storms of life and a triumphant entry into the haven of our eternal rest and glory in the presence of God.

If we are unhappy and depressed Christians it is more than likely that it is all due to that lack of discipline. Let us therefore be up and doing, and giving all diligence, let us supplement our faith and not be afraid. Let us get our ideas clear and then put them into practice, and supplement our faith with this strength and vigour, with this knowledge, with this temperance, with this patience, godliness, brotherly kindness and love. Let us begin to enjoy our Christian life and to be useful and helpful to others. Let us grow in grace and knowledge and so be an attraction to all who know us to come and join with us in the like precious faith, and to experience the blessedness of these exceeding great and precious promises which never fail.

Spiritual Depression, p. 216

September 25

Whom have I on earth below?
Thee, and only Thee, I know;
Whom have I in heaven, but Thee?
Thou art all in all to me

(Charles Wesley)

Can you say quite honestly, 'Whom have I in heaven but thee? and there is none upon earth that I desire beside thee'? [Psalm 73:25] . . . That is how the Psalmist can speak of his relationship to God . . . the whole business of the New Testament gospel and its salvation is simply to bring us to this. . . . Whatever else we may have, whatever else we may be able to say, we must never be satisfied until we can come to this. This is the goal, this is the objective. To be satisfied with anything short of this, however good, is in a sense to deny the gospel itself, for the great and grand end and object of the whole gospel is to bring us . . . to this particular position.

Let us then face this tremendous statement. . . . What does he mean? What is he saying? I am sure the first thing in his mind was a negative and that he was making a negative statement. By his very question he is saying that, as the result of his experience, he has found that there is no one else anywhere who can help him, that nowhere is there any other Saviour. 'Who is there who can help me in heaven or earth but thou?' he asks. There is no one else. When things have gone wrong, when he is really at the end of his tether, when he does not know where to go or to whom to turn, when he needs comfort and solace and strength and assurance, and something to hold on to, he has found that there is no one apart from God.

Faith on Trial, pp. 107–8

The Hebrew word 'revive' has the primary meaning of 'preserve', or 'keep alive'. Habakkuk's great fear was that the Church was going to be destroyed altogether, so he prayed, 'Preserve it, O God, keep it alive, don't let it be overwhelmed'. But to revive means not only to keep alive or to preserve, but also to purify and correct, to get rid of the evil. This is always an essential accompaniment whenever God revives. In the history of every revival, we read of God purifying, getting rid of the sin, the dross, and the things that were hindering His cause . . . while the Church is being preserved, purified and corrected, she is at the same time being prepared for deliverance. The prophet looks at the approaching calamity and says, 'O Lord, even while we are being chastised, prepare us for the deliverance that is to come. Make all thy people worthy of Thy blessings'. . . .

Habakkuk's final appeal is most touching [chapter 3, verse 2] —'In wrath', he says, 'remember mercy'. . . . He does not ask God to remember them because of any of their merits. . . . The only thing he does is to remind God of His own nature, and of that other aspect of His holy being—His mercy. He seems to say, 'Temper wrath with mercy. We have nothing to say but to ask that Thou shouldest act like Thyself, and in the midst of wrath shouldest have pity upon us.'

Here we have the model prayer for just such a time as this.* In all our 'national days of prayer' during the last war there seemed to be an assumption that *we* were all right, and all we had to do was to ask God to defeat our enemies who alone were all wrong. No place seemed to be given for any real humiliation, or confession of sin. . . . The message of this book [Habakkuk] is that until we truly humble ourselves . . . until we see ourselves as we are in the sight of God . . . we have no right to look for peace and happiness. Until the world learns these mighty lessons from the Word of God there is no hope for it.

From Fear to Faith, pp. 64–6

*1953.

The people listening to Him [said]. . . . 'This man teaches with authority, not as the Pharisees and scribes.' 'Did you notice', they said, 'that He did not spend His time saying, "Well, now, Hillel has taught this, but on the other hand Gamaliel suggests that"?' He did not quote a lot of authorities, explain their positions and then end with some kind of deduction of His own. Not at all. He just spoke directly with authority.

Do you remember the soldiers who were sent . . . to arrest Him? They came back without the prisoner, and their leaders looked at them and said, '. . . where is the prisoner?'. The only thing they could say in reply was this, 'Never man spake like this man' (John 7:46). There was something about [Him] . . . that kept them from laying hands on Him. . . .

Sometimes the disciples themselves reacted to a miracle by being filled with fear. . . . Why? They had sensed the power and the presence of God. . . . A sense of awe spread over the people. . . . But we are told that even the devils acknowledged Him. . . . They knew Him, and they were afraid of Him and of His authority. Think of the devils tormenting the man in the country of the Gadarenes. . . . At once they recognized Him. They proclaimed Him, and . . . they trembled at His authority. . . .

Indeed, even His enemies recognized it clearly. They saw that He claimed to be God. See, for example, John 10:33. . . . His stumbling, fumbling disciples *themselves* eventually confessed it. Peter made the great statement at Caesarea Philippi, 'Thou art the Christ, the Son of the living God' (Matthew 16:16). On another occasion, our Lord . . . turned to the disciples and said, 'Will ye also go away?' Peter answered, again perhaps not knowing fully what he said, 'To whom shall we go?' Where else is there an authority? (John 6:66–69) . . . the apostles recognized, 'There is no one else. You are the last, the final Authority.'

Authority, pp. 22–3

271

If you really do want to help others, and to help to rid them of these blemishes and faults and frailties and imperfections, first of all realize that your spirit and your whole attitude has been wrong. This spirit of judging and hypercriticism and censoriousness that is in you is really like a beam, contrasted with the little mote in the other person's eye.... 'Start with your own spirit . . . [says Jesus] face yourself quite honestly and squarely and admit to yourself the truth about yourself.' How are we to do all this in practice? Read 1 Corinthians 13 every day; read this statement of our Lord's every day [Matthew 7:1–5]. Examine your attitude towards other people; face the truth about yourself. . . . It is a very painful and distressing process. But if we examine ourselves and our judgements and our pronouncements honestly and truly, we are on the highroad to getting the beam out of our eye. Then having done that we shall be so humbled that we shall be quite free from the spirit of censoriousness and hypercriticism.

What a wonderful piece of logic this is! When a man has truly seen himself he never judges anybody else in the wrong way. All his time is taken up in condemning himself, in washing his hands and trying to purify himself. . . . You cannot be a spiritual oculist until you yourself have clear sight. Thus, when we face ourselves and have got rid of this beam, and have judged and condemned ourselves and are in this humble, understanding, sympathetic, generous, charitable state, we shall then be able . . . to 'speak the truth in love' to another and thereby to help him. . . . Judge not, except you judge yourself first.

Studies in the Sermon on the Mount, ii, pp. 180–2

To hunger and thirst after righteousness is nothing but the longing to be positively holy. . . . The man who hungers and thirsts after righteousness is the man who wants . . . to show the fruit of the Spirit in his every action . . . [It] . . . is to long to be like the New Testament man, the new man in Christ Jesus. . . . It means that one's supreme desire in life is to know God and to be in fellowship with Him, to walk with God the Father, the Son and the Holy Spirit in the light. 'Our fellowship', says John, 'is with the Father, and with his Son Jesus Christ.' He also says, 'God is light, and in him is no darkness at all' . . . In the end [it] is nothing but a longing and a desire to be like the Lord Jesus Christ Himself. Look at Him; look at His portrait in these Gospels; look at Him when He was here on earth in His incarnate state; look at Him in His positive obedience to God's holy law; look at him in His reaction to other people, His kindness, His compassion, His sensitive nature; look at Him in His reaction to His enemies and all that they did to Him. There is the portrait, and you and I, according to the New Testament doctrine, have been born again and have been fashioned anew after that pattern and image. The man, therefore, who hungers and thirsts after righteousness is the man who wants to be like that. His supreme desire is to be like Christ.

Studies in the Sermon on the Mount, i, pp. 79–80

How important this is—the precious character of faith.
[Peter] brings out that in his comparison with gold. Look at
gold, he says in effect. Gold is precious but not as precious as
faith . . . gold is something that ultimately is going to vanish
. . . there is nothing permanent about it, though it is wonderful
and very precious. But faith is eternal. Gold perishes but faith
does not. Faith is something that is everlasting and eternal. The
thing by which you live, says the Apostle, is the thing which
accounts for your being in the Christian life. . . . We walk by
faith, the whole of our life is a matter of faith, and you see, says
the Apostle, this is so precious in the sight of God, it is so
marvellous, it is so wonderful that God wants it to be absolutely
pure. You purify your gold by means of fire. You get rid of the
alloy and all the impurities by putting gold in the crucible and
applying great heat to it, and so these other things are removed
and the gold remains. His argument, therefore, is that if you
do that with gold that perishes, how much more does it need
to be done with faith. Faith is this extraordinary principle
which links man to God; faith is this thing that keeps a man
from hell and puts him in heaven; it is the connexion between
this world and the world to come; faith is this mystic, astounding thing that can take a man dead in trespasses and sins and
make him live as a new being, a new man in Christ Jesus. That
is why it is so precious. It is so precious that God wants it to
be absolutely perfect. That is the Apostle's argument. So you
are in these manifold temptations (1 Peter 1:6) because of the
character of faith.

Spiritual Depression, pp. 226–7

. . . what this man is saying Psalm 73:25 is that, despite his imperfections, despite his failure, when he was away from God, and more or less turning his back on Him, he could find no satisfaction. In his experience, when he was wrong with God he was wrong everywhere. There was an emptiness about his life— no satisfaction, no blessing, no strength—and even though he was not able to make any positive statement about God, he could at least say that there was nothing and no one else! . . . Can we say that we have seen through everything in this life and world? Have we yet come to see that everything that the world offers is 'a broken cistern'? Have we really been enabled to see through the world and its ways and all its supposed glory? Have we come to the point where we can say: Well, I know this much at any rate; there is nothing else that can satisfy me. I have tried what the world has to offer, I have experimented with all those things, I have played with them and I have come to this conclusion, that when I am away from God, to quote Othello, 'chaos is come again'.

. . . Anyone who has been a backslider knows exactly what I am saying. . . . The backslider is a man who, because of his relationship to God, can never really enjoy anything else. He may try, but he is miserable while it lasts. He has seen through it. This, therefore, is something by which we may always test ourselves. In a remarkable way we have in this confession a striking test of our Christian faith and belief. That is often the first step in our recovery—a realization that everything has actually become different. . . . Things of the world do not seem to possess the charm and value they once seemed to have. We discover that when we are not in the right relationship to God the very foundations seem to have gone. We may travel to the ends of the earth in an attempt to find satisfaction without God. But we find that there is none.

Faith on Trial, p. 108

Simply trusting every day,
Trusting through a stormy way

Our faith . . . needs to be perfected. . . . There are differences in the quality of faith. Faith is many-sided. There is generally at the beginning a good deal of admixture in what we call our faith; there is a good deal of the flesh that we are not aware of. And as we begin to learn these things, and as we go on with the process, God puts us through His testing times. He tests us by trials as if by fire in order that the things which do not belong to the essence of faith may fall off. We may think that our faith is perfect and that we can stand up against anything. Then suddenly a trial comes and we find that we fail. Why? Well, that is just an indication that the trust element in our faith needs to be developed; and God develops the trust element . . . by trying us in this way.

The more we experience these things, the more we learn to trust God. We naturally trust Him when He is smiling on us, but a day comes when the clouds are blackening the heavens and we begin to wonder whether God loves us any longer and whether the Christian life is what we thought it to be. Ah, our faith had not developed the element of trust, and God so deals with us in this life as to bring us to trust Him in the dark when we can see no light at all, and to bring us to the point where we can confidently say:

> When all things seem against us,
>   To drive us to despair,
> We know one gate is open
>   One ear will hear our prayer.

That is true faith, that is real trust. Look at a man like Abraham. . . . He trusted God absolutely when every appearance was to the contrary. And that needs to be developed in us. We do not start like that, but as we go through these experiences we find that 'behind a frowning providence He hides a Father's face', and the next time the trials come we remain calm and collected.

Spiritual Depression pp. 227–8

I cannot imagine a better, more cheering or a more comforting statement with which to face all the uncertainties and hazards of our life in this world of time than that contained in Matthew 7 verses 7–11. It is one of those great comprehensive and gracious promises which are to be found only in the Bible . . . this is the promise that comes to us: 'Ask, and it shall be given you; seek, and ye shall find; knock, and it shall be opened unto you.' . . . There is no doubt about it, it is certain; it is an absolute promise . . . made by the Son of God Himself, speaking with all the fullness and authority of His Father.

The Bible teaches us everywhere that that is the one thing that matters in life . . . it emphasizes that what really matters in life is not so much the various things that come to meet us . . . as our readiness to meet them. The whole of the Biblical teaching with regard to life is . . . summed up in that one man Abraham, of whom we are told, 'he went out, not knowing whither he went'. But he was nevertheless perfectly happy, at peace and at rest. He was not afraid. Why? An old Puritan who lived three hundred years ago answers that question for us: 'Abraham went out, not knowing whither he went; but he did know with whom he went.' That is the thing that matters. . . . He was not alone, there was One with him who had told him that he would never leave him, nor forsake him; and though he was uncertain as to the events that were coming to meet him, and the problems which would arise, he was perfectly happy because he knew his Travelling Companion. . . . Our Lord does not promise to change life for us; He does not promise to remove difficulties and trials and problems and tribulations; He does not say that He is going to cut out all the thorns and leave the roses with their wonderful perfume. No; He faces life realistically, and tells us that these are things . . . which are bound to come. But He assures us that we can so know Him that, whatever happens, we need never be frightened, we need never be alarmed.

Studies in the Sermon on the Mount, ii, pp. 195–6

When the great day comes, the genuineness of your faith will be made manifest. There will be praise and honour and glory. Your little faith, the faith you think is so little, will stand out as something tremendous. It has stood the test and it is going to minister unto 'praise and honour and glory'. Whose honour and praise and glory? First of all His. . . . The Lord Jesus Christ . . . will stand at that great day and look with a sense of satisfaction at Christian people, those whom He called. They have not faltered, He will look at them and He will be proud of them. . . .

But it will also be to our honour and glory and praise, yours and mine . . . we shall hear Him praising us and saying, 'Well done, thou good and faithful servant, enter thou into the joy of thy Lord'. He will clothe us with His own glory and we shall spend our eternity enjoying it with Him: and the greater and the more genuine our faith the greater will our glory be. . . .

We may be in heaviness through many temptations and trials at this present time, and we may be weeping as we go along. It does not matter. We are promised that the day will come when . . . God Himself 'shall wipe away all tears from our eyes', and we shall be with Him in glory everlasting.

That is the Christian way of facing trials. Thank God we are in His hands. It is His way of salvation and not ours. Let us submit ourselves to God, let us be content to be in His hands, and let us say to Him: Send what Thou wilt, our only concern is that we may ever be well-pleasing in Thy sight.

Spiritual Depression, pp. 231–2

. . . the Christian and the non-Christian belong to two entirely different realms . . . the first thing you have to realize about yourself is that you belong to a different kingdom. You are not only different in essence; you are living in two absolutely different worlds. You are in this world; but you are not of it . . . you are citizens of another kingdom. . . .

What is meant by this kingdom of heaven? . . . It means, in its essence, Christ's rule or the sphere and realm in which He is reigning. . . . Many times when He was here in the days of His flesh our Lord said that the kingdom of heaven was already present. Wherever He was present and exercising authority, the kingdom of heaven was there. You remember how on one occasion, when they charged Him with casting out devils by the power of Beelzebub, He showed them the utter folly of that, and then went on to say, 'If I cast out devils by the Spirit of God, then the kingdom of God is come unto you'. (Matthew 12:8.) Here is the kingdom of God. His authority, His reign was actually in practice. Then there is His phrase when He said to the Pharisees, 'the kingdom of God is within you', or 'the kingdom of God is among you'. It was as though He were saying, 'It is being manifested in your midst. Don't say, "look here" or "look there". Get rid of this materialistic view. I am here amongst you; I am doing things. It is here'. Wherever the reign of Christ is being manifested, the kingdom of God is there. And when He sent out His disciples to preach, He told them to tell the cities which received them not, 'Be ye sure of this, that the kingdom of God is come nigh unto you'.

Studies in the Sermon on the Mount, i, pp. 39–40

God uses varied methods in the process of our sanctification. He is our Father who has 'loved us with an everlasting love'. . . . [His] great concern for us primarily is not our happiness but our holiness . . . and He employs many differing means to that end.

Our failure to realize that often causes us to stumble and, in our sin and folly, at times even to misunderstand completely some of God's dealings with us. Like foolish children we feel that our heavenly Father is unkind to us and we . . . feel that we are being dealt with harshly . . . it is all due to our failure to realize God's glorious purposes with respect to us. . . .

Sometimes God promotes sanctification in His children by chastizing them (Hebrews 12:5–11), and especially by enabling them to understand the meaning of chastisement. . . . 'Look at the things you are suffering', says the writer. 'Why are you suffering them?' The answer is that they are suffering these things because they are children of God . . . God is doing these things to them for their good. . . . What this man is really saying is that the whole of salvation is God's work from beginning to end, and that God has His ways of producing it. Once God starts working He goes on with that work . . . when God starts His work upon His people He is going to complete that work. God has an ultimate objective and purpose for them and that is that they might spend eternity with Him in glory. Much that happens to us in this world is to be understood and explained in the light of that fact; and it is as definite as this, according to this man's argument, that God will bring us to that condition, and nothing shall prevent us coming into that condition.

Spiritual Depression, pp. 235–6

Everything we do in this world is of tremendous significance, and we cannot afford to take anything for granted . . . our Lord . . . starts with the question of judging other people. We must be careful about that because we ourselves are under judgement. But why then does our Lord utter this promise of [Matthew 7] verses 7–11 at this point? Surely the answer is this. In verses 1–6 He has shown us the danger of condemning other people as if we were the judges, and of harbouring bitterness and hatred in our hearts. He has also told us to see to it that we remove the beam out of our own eye before trying to extract the mote out of our brother's eye. The effect of all that upon us is to reveal us to ourselves and to show us our terrible need for grace . . . we are humbled and begin to ask, 'Who is sufficient for these things? How can I possibly live up to such a standard?' . . . we realize how unworthy and sinful we are. And the result of this is that we feel utterly hopeless and helpless. We say, 'How can we live the Sermon on the Mount? How can anybody come up to such a standard? We need help and grace. Where can we get it?' Here is the answer: 'Ask, and it shall be given you; seek, and ye shall find; knock, and it shall be opened unto you'. That is the connexion and we should thank God for it, because standing face to face with this glorious gospel we must all feel undone and unworthy. Those foolish people who think of Christianity only in terms of a little morality which they themselves can produce have never really seen it. The standard by which we are confronted is that found in the Sermon on the Mount, and by it we are all crushed to the ground and made to realize our utter helplessness and our desperate need of grace. Here is the answer; the supply is available, and our Lord repeats it (v. 8).

Studies in the Sermon on the Mount, ii, pp. 198–9

Another danger is the danger of self-confidence. God has given gifts to man and the danger is for man to rely upon himself and his gifts and to feel . . . that he does not need God. Pride and self-assurance are a constant danger. . . . Then there is always the danger of being attracted by the world and its outlook and its way . . . these things are so subtle. It is not that a man deliberately sits down and decides that he is going back into the world. It is something that happens almost imperceptibly. The world and its attractions are always there and a man slips into them almost without knowing it. . . .

Yet another danger is that of resting on our oars . . . and so we do not grow. If we compare ourselves with what we were ten years ago, there is really no difference. We do not know God any more intimately, we have not advanced one step, we have not 'grown in grace and in the knowledge of the Lord'. We are resting in a state of self-satisfaction. . . . As we go on year by year in the Christian life we ought to be able to say that we know God better than we used to, we should be able to say that we love Him more than once we did. . . . Do we know God better, are we really seeking Him more and more? God knows, the danger is to forget Him because we are interested in ourselves. . . . And so God in His infinite love chastises us in order . . . to bring us back to Himself, in order to safeguard us against these terrible dangers that are constantly threatening us and surrounding us. Let me put it to your experience. Can you say that you thank God for things that have gone against you? . . . can you look back and say, 'It is good for me that I was afflicted', like the Psalmist in Psalm 119:71?

Spiritual Depression, pp. 243–4

Thy gifts alone cannot suffice
                                        Unless Thyself be given

'If you ask me', says Paul, 'what my greatest desire is, it is this: "That I may know him" ' [Philippians 3:10]. You notice his supreme ambition . . . not to be a great soul winner. That was one ambition of his, and a right one. It was not even to be a great preacher. . . . Because, as the Apostle reminds us elsewhere, if you put the other things first you may find yourself, even as a preacher, becoming . . . a castaway. But when we put Paul's desire at the centre there is no danger. Paul had seen the face of the living Christ, the risen Lord. Yet what he hungers for and pants after is this further, deeper, more intimate knowledge of Him, a personal knowledge, a personal revelation of the living Lord. . . .

There is nothing higher than this. Look at the aged John writing his farewell letter to Christians. His great desire, he tells them in 1 John 1:4, is 'that your joy may be full'. How is it to be full? . . . that you may share with us as partners the blessed experience we enjoy. . . . [This] does not just mean that you are engaged in God's work. It means that, of course; but that is the lowest level. The highest level is really to know God Himself. 'This is life eternal, that they might know thee the only true God, and Jesus Christ, whom thou hast sent' (John 17:3). . . . When a man asked [Jesus] which was the greatest commandment of all, He said, 'Thou shalt love the Lord thy God with all thy heart, and with all thy soul, and with all thy mind . . .' (Matthew 22:37). The first thing, the most important thing in life, is that we so know God that we love Him with the whole of our being. To be satisfied with anything short of that . . . is to misunderstand the whole end and object and purpose of Christian salvation. Do not stop at forgiveness. Do not stop at experiences. The end is to know God, and nothing less. This Psalmist [Psalm 73] is able to say that he now desires God for His own sake, and not merely for what God gives and does.

Faith on Trial, pp. 110–11

Let us look briefly at what is promised to the people who
[hunger and thirst after righteousness]. It is one of the most
gracious, glorious statements to be found in the entire Bible.
'Happy', 'blessed', 'to be congratulated' are those who
thus hunger and thirst. . . . Why? Well, 'they shall be filled',
they shall be given what they desire. The whole gospel is there.
That is where the gospel of grace comes in; it is entirely the
gift of God. You will never fill yourself with righteousness,
you will never find blessedness apart from Him. To obtain this,
'all the fitness He requireth, is to see your need of Him',
nothing more. When you and I know our need, this hunger and
starvation, this death that is within us, then God will fill us,
He will give us this blessed gift. 'Him that cometh to me I will
in no wise cast out.' Now this is an absolute promise. . . .
Hunger and thirst after righteousness, long to be like Christ,
and then you will have that and the blessedness.

How does it happen? . . . it happens immediately, thank God.
'They shall be filled' at once, in this way—that immediately
we desire this truly, we are justified by Christ and His righteousness and the barrier of sin and guilt between us and God is
removed. I trust there is no one who is uncertain or unhappy
about that. If you believe truly on the Lord Jesus Christ, if
you believe that on that cross He was dying for you and for
your sin, you have been forgiven; you have no need to ask for
forgiveness, you have been forgiven. You have to thank God
for it, you are filled with that righteousness immediately. . . .
God looks at you in the righteousness of Christ and He no
longer sees the sin. He sees you as a sinner whom He has
forgiven . . . glorious, wondrous truth.

Studies in the Sermon on the Mount, i, pp. 81–2

I cannot understand how any one who has read the Scriptures can accept . . . any idea of passivity with respect to the way of holiness. Here is a man who tells us to yearn after holiness with all our might until we have it, to follow after it, pursue it, to hunt after it. . . . Those are the exercises through which God puts us in the gymnasium; that is God's way of making us to be really His children. . . . This process is very painful at the time, but listen to the promise; 'afterward it yieldeth the peaceable fruit of righteousness' [Hebrews 12:11]. Do not worry about the pain, keep on moving those stiff muscles and you will find that they will soon become supple. . . . The more we are put through this training in the gymnasium the better, because God is preparing us, not for time only, but for eternity. . . . It is not this world that matters, it is the next; it is not the here and now that are important, it is the eternal. God in this life is preparing us for everlasting bliss and glory.

Remember also in that connexion the One to whom we are going—'without holiness no man shall see the Lord'. If we want to see God we had better do the exercises in the gymnasium very thoroughly. . . . God is putting us through these exercises in order to make us holy. If you and I, therefore, do not pay attention to this treatment that God is giving us, it just means that we do not realize who we are, or it means that we are not children of God at all. If we really want to go on to God and heaven we must submit and do exactly what He tells us, because He is putting us through all this treatment in order to promote our holiness. It is all for our profit and that we may become sharers and partakers of His holiness.

Spiritual Depression, pp. 257–8

Why are we all what we are in view of such promises?
[Matthew 7:7.] Why is the quality of our Christian living so
poor? . . . Everything we need is available; why then are we
what we are? Why are we not exemplifying this Sermon on the
Mount more perfectly? Why are we not conforming more and
more to the pattern of the Lord Jesus Christ Himself? All that
we need is offered us; it is all promised us here in this comprehensive promise. Why are we not availing ourselves of it as we
should? . . . there are certain conditions which must be observed
before we can rejoice in these great benefits that are offered
us in Christ. What are they?

. . . If we want to go through life triumphantly, with peace
and joy in our hearts, ready to face whatever may come to
meet us, and to be more than conquerors in spite of everything,
there are certain things we have to realize. . . . The first is, we
must realize our need . . . the effect of sin upon us is such that
we shall never fly to Christ until we realize that we are paupers.
But we hate to regard ourselves as paupers, and we do not
like to feel our need. People are ready to listen to sermons
which present Christ to them, but they do not like to be told
that they are so helpless that He had to go to the cross and
die before they could be saved. . . . We must be brought to
realize our need. The first two essentials to salvation and rejoicing in Christ are the consciousness of our need, and the
consciousness of the riches of grace that are in Christ. It is
only those who realize these two things who 'ask' truly. . . .
The other man is not aware of his need. It is the man who
knows that he is 'down and out' who begins to ask. And then
he begins to realize the possibilities that are in Christ.

Studies in the Sermon on the Mount, ii, pp. 199–200

Man by nature always wants to break away and to get away from God . . . [because of his] pride. 'They became vain in their reasonings, and their foolish heart was darkened. Professing themselves to be wise, they became fools' . . . the final step is to reject God's revelation altogether and to substitute their own ideas and reasonings instead. They refuse the knowledge of God which is offered and given . . . but, feeling still the need and the necessity of a religion, they proceed to make their own god or gods and then worship them and serve them. Man believes in his own mind and his own understanding, and the greatest insult that can ever be offered to him is to tell him, as Christ tells him, that he must become as a little child and be born again. . . .

Man rebels against God as He is and as He reveals Himself. He even hates Him for His goodness. And then he proceeds to make his own gods. . . . Whatever we may propose to do about our world, whatever plans and ideas we may have with regard to the future, if we ignore this basic fact all will be in vain . . . to invite [man] just as he is to follow Christ is not enough. . . . He must face the naked, terrible truth about himself and his attitude towards God. It is only when he realizes that truth that he will be ready truly to believe the gospel and return to God.

That is the task of the Church; that is our task. Shall we commence upon it by examining ourselves? Do we accept the revelation of God as given in the Bible or do we base our views upon some human philosophy? Are we afraid of being called old-fashioned or out of date because we believe the Bible? Further, is God central and supreme in our lives, do we really glorify Him and show others that we are striving constantly to be well-pleasing in His sight? And finally, are we doing all this . . . as men and women, who . . . are so full of thankfulness and gratitude that we can gladly say

> 'Love so amazing, so divine,
> Demands my soul, my life, my all.'

The Plight of Man and the Power of God, pp. 21–4

. . . Beyond all else for our encouragement, look at the One who subjected Himself to it all, though He need not have done so—'Looking unto Jesus the Author and Finisher of our Faith who for the joy that was set before Him endured the Cross, despising the shame'. [Hebrews 12:2.] He knew what it meant. He said, 'Father, if it be possible let this cup pass from me, nevertheless not my will but thine be done'. He endured it all for the joy that was laid up for Him and for your salvation and mine. So, when you may feel that the discipline is too much and that it is very painful, look unto Him, keep looking at Him and follow Him. And as certainly as we do so we shall find that this which for the moment is so painful and grievous will afterward yield, even in this life and world, and still more in glory, this wonderful fruit of health and righteousness, of peace and of the enjoyment of God. I do not know what you feel, but as I have meditated this last fortnight upon this great word, I say honestly and in the presence of God, that there is nothing that gives me greater comfort and greater solace than this, to know that I am in God's hands, and that He so loves me and is so determined upon my holiness and upon bringing me to heaven. . . . 'Nothing shall be able to separate us from the love of God which is in Christ Jesus our Lord.' Take the exercises, my friend, hurry to the gymnasium,* do what He tells you, examine yourself, practise it all whatever the cost, however great the pain, and enter into the joy of the Lord.

Spiritual Depression, pp. 258–9

* October 11

Thank God [His forgiveness and acceptance is something that] happens immediately. But it is also a continuing process . . . the Holy Spirit . . . begins within us His great work of delivering us from the power of sin and from the pollution of sin. We have to hunger and thirst for this deliverance, from the power and from the pollution. And if you hunger and thirst for that you will get it. The Holy Spirit will come into you and He will work in you 'both to will and to do of his good pleasure'. Christ will come into you, He will live in you; and as He lives in you, you will be delivered increasingly from the power of sin and from its pollution. You will be able to be more than conqueror over all these things that assail you, so that not only do you get this answer and blessing immediately, it goes on continuously as you walk with God and with Christ, with the Holy Spirit living in you. You will be enabled to resist Satan, and he will flee from you; you will be able to stand against him and all his fiery darts, and the whole time the work of getting rid of the pollution will be going on within you.

But of course, this promise is fulfilled perfectly and absolutely in eternity. There is a day coming when all who are in Christ and belong to Him shall stand in the presence of God, faultless, blameless, without spot and without wrinkle. All blemishes will have gone. A new and perfect man in a perfect body. . . . We shall stand in the presence of God, absolutely perfect in body, soul and spirit, the whole man filled with a perfect, complete, and entire righteousness which we shall have received from the Lord Jesus Christ.

Studies in the Sermon on the Mount, i, pp. 82–3

What are you looking for and hoping for in heaven? . . . Do you ever look forward to being in heaven? . . . I like the way in which Matthew Henry put it: 'We are never told in the Scriptures that we should look forward to death; but we are told very frequently that we should look forward to heaven.' The man who looks forward to death simply wants to get out of life because of his troubles. That is not Christian; that is pagan. The Christian has a positive desire for heaven. . . . But, more than this, what do we look forward to when we get to heaven? . . . Is it the rest of heaven? Is it to be free from trouble and tribulations? Is it the peace of heaven? Is it the joy of heaven? All these things are to be found there, thank God; but that is not the thing to look forward to in heaven. It is the face of God. 'Blessed are the pure in heart: for they shall see God.' The Vision Splendid, the *Summum Bonum*, to stand in the very presence of God—'To gaze and gaze on Thee'. Do we long for that? Is that heaven to us? Is that the thing we want above everything else? It is the thing to covet and to long for.

The Apostle Paul tells us that to die is 'to be with Christ'. There is no need to add anything to that. That is why, I believe, we are told so little in a detailed sense about the life in heaven and in glory. People often ask why we are not told more about it. I think there are two answers to that. One is that because of our sinful state any description we might be given would be misunderstood by us. . . . The second reason is more important; it is that it is often idle curiosity that desires to know more. I will tell you what heaven is. It is 'to be with Christ' and if that does not satisfy you, then you do not know Christ at all. . . . I do not want anything else. 'Where Thou art is heaven. Just to look at Thee is sufficient.'

Faith on Trial, p. 111

There is no reason that is so frequently adduced today for the rejection of the gospel as the fact that it is so old . . . such an attitude is utterly unreasonable, and is nothing but the manifestation of sheer prejudice . . . what is important when we are discussing truth, is not the age of truth, but its veracity. . . . If I say that that alone can be true which is new and modern . . . then clearly my whole idea of truth is changed, and I have set up a standard which is become more important than truth itself—namely, modernity. . . .

What is the truly scientific method of research? It is almost invariably something like this. A young man who is given a piece of scientific research work is generally placed under the care . . . of an older man. . . . What has the old man to say to the young man? Does he tell him to start by burning and destroying every book that has ever been written on the subject in the past? No, he does the exact opposite. He advises the young man, before he makes a single experiment, to go to the library, and to read and study all the past literature on the subject, to understand it, grasp it, make full use of it. . . . The truly scientific method is not one which turns its back upon the past. It is one which starts with the past, studies it, and builds upon it. . . . There is nothing which is more thoroughly unscientific than the way in which the average person today dismisses the Bible, and the whole of the Christian gospel and the Christian Church, without ever reading the Bible, without being familiar with the case for the gospel, without reading the history of the Church. Whatever else may be claimed for the method of such an individual, it stands convicted as the very antithesis of the truly scientific one.

Truth Unchanged, Unchanging, pp. 99–106

This [Philippians 4:6, 7] is undoubtedly one of the noblest, greatest and most comforting statements . . . in any extant literature . . . there is nothing that has greater comfort for God's people than these two verses. . . . Here in these verses he goes on to consider another factor that is perhaps more problematical than any of the others which tend to rob us of the joy of the Lord, and that is what we may well describe as the tyranny of circumstances, or the things that happen to us. How many they are, and how often do they come! . . . all the New Testament epistles face this particular problem, and were designed to help the first Christians to overcome the tyranny of circumstances. They lived in a very difficult world and had to suffer and to endure a great deal; and these men called of God wrote their letters in order to show them how to overcome these things. It is the great theme of the New Testament; but you find it also in the Old Testament. Take the third and fourth Psalms, for instance. How perfectly they put it all. The great problem in life is, in a sense, how to lay oneself down to rest and to sleep. 'I laid me down and slept', said the Psalmist. Anybody can lie down, but the question is can you sleep? The Psalmist describes himself surrounded by enemies and by difficulties and trials, and his mighty testimony is that in spite of that, because of his trust in the Lord, he both laid him down and slept, and he awaked safe and sound in the morning. Why? Because the Lord was with him and looking after him.

Spiritual Depression, pp. 261–2

The importance of [the] element of persistence cannot be exaggerated. You find it not only in biblical teaching, but also in the lives of all the saints. . . . If we really want to be men of God, if we really want to know Him, and walk with Him, and experience those boundless blessings which He has to offer us, we must persist in asking Him for them day by day. We have to feel this hunger and thirst after righteousness, and then we shall be filled. And that does not mean that we are filled once and for ever. We go on hungering and thirsting. Like the Apostle Paul, leaving the things which are behind, we 'press toward the mark'. 'Not as though I had already attained', says Paul, 'but I follow after.' That is it. This persistence, this constant desire, asking, seeking, and knocking. This, we must agree, is the point at which most of us fail.

Let us then hold on to that first principle. Let us examine ourselves in the light of these Scriptures and the pictures given of the Christian man in the New Testament. Let us look at these glorious promises and ask ourselves, 'Am I experiencing them?' And if we find we are not, as we must all confess, then we must go back again to this great statement. That is what I mean by the possibilities. While I must begin by asking and seeking, I must go on doing so until I am aware of an advance and a development and a rising to a higher spiritual level. We must keep on at it. It is a 'fight of faith'; it is 'he that endureth to the end' that will be saved in this sense. Persistence, continuance in well-doing, 'always to pray and not to faint'. Not just pray when we want a great blessing and then stop; always pray. Persistence; that is the first thing. The realization of the need, the realization of the supply, and persistence in seeking after it.

Studies in the Sermon on the Mount, ii, pp. 201–2

We must face our personal situation . . . by asking: Is there something in my life that is meriting the chastisement of God? Have I been what I ought to be? . . . The trouble is that we always look at the situation and the problem instead of trying to discover whether there is anything in our soul that leads God so to deal with us. The moment I become really concerned about the state of my soul, instead of my affliction, I am on the high road to God's blessing. The Epistle to the Hebrews declares that chastisement is a proof that we are God's children. 'Whom the Lord loveth He chasteneth.' If we do not know what chastisement means we ought to be alarmed because, if we are children of God, He is concerned about us and is bringing us to perfection. . . . When things are apparently going against us, the thing to do is . . . to look at ourselves and say, 'What of my soul? What is God saying to me and doing to me? What is it in me that is meriting all this?' After examining ourselves, and humbling ourselves, we should place ourselves in the hands of God and say, 'Thy way, not mine, O Lord, however hard it be. My one concern is that my soul should be right. I ask only that in wrath Thou shouldest remember mercy [Habakkuk 3:2]. But, above all, go on with Thy work that my soul may be revived, and that I may become well-pleasing in Thy sight'.

From Fear to Faith, pp. 66–7

October 21 '*The sea broke over . . . and poured in between the decks. . . . The Germans [Moravians] calmly sang on. I asked one of them afterwards, "Were you not afraid?" He answered, "I thank God, no".*'
(Wesley's *Journal*, 1736)

It is one thing to say that you subscribe to the Christian faith, it is one thing, having read your Bible . . . to say, 'Yes, I believe all that, it is the faith by which I live'. But it is not always exactly the same thing to find that faith triumphant and victorious and maintaining you in a state of joy, when everything seems to have gone against you and well nigh driven you to despair. . . . It is far removed from the realm of mere theory. You are *in* the position, you are *in* the situation, these things are happening to you, and the question is, what is your faith worth at that point? Does it differentiate you from people who have no faith? . . . People today tell us that they are realists and practical. They say that they are not interested in doctrine, and not interested to listen very much to what we say, but if they see a body of people who seem to have something that enables them to triumph over life, they become interested at once. This is so because they are unhappy, and frustrated and uncertain, and fearful. If, when in that condition themselves, they see people who seem to have peace and calm and quiet, then they are ready to look at them and to listen to them. So that from the standpoint of our own personal happiness and our maintenance of the joy of the Lord, and also from the standpoint of our witness and our testimony in these difficult days, it behoves us to consider very carefully what the Apostle has to say in these masterly statements [Philippians 4:6, 7] about the way to deal with the tyranny of circumstances and conditions.

Spiritual Depression, pp. 262–3

. . . God is your Father only when you satisfy certain conditions. He is not the Father of any one of us as we are by nature.

How then does God become my Father? According to the Scriptures it is like this. Christ 'came unto his own, and his own received him not. But as many as received him, to them gave he power (i.e., authority) to become the sons of God' [John 1:11, 12]. You become a child of God only when you are born again, when you receive a new life and a new nature. The child partakes of the nature of the Father. God is holy, and you and I are not children of God until we have received a holy nature; and that means we must have a new nature. . . . Now that is what is offered to us. And there is no contact and communion with God, nor are we heirs to any of these promises of God, until we become His children. . . . And believing in Him, we receive a new life and nature and we become children of God. Then we can know that God is our Father; but not until then. He will also give us His Holy Spirit, 'the Spirit of adoption, whereby we cry, Abba, Father'; and the moment we know this we can be certain that God as our Father accepts a specific attitude with respect to us. It means that, as my Father, He is interested in me, that He is concerned about me, that He is watching over me, that He has a plan and purpose with respect to me, that He is desirous always to bless and to help me. Lay hold of that; take a firm grasp of that. Whatever may happen to you, God is your Father, and He is interested in you, and that is His attitude towards you.

Studies in the Sermon on the Mount, ii, p. 203

We must have the full message . . . 'deliver the whole counsel of God'. . . . It starts with the Law. The Law of God . . . the demands of a righteous God, the wrath of God. That is the way to bring men and women to conviction; not by modifying the Truth. . . . We must confront them with the fact that they are men, and that they are fallible men, that they are dying men, that they are sinful men, and that they will all have to stand before God at the Bar of Eternal Judgement. . . .

And then we must present to them the full-orbed doctrine of the Grace of God in Salvation in Jesus Christ. We must show that no man is saved 'by the deeds of the Law', by his own goodness or righteousness, or church membership or anything else, but solely, utterly, entirely by the free gift of God in Jesus Christ His Son. . . . We must preach the full-orbed doctrine leaving nothing out—conviction of sin, the reality of Judgement and Hell, free grace, justification, sanctification, glorification.

We must also show that there is a world view in the Bible . . . that here alone you can understand history—past history, present history, future history. Let us show this great world view, and God's Eternal purpose. . . .

Let us at the same time be very careful that we are giving it to the whole man . . . the gospel is not only for a man's heart, that you start with his head and present Truth to it. . . . Let us show that it is a great message given by God which we in turn pass on to the mind, to the heart, to the will. There is ever this danger of leaving out some part or other of man's personality. . . . Let us be certain that we address the whole man—his mind, his emotions and his will.

The Weapons of our Warfare, pp. 21–2

'This condition of anxiety', says Paul, 'is something which is in a sense outside your own control, it happens apart from you and in spite of you'. . . . The heart and the mind are outside our control. . . . Here the 'heart' does not mean only the seat of emotions, it means the very central part of one's personality. The 'mind' can be translated . . . by the term 'thought'. . . . The heart has feelings and emotions. If a dear one is taken ill how the heart begins to work! . . . Not only that, the imagination! What a prolific cause of anxiety is the imagination. . . . In this state of anxiety we spend the whole of our time reasoning and arguing and chasing imaginations. And in that state we are useless. . . . And so, alas, our testimony is useless. We are of no value to others and above all we lose the joy of the Lord. . . .

What have we to do in order to avoid that inner turmoil? . . . [Paul] does not just say, 'Stop worrying' . . . [for that] is useless. Incidentally it is also bad psychology. . . . In the same way the Bible does not say, 'Do not worry, it may never happen' . . . when I am in this state, my reaction is, 'Yes, but it *may* happen' . . . all these methods fail to deal with my situation because they never realize the power of what Paul calls 'the heart' and 'the mind' . . . [Paul] puts his remedy in the form of a positive injunction. 'Let your requests be made known unto God' . . . and he has given us particular instructions for the carrying out of his injunction. . . . First he tells us to pray. . . . This is the most general term and it means worship and adoration. If you have problems that seem insoluble, if you are liable to become anxious and overburdened, and somebody tells you to pray, do not rush to God with your petition. . . . Before you make your requests known unto God, pray, worship, adore. Come into the presence of God and for the time being forget your problems. Do not start with them. Just realize that you are face to face with God.

Spiritual Depression, pp. 264–7

We must remember increasingly the good gifts which He has for us. 'How much more shall your Father which is in heaven give good things to them that ask him?' This is the theme of the whole Bible. What are the good things? Our Lord has given us the answer. . . . 'If ye then, being evil, know how to give good gifts unto your children; how much more shall your heavenly Father give the Holy Spirit to them that ask him?' [Luke 11:13]. That is it. And in giving the Holy Spirit He gives us everything; every fitness we require, every grace, every gift . . . (2 Peter 1:3). You see now why we should thank God that asking, and seeking, and knocking do not just mean that if we ask for anything we like we shall get it. Of course not. What it means is this. Ask for any one of these things that is good for you, that is for the salvation of your soul, your ultimate perfection, anything that brings you nearer to God and enlarges your life and is thoroughly good for you, and He will give it you. He will not give you things that are bad for you. You may think they are good but He knows they are bad. He does not make a mistake, and He will not give you such things . . . the promise literally is this, that if we seek these good things, the fullness of the Holy Spirit, the life of love, joy, peace, long-suffering, etc., all these virtues and glories that were seen shining so brightly in the earthly life of Christ, He will give them to us. If we really want to be more like Him, and like all the saints, if we really ask for these things, we shall receive. . . .

That is the way to face the future. Find out from the Scriptures what these good things are and seek them. The thing that matters supremely . . . is to know God . . . and if we . . . 'seek first the kingdom of God and his righteousness' then we have the word of the Son of God for it that all these other things shall be added unto us.

Studies in the Sermon on the Mount, ii, pp. 204–5

[Paul] tells us that we can take particular things to God, that petition is a legitimate part of prayer. . . . But wait, there is still one other thing—'by prayer and supplication, with thanksgiving'. (Philippians 4:6.) That is one of the most vital of all these terms. . . . If, while we pray to God, we have a grudge against Him in our hearts, we have no right to expect that the peace of God will keep our hearts, we have no right to expect that the peace of God will keep our heart and our mind. If we go on our knees feeling that God is against us, we may as well get up and go out. No, we must approach Him 'with thanksgiving'. There must be no doubt as to the goodness of God in our heart. . . . We must say, 'I may be in trouble at the moment, but I can thank God for my salvation and that He has sent His Son to die on the Cross for me and for my sins. There is a terrible problem facing me, I know, but He has done that for me . . . I will thank Him for the many blessings I have received in the past'. We must just work out with all our mind and with all our energy the reasons for thanking and praising God. We must remind ourselves that He is our Father, that He loves us so much that the very hairs of our head are all numbered. And when we have reminded ourselves of these things we must pour out our heart in thanksgiving . . . we must come into His presence with a loving, praising, worshipping adoration, and confident faith, and then make our requests known unto Him. The prayer that Paul advocates, in other words, is not a desperate cry in the dark, not some frantic appeal to God without any real thought. No, no, we first realize and recollect that we are worshipping a blessed, glorious God. We worship first and then we make our requests known.

Spiritual Depression, pp. 267–8

[The golden rule] is nothing, of course, but an epitome of the commandments which our Lord has summed up elsewhere in the words, 'Love thy neighbour as thyself'. . . . You do not start with the other person; you start by asking yourself, 'What is it I like? What are the things that please me? What are the things that help and encourage me?' Then you ask yourself, 'What are the things I dislike? What are the things that upset me, and bring out the worst in me? What are the things that are hateful and discouraging?' You make a list of both these things, your likes and dislikes, and you work them out in detail—not only in deeds, but also in thoughts and in speech—with respect to the whole of your life and activities. 'What do I like people to think about me? What is it that tends to hurt me?'

. . . Having drawn up this list of all our likes and dislikes, when we come to deal with other people we have nothing to do but to say quite simply, 'That other person is exactly as I am in these matters'. We must put ourselves constantly in their position. In our conduct and behaviour with respect to them we must be careful to do, and not to do, all the things which we have found to be pleasing or displeasing to ourselves. . . . You do not like unkind things said about you? Well, do not say them about others. You do not like people who are difficult, and who make your life difficult, and bring problems into your life, and constantly put you on edge? Well; in exactly the same way, do not let your behaviour be such that you become like that to them. It is quite as simple as that, according to our Lord. All the great textbooks on ethics and social relationships and morality, and on all the other subjects which deal with the problems of human relationships in the modern world can really be reduced to that.

Studies in the Sermon on the Mount, ii, pp. 207–8

'O, yes,' says this man [Psalm 73] 'I know that . . . even though a day may come when I shall feel the foundations of life shaking beneath me, God will be a rock that will hold me. He cannot be moved; He cannot be shaken. He is the Rock of ages, and wherever I am, and whatever may be happening, however my physical frame is behaving, and even when the things of earth are passing away, God the Rock will sustain me and I shall never be moved. God is the Rock, the strength of my heart, and my portion for ever.'

The Bible is never tired of saying this. . . . Listen to Isaiah. . . . He talks about that 'foundation stone'; that 'tried stone . . . a sure foundation' that has been set, and what he says is, 'He that believeth shall not make haste'. . . . Or according to another possible translation, 'He that believeth shall never be put to shame'. Why not? He is on the Rock, he has this support, he has this foundation, and it cannot be moved, for it is God Himself. . . .

> My hope is built on nothing less
> Than Jesu's blood and righteousness;
> I dare not trust my sweetest frame,
> But wholly lean on Jesu's name.
>> On Christ, the solid Rock, I stand;
>> All other ground is sinking sand . . .

Do you know this? Are you on the Rock? Do you know Him? Do not try to live on your family; do not live on your business, or on your own activity; do not live on your experiences, or anything else. They will all come to an end and the devil will suggest that even your highest experiences can be explained psychologically. Let us live on nothing, let us trust nothing, but Him. He is the Rock of Ages, the everlasting God:

> On Christ, the solid Rock, I stand;
> All other ground is sinking sand.

Faith on Trial, pp. 114–15

Have you noticed the apparent contradiction in Philippians 3? Paul says, 'Not as though I had already attained, either were already perfect', and then a few verses further on he says, 'Let us therefore, as many as be perfect. . . .' Is it a contradiction of what he has just been saying? Not at all; you see the Christian is perfect, and yet he is to become perfect. . . . At this moment I am perfect in Christ, and yet I am being made perfect. 'Not as though I had already attained, either were already perfect; but I follow after. . . . I press toward the mark.' Yes, he is addressing those who are Christians, those who are already perfect in this matter of understanding concerning the way of righteousness and justification. Yet his exhortation to them in a sense is, 'let us therefore go on to perfection'.

I do not know what you feel about this, but to me it is fascinating. You see the Christian is one who at one and the same time is hungering and thirsting, and yet he is filled. And the more he is filled the more he hungers and thirsts. That is the blessedness of this Christian life. It goes on. You reach a certain stage in sanctification, but you do not rest upon that for the rest of your life. You go on changing from glory into glory 'till in heaven we take our place'. 'Of his fullness have we received and grace upon grace', grace added to grace. It goes on and on; perfect, yet not perfect; hungering, thirsting, yet filled and satisfied, but longing for more, never having enough because it is so glorious and so wondrous; fully satisfied by Him and yet a supreme desire to 'know him, and the power of his resurrection'. . . . Are you filled? are you blessed in this sense? are you hungering and thirsting? Those are the questions. This is the gracious, glorious promise of God to all such: 'Blessed are they which do hunger and thirst after rightousness, for they shall be filled.'

Studies in the Sermon on the Mount, i, p. 83

Never does the Apostle say that if we pray, our prayer in and of itself will make us feel better. It is a disgraceful thing that people should pray for that reason. That is the psychologists' use of prayer. They tell us that if we are in trouble it will do us good to pray. . . . Prayer is not auto-suggestion.

Neither does he say, 'Pray, because while you are praying you will not be thinking about that problem, and therefore you will have temporary relief'. . . . Neither does he say, 'If you fill your mind with thoughts of God and Christ these thoughts will push out the other things'. . . . Neither does he say. . . . 'Pray, because prayer changes things'. No, it does not. Prayer does not 'change things'. . . . It is not your prayer that is going to do it, it is not you who are going to do it, but God. 'The peace of God that passeth all understanding'—He, through it all, 'will keep your hearts and minds in Christ Jesus'.

I must say a word about that expression 'keeping' your hearts and minds. It means garrisoning, guarding—a number of words can be used. It conjures up a picture. What will happen is that this peace of God will walk round the ramparts and towers of our life. We are inside, and the activities of the heart and mind are producing those stresses and anxieties and strains from the outside. But the peace of God will keep them out and we ourselves inside will be at perfect peace. It is God that does it. It is not ourselves, it is not prayer, it is not some psychological mechanism. We make our requests known unto God, and God does that for us and keeps us in perfect peace.

Spiritual Depression, pp. 269–70

(from the annual 'mottos' of the Wesley Guild)

The failure of man to live by, and to keep, the golden rule is due to the fact that he is self-centred. That, in turn, leads to self-satisfaction, self-protection, self-concern. Self is in the forefront the whole time, for man wants everything for himself. In the last analysis is not that the real cause of the trouble in your labour disputes? . . . One side says, 'I am entitled to have more'. The other side says, 'Well, if he has more, I shall have less'. And so they both object to each other and there is a quarrel, because each one is thinking only of himself. I am not entering into the particular merits of particular disputes . . . but the bitterness always comes in because of sin and self. If we were only honest enough to analyse our attitude towards all these questions, whether political, social, economic, national or international, we should find that it all comes to that. You see it in the nations. Two nations want the same thing, so each one is watching the other. All nations try to see themselves simply as the guardians and the custodians of the general peace of the world. There is an element of selfishness in patriotism always. It is 'my country', 'my right'; and the other nation says the same; and because we are all so self-centred there are wars. All disputes are quarrelling and unhappinesses, whether between individuals, or between divisions of society, or between nations or groups of nations, all in the end come down to just that. The solution for the problems of the world today is essentially theological. All the conferences and all the proposals about disarmament and everything else will come to nothing while there is sin in the human heart controlling individuals and groups and nations. The failure to implement the golden rule is due solely to the Fall and to sin.

Studies in the Sermon on the Mount, ii, p. 213

Another translation [of Psalm 73:28] could be this, 'But as for myself, nearness to God is good for me' . . . His chief ambition is going to be just that, to keep near to God. . . . We are all either far from God or near to Him . . . so that it is vitally important that we should arrive at this man's resolve, to be near to God.

. . . what was uppermost in his mind was something like this. Reviewing his sad experience he came to the conclusion that what had really been wrong with him . . . was just the fact that he did not keep near to God. He had thought it was the fact that the ungodly seemed to prosper while he experienced nothing but troubles. But now, having been given the enlightenment which he had in the sanctuary of God, he sees quite clearly that this was not the root cause of his trouble at all. There is only one thing that matters and that is man's relationship to God. If I am near to God, says this man, it does not really matter what happens to me; but if I am far from God, nothing can eventually be right. . . .

This is the beginning and the end of wisdom in the Christian life. The moment we move away from God everything goes wrong. The one secret is to keep near to God. When we fail, we are like a ship at sea that loses sight of the North star, or whose compass fails. If we lose our bearings, we must not be surprised at the consequences. That is what this man discovered. 'This is what I need,' he says; 'not blessings, not the prosperity other people have. . . . Therefore, this is my resolution. For myself, I am going to live near God. That is always going to be the big thing in my life. I am going to start with that every day as it comes. I am going to say to myself, Whatever else happens that this is the essential thing, to be near to God.'

Faith on Trial, pp. 117–18

[Psalm 42:11] is an extraordinarily accurate picture of
spiritual depression . . . you can almost see the man . . . the
man who is dejected and disquieted and miserable, who is
unhappy and depressed always shows it in his face. He looks
troubled and he looks worried. You take one glance at him and
you see his condition. Yes, says the Psalmist in effect, but when
I really look at God, as I get better, my face gets better also—
'He is the health of my countenance'. I lose that drawn,
haggard, vexed, troubled, perplexed, introspective appearance
and I begin to look composed and calm, balanced and bright.
This is not the putting on of a mask, but something that is
inevitable. If we are depressed or unhappy, whether we like it
or not, we will show it in our face. On the other hand, if we are
in the right relationship to God, and in a true spiritual condition
that again quite inevitably must express itself in our countenance, though I am not suggesting that we should perpetually
have* that inane grin upon our faces that some people think
is essential to the manifestation of true Christian joy. You need
not put anything on, it will be there; it cannot help expressing
itself—'He is the health of my countenance'.

Spiritual Depression, pp. 13–14

---

*"The truly happy do not laugh' (Maeterlinck) [Ed.].

> *The most impossible of all*
> *Is, that I e'er from sin should cease;*
> *Yet shall it be, I know it shall:*
> *Jesus, look to Thy faithfulness!*

It is very interesting to observe how people, when they have the gospel presented to them, generally have two main objections to it, and . . . the two objections are so often found in the same people. . . . First of all, when they hear this announcement, 'Blessed are they which do hunger and thirst after righteousness: for they shall be filled', when they are told that salvation is altogether of grace, that it is something that is given by God, which they cannot merit, which they can never deserve, and about which they can do nothing except receive it, they immediately begin to object and say, 'But that is making the thing much too easy . . . surely salvation cannot be as easy as that'. . . .

Then, when one points out to them that it must be like that because of the character of the righteousness about which the text speaks, they begin to object and to say that that is making it much too difficult, indeed so difficult as to make it impossible . . . They go astray, you see, about this whole question of righteousness. Righteousness to them means just being decent and moral up to a certain level. But . . . righteousness ultimately means being like the Lord Jesus Christ. . . . That is what we have to attain unto. And, of course, the moment we realize that then we see that it is something we ourselves cannot do, and realize that we must therefore receive it as helpless paupers, as those who have nothing in our hands at all, as those who take it entirely as a free gift . . . to object to the gospel because it 'makes things too easy', or to object to it because it makes things too difficult, is just virtually to confess that we are no Christians at all. The Christian is one who admits that the statements and the demands of the gospel are impossible, but thanks God that the gospel does the impossible for us.

Studies in the Sermon on the Mount, i, pp. 84–

Beloved Christian, whatever it is that is tending to get you down, tending to make you a victim of this anxiety, this morbid care, harassing and spoiling your Christian life and witness, whatever it is, let it be known unto God . . . and if you do so it is absolutely guaranteed that the peace of God . . . shall guard, keep, garrison your heart and mind. . . . Like the Psalmist you will lay yourself down and you will sleep, you will know this perfect peace. Do you know this, have you got this peace? Is this another bit of theory or does it actually happen? I assert that nearly two thousand years of Christian history . . . proclaim that this is a fact. Read the stories of the saints and the martyrs and the Confessors. . . . John George Carpenter, until a few years ago the General of the Salvation Army, tells how he and his wife had to part with their daughter, a lovely girl, of whom they were so fond and proud and who had dedicated her young life to foreign mission work in the East. Suddenly she was taken ill with typhoid fever. Of course, they began to pray, but John Carpenter and Mrs Carpenter somehow felt, although they could not explain it, that they could not pray for that child's recovery. They went on praying but their prayer was— 'Thou canst heal her if Thou wilt'—they could not positively ask God to heal her. . . . They went on like that for six weeks and then this beautiful girl died. The very morning she died John Carpenter said to Mrs Carpenter, 'You know, I am aware of a strange and curious calm within', and she replied and said, 'I feel exactly the same'. And she said to him, 'This must be the peace of God'. And it was the peace of God. . . . There they were, they had made their request known in the right way, and . . . this amazing calm and peace had come to them. . . . 'it must be the peace of God'. It was. Thank God for it.

Spiritual Depression, pp. 271–2

How can our attitude and conduct ever conform to what our Lord says here [Matthew 7:12]? The answer of the gospel is that you must start with God. What is the greatest commandment? It is this: 'Thou shalt love the Lord thy God. . . .' And the second is like unto it: 'Thou shalt love thy neighbour as thyself.' You notice the order. You do not start with your neighbour, you start with God. And relationships in this world will never be right, whether between individuals, or groups of nations, until we all start with God. You cannot love your neighbour as yourself until you love God. You will never see yourself or your neighbour aright until you have first of all seen both in the sight of God. . . .

So then we start with God. We turn from all the quarrelling and disputes and problems and we look into His face. We begin to see Him in all His holiness and almightiness, and in all the power of His creatorship, and we humble ourselves before Him. . . . The knowledge of God humbles us to the dust; and in that position you do not think about your rights and your dignity. You have no need any longer to protect yourself, because you feel you are unworthy of everything.

But, in turn, it also helps us to see others as we should see them. We see them now, no longer as hateful people who are trying to rob us of our rights . . . we see them, as we see ourselves, as the victims of sin and of Satan. . . . We have an entirely new view of them. We see them to be exactly as we are ourselves, and we are both in a terrible predicament. And we can do nothing; but both of us together must run to Christ and avail ourselves of His wonderful grace. We begin to enjoy it together and we want to share it together. That is how it works. It is the only way whereby we can ever do unto others as we would that they should do unto us.

Studies in the Sermon on the Mount, ii, pp. 213-15

November 6   *I have learned, in whatsoever state I am,
therewith to be content. I know both how to be
abased and I know how to abound; everywhere
and in all things I am instructed both to be full
and to be hungry, both to abound and to suffer
need*   (Philippians 4:11–12)

There are two big principles here. The first of course is the
condition at which the Apostle had arrived. The second is the
way in which he had arrived at that condition. . . . Let us first
look at the condition to which the Apostle had attained. He
describes it by the word that is translated here as 'content'. . . .
But . . . the word 'content' does not fully explain it; it really
means that he is 'self-sufficient', independent of circumstances
or conditions or surroundings, 'having sufficiency in oneself'.
. . . The affirmation made by the Apostle is that he has arrived
at a state in which he can say quite honestly and truthfully that
he is independent of his position . . . and of everything that is
happening to him. Now that that was no mere rhetorical statement on the part of the Apostle is made very clear in the
records that we have of this man and of his life in different
parts of the New Testament. . . . You remember how he and
Silas were arrested [at Philippi] and beaten and thrown into
prison with their feet made fast in the stocks. Their physical
conditions could not very well have been worse, yet so little
effect did that have upon Paul and Silas that 'at midnight [they]
prayed and sang praises unto God' (Acts 16:25). Independent
of circumstances, 'content in whatsoever state I am', to be self-
satisfied, independent of surroundings. That is what you find
also in the famous passage in the Second Epistle to the Corinthians, chapter twelve, where Paul tells us how he learned to be
independent of 'the thorn in the flesh', self-sufficient in spite of
it. You remember also how he exhorts Timothy to take hold of
this principle by saying: 'Godliness with contentment is great
gain' (1 Timothy 6:6). There is nothing like it, he says in effect;
if you have that you have everything.

Spiritual Depression, pp. 277–8

When we look to God and realize something of the truth about Him, and ourselves in relationship to Him, the one thing we are conscious of is that God never deals with us according to our deserts . . . [He] gives us His good things in spite of our being what we are. He does not merely look at us as we are. Were He to do so we should all be condemned. . . . But He is interested in us in spite of these externals: He sees us as a loving Father. He looks upon us in His grace and mercy. So He does not deal with us merely as we are. He deals with us in grace.

. . . 'Now', [Jesus] says in effect, 'you deal like that with your fellow men. Do not merely see the offensive and the difficult and the ugly. See behind all that.' Let us then observe human beings in their relationship to God, destined for eternity. Let us learn to look at them in this new way, in this divine way. 'Look on them', says Christ . . . 'as I have looked upon you, and in the light of the thing that brought Me from heaven for you, to give My life for you.' Look at them like that. The moment you do so you will find that it is not difficult to implement the golden rule, because at that point you are delivered from self and its terrible tyranny, and you are seeing men and women with a new eye and in a different way . . . a spiritual way. It is only when we come to this, after having started with God and sin and self and others, that we shall indeed be able to implement this amazing summary of the law and the prophets: 'Whatsoever ye would that men should do to you, do ye even so to them.' That is the thing to which we are called in Christ Jesus. We are to implement it, we are to practise it. And as we do so we shall be showing the world the only way in which its problems can be solved. We shall at the same time be missionaries and ambassadors for Christ.

Studies in the Sermon on the Mount, ii, pp. 215–16

We must surely ask ourselves questions such as these: Are we filled? Have we got this satisfaction? Are we aware of this dealing of God with us? Is the fruit of the Spirit being manifested in our lives? Are we concerned about that? Are we experiencing love to God and to other people, joy and peace? Are we manifesting long-suffering, goodness, gentleness, meekness, faith and temperance? They that do hunger and thirst after righteousness shall be filled. They are filled, and they are being filled. Are we, therefore, I ask, enjoying these things? Do we know that we have received the life of God? Are we enjoying the life of God in our souls? Are we aware of the Holy Spirit and all His mighty working within, forming Christ in us more and more? If we claim to be Christian, then we should be able to say yes to all these questions. Those who are truly Christian are filled in this sense. Are we thus filled? Are we enjoying our Christian life and experience? Do we know that our sins are forgiven? Are we rejoicing in that fact, or are we still trying to make ourselves Christian, trying somehow to make ourselves righteous? Is it all a vain effort? Are we enjoying peace with God? Do we rejoice in the Lord always? Those are the tests that we must apply. If we are not enjoying these things, the only explanation of that fact is that we are not truly hungering and thirsting after righteousness. For if we do hunger and thirst we shall be filled. There is no qualification at all, it is an absolute statement, it is an absolute promise— 'Blessed are they which do hunger and thirst after righteousness: for they shall be filled'.

Studies in the Sermon on the Mount i p. 87

What was there to sustain [Habakkuk] when the Chaldeans arrived and began to destroy the city? . . . It was not merely resignation or saying, 'Well, there is no use crying over spilt milk, or getting alarmed and excited, because we cannot do anything about it'. Nor was it just applying the principle of psychological detachment. It was not . . . saying, 'The best thing is not to think about it! Go to the pictures, read novels and don't think!'—a sort of escapism. Neither was it an attempt at being courageous . . . 'psychological' treatment differs greatly from the scriptural method. It is often sheer cruelty to a man who is in a state of uncontrolled fear to say to him, 'Pull yourself together'. If he could, he would, and the trembling would stop. . . . The methods which the world offers at such a time are effective only for certain people, and at a stage when their help is hardly necessary. They are of no value when a person is in this stage of utter physical alarm [Habakkuk 3:16]. Instead of mere resignation, or plucking up one's courage, the Scripture shows that it is possible even under such conditions to be in a state of actual rejoicing (Habakkuk 3:17–18). The Christian claims nothing less than that. Your man of the world may, if he is in a physically good condition, school himself to a state of resignation. He may put on a courageous air as many did during the last war . . . and that as far as it goes is a commendable spirit. But, in contrast to that, the Christian is assured that though he may be a person who is physically disposed to be thoroughly alarmed, he may experience not only strength but positive joy in the midst of danger. He may 'rejoice in tribulation' and be triumphant in the midst of the worst circumstances. That is the challenge of the Christian position. Herein we as Christians are to differ from the world. When hell is let loose . . . we are to be 'more than conquerors'. . . . We are to rejoice in the Lord. . . . Such a time is a test for our Christian profession. If we are not then more than conquerors we are failing as Christians.

From Fear to Faith, pp. 70–1

What is eternal life? Our Lord has defined it. 'This is life eternal, that they might know thee the only true God, and Jesus Christ, whom thou hast sent' (John 17:3). Or, as John puts it in his First Epistle, where he writes in order that his readers 'may have fellowship with us: and truly our fellowship is with the Father, and with His Son Jesus Christ' (1 John 1:3). Now the Psalmist says [73:28], 'This is my resolve. I want to keep near this God; I want to keep in touch with Him; I want to spend all my time with Him; I want to live as always in His presence. I like to think of His power and His promises, to remember His constancy'. And is not this a comforting and consoling, as well as an uplifting, thought? We do not know what is awaiting us, we live in a world that is full of change and we ourselves are inconsistent. The best of us are changeable creatures. And there is nothing so characteristic of our world as its instability and uncertainty. Is there anything more wonderful than to know that, at any moment, we can enter into the presence of One who is everlastingly the same . . . [James 1:17] . . . the same in His might, His majesty, His glory, His love, His mercy, His compassion, and the same in all that He has promised! Do you not understand this man now? 'I do not care about the others', he says; 'but I, as for me, nearness to God is good for me.' Let us think more about God. Let us meditate upon Him; let us turn our minds and our hearts towards Him. Let us realize that in Christ He offers us His fellowship, His companionship, and that constantly and always.

Faith on Trial, p. 121

The Christian's concern is to view life in this world in the light of the gospel. . . . If you are anxious about the state of the world and the threat of possible wars, then . . . the most direct way of avoiding such calamities is to observe words such as these. . . . 'Blessed are they which do hunger and thirst after righteousness. . . .' If every man and woman in this world knew what it was to 'hunger and thirst after righteousness' there would be no danger of war. Here is the only way to real peace . . . all the denunciations that are so constantly made of various countries and peoples and persons will not have the slightest effect upon the international situation. Thus we often waste our time, and God's time, in expressing our human thoughts and sentiments instead of considering His Word. . . . The greatest need in the world now is for a greater number of Christians, individual Christians. If all nations consisted of individual Christians there would be no need to fear atomic power or anything else. So the gospel, which seems to be so remote and indirect in its approach, is actually the most direct way of solving the problem. One of the greatest tragedies in the life of the Church today is the way in which so many are content with those vague, general, useless statements about war and peace instead of preaching the gospel in all its simplicity and purity. It is righteousness that exalts a nation, and the most important thing for all of us is to discover what righteousness means.

Studies in the Sermon on the Mount, i, p. 73

November 12   *Beware lest thou forget the Lord, which brought thee forth out of the land of Egypt*

(Read Deuteronomy 6)

[Paul] was anxious to make the all-inclusiveness of his claim perfectly clear (Philippians 4:10–12). . . . He knows how to be abased, he knows how to be hungry and to suffer need; on the other hand he knows how to abound, how to be full and to have plenty. It would be interesting to discuss the relative difficulty of these two things. Which is the more difficult, to be abased or to abound without losing the contented mind? I do not know whether we can ever answer the question. They are both extremely difficult and one is as difficult as the other. Can I be abased without feeling a sense of grudge, or without being worried, or without being anxious? Can I suffer the need of food and clothing, can I be abased in my profession or office or work, can I somehow or another be put down and still remain in spirit exactly as I was before? What a difficult thing this is . . . Paul . . . had experienced every kind of trial and tribulation and yet he is unaffected by them.

Then take the other side. 'I know how to abound', says Paul, 'I know how "to be full", I know how to enjoy plenty.' What a difficult thing this is. How difficult it is for the wealthy person not to feel complete independence of God. . . . Most of us remember Him when we are down . . . but, when we have everything we need, how easy it is to forget God. . . . What Paul says is that in either of these positions he is perfectly free. Poverty does not get him down, riches do not carry him away and make him lose his hold. He says that he is not dependent upon either, that he is self-sufficient in this sense, that his life is not controlled by these things, that he is what he is apart from them. Whether he is 'to abound' or to 'suffer need' it does not matter.

Spiritual Depression, pp. 280–1

[Jesus'] object in this Sermon . . . is to bring Christian people to realize first of all their nature, their character as a people, and then to show them how they are to manifest that nature and character in their daily life. Our Lord, the Son of God, has come from heaven to earth in order to found and establish a new kingdom, the kingdom of heaven. . . . Therefore it is essential that He should make it quite plain and clear that this kingdom He has come to establish is entirely different from anything that the world has ever known, that it is to be the kingdom of God, the kingdom of light, the kingdom of heaven. His people must realize that it is something unique and separate; so He gives them a description of it . . . We have looked at His general portrait of the Christian in the Beatitudes. We have listened to Him telling these people that, because they are that kind of person, the world will react to them in a particular way; it will probably dislike them and persecute them. . . . [Yet] they are to remain in society as salt and as light. They are to keep society from putrefaction and from falling to pieces, and they are to be . . . that light, apart from which the world remains in a state of gross darkness.

. . . He then comes to the practical application and outworking of it all . . . giving detailed instructions as to how we are to do our almsgiving, and how to pray and how to fast. Finally He deals with our whole attitude towards life in this world. . . . 'There', He says, . . . 'is the character of this kingdom which I am forming. That is the type of life I am going to give you, and I want you to live and manifest it' . . . Having done that, He pauses, and looks at His congregation and says, 'Well, now; there is My purpose. What are you going to do about it? There is no point in listening to this Sermon, there is no purpose in your having followed Me through all this delineation of the Christian life, if you are only going to listen. What are you going to do about it?'

Studies in the Sermon on the Mount, ii, pp. 217–18

. . . the need for repentance and the importance of it is something that is taught in the Scriptures everywhere. The classic example of this teaching is, of course, to be found in the parable of the Prodigal Son. . . . Or take that wonderful statement in 2 Corinthians 7:9–11. These Christians in Corinth had committed a sin and Paul had written to them about it, and had sent Titus to preach to them about it. Their subsequent action provides us with a definition of what is really meant by a true spirit of repentance. What pleased the great Apostle about them was the way in which they dealt with themselves. . . . These Corinthian people had dealt severely with themselves and had condemned themselves; they had 'sorrowed after a godly sort', and because of that Paul tells them that they are again in the place of blessing.

Another wonderful example of the same thing comes in the book of Job. You remember how Job throughout the main part of that book is justifying himself, defending himself and sometimes feeling sorry for himself. But when he came truly into the presence of God, when he was in the place where he met with God, this is what he said, 'Wherefore I abhor myself, and repent in dust and ashes' (42:6). . . . I wonder whether we know that experience. . . . The popular doctrine of our times does not seem to like that, because it teaches that we have passed out of Romans 7. We must not talk about sorrow for sin because that would mean that we are still in the very early stages of the Christian life. So we pass over Romans 7 and turn to Romans 8. But have we ever been in Romans 7? . . . Have we ever really abhorred ourselves and repented in dust and ashes? This is a very vital part of the discipline of the Christian life. Read the lives of the saints throughout the centuries and you will find that they did it very frequently. Go back to Henry Martyn, for example; go back to any of those mighty men of God, and you will find that they frequently abhorred themselves. . . . And it was because of this that they were so mightily blessed of God.

Faith on Trial, pp. 68–9

'Tis all my business here below
To cry: Behold the Lamb!

People who really want something always give some evidence of that fact. People who really desire something with the whole of their being do not sit down, passively waiting for it to come. And that applies to us in this matter. . . . The person who is truly hungering and thirsting after righteousness obviously avoids everything that is opposed to such a righteousness. I cannot obtain it myself, but I can refrain from doing things that are obviously opposed to it. I can never make myself like Jesus Christ, but I can stop walking in the gutters of life. That is a part of hungering and thirsting.

Let us subdivide that. There are certain things in this life that are patently opposed to God and His righteousness. There is no question about that at all. We know they are bad; we know they are harmful; we know they are sinful. I say that to hunger and thirst after righteousness means avoiding such things just as we would avoid the very plague itself. If we know there is an infection in a house, we avoid that house. We segregate the patient who has a fever, because it is infectious, and obviously we avoid such persons. The same is equally true in the spiritual realm.

But it does not stop at that. I suggest that if we are truly hungering and thirsting after righteousness we shall not only avoid things that we know to be bad or harmful, we shall even avoid things that tend to dull or take the edge off our spiritual appetites. There are so many things like that, things that are quite harmless in themselves and which are perfectly legitimate. Yet if you find that you are spending too much of your time with them, and that you desire the things of God less, you must avoid them. . . . I think it is a commonsense argument.

Studies in the Sermon on the Mount, i, pp. 89–90

If we advocate godliness simply because it leads to the true morality, if we commend religion because it leads to the best state of society, then we are reversing the order actually and insulting God. God must never be regarded as a means to an end; and religion is not to be commended primarily because of certain benefits which follow its practice. . . . Hence the temptation to statesmen and leaders to pay lip service to religion, and to believe in its maintenance in a general form. . . . God is to be worshipped because He is God, because He is the Creator, because He is the Almighty, because He is the 'high and lofty One that inhabiteth eternity', because His Name is Holy. And in His presence it is impossible to think of anything else. All thoughts of self and of benefits that may accrue, all ideas concerning the possible results and advantages to ourselves, or to our class or country, are banished. He is supreme and He is alone. . . . The results and blessings of salvation, the moral life and the improved state of society—all these things are the consequence of true belief and they must never be allowed to usurp the supreme position. . . .

This is one of the most subtle dangers that faces us as we try to think out and plan a new state of society for the future. It is a danger which can be seen in the writings of a number of writers today who are concerned about the state of this country. . . . They advocate a religious society and a Christian education . . . simply because they have found all else to fail, and because they think that this is more likely to be successful. But . . . before you can have a Christian society and Christian education you must first of all have Christians. No education or culture, no mode of training, will ever produce Christians and the corresponding morality. To do that we must come face to face with God and see our sin and helpless plight . . . we must repent before Him and then receive His gracious offer of salvation in Jesus Christ His Son. . . . God must be worshipped for His own sake.

The Plight of Man and the Power of God, pp. 31–2

*A wonderful fashion of teaching He hath
And wise to salvation He makes us
through faith.*

[The apostle] says: 'I have learned', or better, 'I have come
to learn'. I thank God that Paul said that. Paul was not always
like this any more than any one of us. He had 'come to learn'.
He has another interesting word also. He says, 'Everywhere
and in all things I am "instructed" both to be full and to be
hungry' . . . what he really says is, 'I have been initiated', 'let
into the secret', 'let into the mystery'.

Paul says that he has come to learn how to be in this condition. Now there are many intimations in the New Testament
that this was particularly difficult for him. Paul was sensitive,
proud by nature, and, in addition, he was an intensely active
being. Nothing could be more galling for such a man than to
lie in prison. He had been brought up as a Roman citizen, but
here he is enduring bondage, not spending his life among great
intellectual people, but among slaves. How does he manage it?
'Ah', he says, 'I have come to learn, I have been let into the
secret, I have been let into the mystery.'

How did he come to learn? . . . In the first place it was by
sheer experience. [2 Corinthians 12:9–10 tell] about 'the thorn
in the flesh'. Paul did not like it. He struggled against it; three
times he prayed that it might be removed. But it was not
removed. He could not reconcile himself to it. He was impatient, he was anxious to go on preaching, and this thorn in
the flesh was keeping him down. But then he was taught the
lesson, 'My grace is sufficient for thee'. He came to a place of
understanding. . . . He had to learn, and experience teaches us
all. Some of us are very slow to learn, but God in His kindness
may send us an illness, sometimes He even strikes us down—
anything to teach us this great lesson and to bring us to this
great position.

Spiritual Depression, pp. 283–4

What hope has the man who is not a Christian? Look at your world; read your newspaper. What can you bank upon? Fifty years ago they used to bank on the fact that man was rapidly improving and getting better. You cannot do that now. You cannot bank on education; you cannot bank on the United Nations any more than you could on the League of Nations. All that has been tried and failed. What hope is there for the world? There is none. There is no comfort for the world now. But for the Christian man who mourns because of sin and because of the state of the world, there is this comfort— the comfort of the blessed hope, the glory that yet remains. So that even here, though he is groaning, he is happy at the same time because of the hope that is set before him. There is this ultimate hope in eternity. In that eternal state we shall be wholly and entirely blessed, there will be nothing to mar life, nothing to detract from it, nothing to spoil it. Sorrow and sighing shall be no more; all tears shall be wiped away; and we shall bask for ever and ever in the eternal sunshine, and experience joy and bliss and glory unmixed and unspoiled. 'Happy are they that mourn: for they shall be comforted.' How true it is. Unless we know that, we are not Christian. If we are Christian, we do know it, this joy of sins forgiven and the knowledge of it; the joy of reconciliation; the joy of knowing that God takes us back when we have fallen away from Him; the joy and contemplation of the glory that is set before us; the joy that comes from anticipation of the eternal state.

Studies in the Sermon on the Mount, i, pp. 61–2

[Jesus] tells us that the first thing we must do after we have read this Sermon is to look at the type and kind of life to which He calls us, and realize what it is.... What would we say is its outstanding characteristic? . . . He answers His own question by saying that the outstanding characteristic of the life to which He calls us is 'narrowness'.... He puts it dramatically before us by saying, 'Enter ye in at the strait gate'. The gate is narrow; and we must also walk along a narrow way.

His illustration is a very useful and practical one. He puts it in a dramatic form and the scene is immediately conjured up in our mind's eye. Here we are, walking along, and suddenly we find two gates confronting us. There is one on the left which is very wide and broad, and a great crowd of people are entering in. On the other hand there is a very narrow gate which takes only one person at a time. We see as we look through the wide gate that it leads to a broad way and that a great crowd is surging along it. But the other way is not only narrow at the beginning, it continues to be narrow, and there are but few to be seen walking along it. We can see the picture quite clearly. That, says our Lord . . . is what I have been talking about. That narrow road is the way along which I want you to walk. 'Enter ye in at the strait gate. Come on to this narrow way where you will find Me walking before you.' At once we are reminded of some of the outstanding characteristics of this Christian life to which our Lord and Saviour Jesus Christ calls us.

Studies in the Sermon on the Mount, ii, p. 220

Paul had come to learn this great truth (Philippians 4: 10–12) by working out a great argument. . . . I think that the Apostle's logic was something like this. He said to himself:

1. Conditions are always changing, therefore I must obviously not be dependent upon conditions.

2. What matters supremely and vitally is my soul and my relationship to God—that is the first thing.

3. God is concerned about me as my Father, and nothing happens to me apart from God. Even the very hairs of my head are all numbered. I must never forget that.

4. God's will and God's ways are a great mystery, but I know that whatever He wills or permits is of necessity for my good.

5. Every situation in life is the unfolding of some manifestation of God's love and goodness. Therefore my business is to look for this peculiar manifestation of God's goodness and kindness and to be prepared for surprises and blessings because 'His ways are not my ways, neither His thoughts my thoughts'. What, for example, is the great lesson that Paul learned in the matter of the thorn in the flesh? It is that, 'When I am weak then am I strong'. Paul was taught through physical weakness this manifestation of God's grace.

6. I must regard circumstances and conditions, not in and of themselves therefore, but as a part of God's dealings with me in the work of perfecting my soul and bringing me to final perfection.

7. Whatever my conditions may be at this present moment they are only temporary, they are only passing, and they can never rob me of the joy and the glory that ultimately await me with Christ.

I suggest that Paul had reasoned and argued it out like that. He had faced conditions and circumstances in the light of the Christian truth and the Christian gospel, and had worked out these steps and stages. And having done so he says, 'Let anything you can think of happen to me, I remain exactly where I was. Whatever may happen to me, I am left unmoved.'

Spiritual Depression, pp. 284–5

. . . unless we day by day voluntarily and deliberately remind ourselves of this righteousness which we need, we are not very likely to be hungering and thirsting after it. The man who truly hungers and thirsts after it makes himself look at it every day. 'But', you say, 'I am so tremendously busy. Look at my agenda. Where have I time?' I say, if you are hungering and thirsting after righteousness you will find time. You will order your life, you will say, 'First things must come first. . . .' 'Where there is a will there is a way.' It is amazing how we find time to do the things we want to. . . .

The man who is hungering and thirsting after righteousness always puts himself in the way of getting it. You cannot create it yourself. . . . But at any rate you do know there are certain ways in which it seems to have come to [the heroes of the Faith] so you begin to imitate their example. You remember that blind man, Bartimaeus. He could not heal himself. . . . But he went and put himself in the way of getting [his sight.] . . . And the man who hungers and thirsts after righteousness is the man who never misses an opportunity of being in those certain places where people seem to find this righteousness. Take, for example, the house of God. . . . I meet people who talk to me about their spiritual problems . . . they so want to be Christian, they say. But somehow or other something is lacking. Quite frequently I find that they do not often go to the house of God, or that they are very haphazard in their attendance. They do not know what it is to hunger and thirst after righteousness. The man who really wants it says, 'I cannot afford to lose any opportunity; wherever this is being talked about I want to be there' . . . And then, of course, he seeks the society of people who have this righteousness. He says, 'The oftener I am in the presence of godly and saintly men the better it is for me. . . . I do not want to spend so much time with others who do me no good. But these people . . . I am going to keep close to them.'

Studies in the Sermon on the Mount, i, pp. 90–1

Let us give our reasons for still believing in the message of the old gospel in the modern world. Our first reason . . . is that man himself as man has not changed at all. All the changes about which men boast so much are external. They are not changes in man himself, but merely in his mode of activity, in his environment. . . . 'But surely', asks someone, 'there is some mistake. Have you not seen the modern man travelling in his aeroplane at four hundred miles an hour? Are you suggesting that he is identical with the man who used to travel on foot at the rate of four miles an hour?' But wait a moment. Let us look at the two men. There they go, one at four hundred miles an hour, the other at four miles an hour. The vital question to answer in each case is what is the object of the travelling? . . . precisely the same in both cases. The individuals are going to make love, or to make war, or to do business, or they are intent upon pleasure. There is but one real difference between the two men. It is the rate at which they travel to the same goal. What, in reality, is the precise difference between the pride which the modern man takes in his culture and sophistication and the pride of those men who, at the very dawn of history, tried to build the tower of Babel into heaven?

. . . It is no part of our purpose to detract or to derogate from the power and the ability of modern man. . . . He has succeeded even in splitting the atom. But . . . he has been quite incapable of thinking of a new sin. All the sins that are being committed in the modern world you will find mentioned in the Old Testament. . . . Man as man does not change at all. He still remains the same contradictory person he has been ever since the original fall. That is our first reason for continuing to present to him the ancient gospel of Jesus Christ.

Truth Unchanged, Unchanging, pp. 110–12
(**continued on November 23**)

Our second reason for [presenting modern man with the ancient gospel of Jesus Christ] is infinitely more important. *God hasn't changed!* And it is when we realize . . . that man's ultimate problem is his relationship to God, that we see the final futility of introducing this question of age and of dates. . . . Someone has well put this point by saying, 'Time writes no wrinkle on the brow of the Eternal'. Of course there have been advances and developments, but do these in any way affect the being and the character of God? Does the fact that we have an internal combustion engine, and that we have succeeded in splitting the atom, in any way abrogate God's laws or in any way lessen His detestation of sin and wrongdoing? No, the most urgent, vital question confronting man is still the question asked of old by Job, 'How should man be just with God?' (Job 9:2). Certainly there is a new setting to problems, whether they are economic, political or educational; whether they deal with the shortage of houses or the proper treatment of strikes. But all these problems are temporary. . . .

The ultimate problem for man is not himself, his happiness, nor the conditions which surround him while he is here on earth. His ultimate problem is his relationship to God both in time and eternity; and God is eternal, changeless, absolute. How foolish it is, therefore, to argue that modern man needs a new remedy or a new type of salvation rather than 'the glorious gospel of the blessed God' (1 Timothy 1:11) which is to be found alone in our Lord and Saviour Jesus Christ.

Truth Unchanged, Unchanging, pp. 112–14 .
(*continued on November 24*)

(continued from November 23)

Our third and last reason [for presenting modern man with the ancient gospel of Christ] . . . is that there is nothing better than it . . . that it is still the only thing in the world which can adequately deal with the problem and the condition of man. Let us agree wholeheartedly with the modern man when he says that he believes always in having the best. . . . Let us by all means have the best, whatever it may cost and whatever its source may be. Further, it is true to say that in many realms and departments of life the latest is undoubtedly the best. Of all the amazing and phenomenal advances which were made in the last* war, there has been none . . . comparable to the advances that were made in the prevention and treatment of the ills of the physical body. We are all aware of the fact that by means of preventive inoculation our children can be safeguarded from the ravages of such diseases as whooping cough and diphtheria . . . [and] of the new chemical treatment of diseases by means of the sulphonamide drugs, and by . . . penicillin. . . . The change is truly astonishing . . . in the treatment of the ills and diseases of the body the latest is the best. But can the same be said about the prevention, treatment and cure of the ills of the soul of man? Is there some wonderful inoculation which can be given to young men and women which will render them immune to the insinuations and suggestions of sin which meet them on the streets, in the movies, in the books and magazines which they read? . . . Is there some wonderful drug which can be given to a man tormented by an accusing conscience . . . ? Is there a tonic which . . . will strengthen his feeble will . . . ? Is there some magical potion that can be given to a man who on his deathbed realizes his sinfulness and is afraid to meet his God and Judge Eternal?

. . . There is but one cure for the ills of man. . . . It is to know that Jesus . . . has forgiven me. . . . It is only from Him . . . that I can be more more than conqueror. . . . It is always, and only, in Christ that I find satisfaction.

Truth Unchanged, Unchanging, pp. 114–17

*The Second World War.

We must learn to depend upon Him and in order to do that we must learn to know Him, we must learn to have communion with Him, we must learn to find our pleasure in Him. The day may come . . . when we shall not be able to read. Then comes the test. Will you still be happy? Do you know Him so well that though you become deaf or blind this fount will still be open? Do you know Him so well that you can talk to Him and listen to Him and enjoy Him always? Will all be well because you have always been so dependent upon your relationship to Him that nothing else really matters? That was the apostle's condition. His intimacy with Christ was so deep and so great that he had become independent of everything else.

. . . I believe that what helped him most to learn this lesson was his looking at the great and perfect example of Christ Himself (Hebrews 12:1–4). Paul 'looked unto Him' and saw Him and His perfect example. And he applied it to his own life. 'While we look, not at the things which are seen, but at the things which are not seen: for the things which are seen are temporal, but the things which are not seen are eternal' (2 Corinthians 4:17, 18).

Christian people, can you say that, do you know that state? Let this become first with us, let this become our ambition, let us strain every nerve and do everything we can to get into this blessed state. Life may force it upon us, but even if circumstances do not, the time is bound to come, soon or late, when earth and every earthly scene will pass away, and in that final isolation of the soul we shall be alone, facing death and eternity. The greatest thing in life is to be able to say with Christ Himself at that hour, 'And yet I am not alone, because the Father is with me' (John 16:32).

Spiritual Depression, pp. 285–6

As we look into the unknown future we do not know what awaits us. Anything may happen. And if there is one thing we, and the whole world, crave for at this moment, it is security and safety. We have been let down so often; we have even let ourselves down. The thoughtful man asks, 'Where can I repose my trust? On what can I bank with absolute sense of safety?' And there is still only one answer. It is God. It is good for me to draw near with God; I have put my trust in this Lord God, this Jehovah, this covenant-keeping God.

The Psalms, of course, constantly emphasize this. You find it also in the Book of Proverbs. 'The name of the Lord is a strong tower: the righteous runneth into it, and is safe' (Proverbs 18:10). A man is outside in the world and the enemy begins to attack him. He cannot deal with him; he does not know what to do; he is alarmed and terrified. Then he runs into the strong tower, the name of the Lord, this Lord Jehovah. The enemy cannot get in there. In the arms of God, these almighty arms, he is safe. . . . Because we are in Christ, we are in God. We are perfectly safe there. Let me quote one of the grandest things the Apostle Paul ever said: 'I am persuaded (he is certain), that neither death, nor life, nor angels, nor principalities, nor powers, nor things present, nor things to come, nor height, nor depth, nor any other creature, shall be able to separate us from the love of God, which is in Christ Jesus our Lord' (Romans 8:38, 39). Safe in the arms of Jesus. If you are there, though hell be let loose it cannot touch you. Nothing can harm those who are in the safe keeping of their covenant-keeping God.

Faith on Trial, p. 123

331

Strong in the strength which God supplies
                      Through His eternal Son

This is a staggering statement—'I can do all things through
Christ which strengtheneth me' (Philippians 4:13). It is a
statement that is characterized at one and the same time by a
sense of triumph and by humility. He sounds at first as if he
were boasting, and yet when you look at his statement again
you will find that it is one of the most glorious and striking
tributes that he has ever paid anywhere to his Lord and
Master. . . . It at one and the same time exhorts us to rejoice,
to make our boast, and yet to be humble and to be lowly. And
there is no contradiction, because the boast of the Christian is
not in himself but in the Lord.

Paul was very fond of saying that. Take, for instance, the
statement: 'God forbid that I should glory save in the Cross of
our Lord Jesus Christ', or again: 'He that glorieth let him glory
in the Lord'. There is the exhortation on the one hand for us
to be boasting; yes, but always boasting in Him.

. . . The Authorized Version . . . does not really bring out the
particular shade of meaning the Apostle was anxious to convey.
It says: 'I can do all things through Christ which strengtheneth
me' . . . a better translation would be: 'I am strong for all
things in the One who constantly infuses strength into me'. . . .
What the Apostle is really saying is not so much that he can do
certain things himself, as that he is enabled to do certain things,
indeed all things, by this One who infuses His strength into
him. . . . The real secret, says Paul, which I have discovered is
that I am made strong for all things in the One who constantly
is infusing strength into me.

Spiritual Depression, pp. 289–91

The long history of the Church can be put in the form of a graph. It starts there at Pentecost in what may be described as a mighty revival. After a lapse of time, you remember, the power appeared to have passed, and the Church went down into a trough. The devil and the world were attacking, and everything seemed to be lost. The Church had no authority and no power. Men became desperate. Suddenly God pours out His Spirit again. There is a mighty revival, and the Church is lifted up to the very crest of the wave once more. That is how the history of the Church has progressed. It has not been a steady level. We might wish it to be like that, but it has never been so. It has always been this up and down, and the ups are the revivals, the 'pouring forth' of the Spirit. . . . Under such mighty out-pourings men have testified that they have learned more of God and of the Lord Jesus Christ in an hour in a meeting during a revival than they had learned in a lifetime of Bible study and reading theology. At the same time men and women who had hitherto belonged to the world and who had never heard the gospel before seemed to be put into the same position immediately.

There is something very wonderful about this . . . 'He that dwelleth in the heavens shall laugh' [Psalm 2:4] and I believe that God sometimes laughs at the Church. He sees us ready to put out our hands to steady the ark. We think that we alone can do it. We are greatly concerned. We hold our conferences and bring out our proposals. But they come to nothing. Then, when we are quite exhausted, after all our great campaigns, conferences and our brilliant organization . . . God unexpectedly—in the last place where you would ever have expected Him to do so and through the last person you would ever have thought of—suddenly sheds forth the Spirit. Then the Church rises to a new period of glory, of power and of influence. Men and women are again converted in masses, and the power of the truth is again upon them.

Authority, pp. 90–2

. . . reading the Bible. Here is the great textbook on this matter. . . . I wonder whether we spend as much time with this Book as we do with the newspaper or with the novels or with the films and all other entertainments—wireless, television and all these things. I am not condemning these things as such. . . . My argument is that the man who is hungering and thirsting after righteousness and has time for such things should have more time for this. . . . Study and read this Book. Try to understand it; read books about it.

And then, prayer. . . . How much time do we spend in His presence? [If you read the biographies of the men of God] you will feel ashamed of yourself. You will find that these saints spent four or five hours daily in prayer, not just saying their prayers at night when they were almost too weary to do so. They gave the best time of their day to God. . . .

And then there is the need for reading the biographies of the saints. . . . The people who hunger and thirst after righteousness are frantic . . . They are like Bartimaeus or like the importunate widow. . . . They come back to the same person until they get it. They are like Jacob struggling with the angel. They are like Luther, fasting, swearing, praying, not finding; but going on increasingly in his helplessness until God gave it to him. The same is true of all the saints of all ages and countries. . . . It seems to work out like this: it is only as you seek this righteousness with the whole of your being that you can truly discover it. You can never find it yourself. Yet the people who sit back and do nothing never seem to get it. That is God's method. God, as it were, leads us on. We have done everything, and having done all we are still miserable sinners: and then we see that, as little children, we are to receive it as the free gift of God. . . . Can I say quite honestly and truly that I desire above everything else in this world truly to know God and to be like the Lord Jesus Christ, to be rid of self . . . and to live only, always and entirely, to His glory and to His honour?

Studies in the Sermon on the Mount, i, pp. 91–3

[For Paul] everything always ends in Christ and with Christ. He is the final point, He is the explanation of Paul's living and his whole outlook upon life . . . Christ is all-sufficient for every circumstance, for every eventuality and for every possibility . . . he is introducing us to what in many ways we may describe as the cardinal New Testament doctrine. The Christian life . . . is not just a philosophy, it is not just a point of view, it is not just a teaching that we take up and try to put into practice. It is all that, but it is something infinitely more. The very essence of the Christian life, according to the New Testament teaching everywhere, is that it is a mighty power that enters into us; it is a life, if you like, that is pulsating in us. It is an activity, and an activity on the part of God. . . .

[Christians] are not just men who have taken up a certain theory and are trying to practise it; it is God doing something in them and through them . . . our highest thoughts, our noblest aspirations, our every righteous inclination is from and of God, is something that is brought into being in us by God Himself. It is God's activity and not merely our activity (Philippians 3: 10). . . . You find [Paul] saying exactly the same thing in other Epistles (Ephesians 1:19, 20; 2:10). . . . You remember also the great statement at the end of the third chapter: 'He is able to do exceeding abundantly above all that we ask or think, according to the power that worketh in us'. Now, that is typical and characteristic New Testament doctrine, and if we have not grasped it we are surely missing one of the most glorious things about the Christian life and position. . . . We come back again to what I am never tired of quoting, namely, John Wesley's favourite definition of a Christian. He found it in that book by Henry Scougal. . . . The life of God in the soul of man. . . . The Christian is not just a good, decent, moral man; the life of God has entered into him, there is an energy, a power, a life in him and it is that that makes him peculiarly and specifically Christian.

Spiritual Depression, pp. 291–2

[The Christian life] is something that is always intensely personal.... We are all of us so much slaves of 'the done thing'. We come into a world full of traditions and habits and customs to which we tend to conform. It is the easy and obvious thing to do; and it is true to say of most of us that there is nothing we hate so much as being unusual or different ... one of the most difficult things that many people have to face when they become Christian is that it is going to involve them in being unusual and exceptional. But it has to happen ... one of the first things that happens to a person who becomes alive to the message of the gospel of Christ is that he says to himself: 'Well; whatever may be happening to the majority, I myself am a living soul and I am responsible for my own life.' ... So when a man becomes a Christian he first begins to see himself as a separate unit in this great world. Formerly he had lost his individuality and identity in the great crowd of people to whom he belonged; but now he stands alone. He had been rushing madly with the crowd, but he suddenly halts. ... He leaves the crowd. You cannot get a crowd through that turnstile all together, it only takes one person at a time. It makes a man realize that he is a responsible being before God, his Judge Eternal. The gate is strait and narrow, it brings me face to face with judgement, face to face with God, face to face with the question of life and my personal being, my soul and its eternal destiny.

But I not only have to leave the crowd, the world and the 'jollity' outside.... I have to leave the *way* of the world outside ... we must leave outside the gate the things that please the world ... the things that belong to and that please our unregenerate nature must be left outside that strait gate.

Studies in the Sermon on the Mount, ii, pp. 221–3
(*continued on p. 337*)

(*continued from p. 336*)

Yes, but still narrower and still straiter; if we really want to come into this way of life, we have to leave our 'self' outside. And it is there of course that we come to the greatest stumbling-block of all. It is one thing to leave the world, and the way of the world; but the most important thing . . . is to leave our self outside. . . . That is not being foolish; it is typical New Testament language. Self is the Adamic man, the fallen nature; and Christ says that he must be left outside. 'Put off the old man', that is, leave him outside the gate. There is no room for two men to go through this gate together, so the old man must be left behind. . . .

The New Testament gospel is very humbling to self and to pride. At the beginning of the Sermon we are confronted by: 'Blessed are the poor in spirit'. No natural man born into this world likes to be poor in spirit. We are by nature the exact opposite to that; we are all born with a proud nature, and the world does its best to encourage our pride from our very birth. The most difficult thing in the world is to become poor in spirit. It is humbling to pride, and yet it is essential. At the entrance to that strait gate there is a notice that says: 'Leave yourself outside'. How can we bless them that curse us, and pray for them which despitefully use us, unless we have done this? How can we possibly follow our Lord, and be children of our Father which is in heaven, and love our enemies, if we are . . . always defending and watching self and being concerned about it. . . . Self cannot possibly exist in this atmosphere; all along it must be crucified. . . . Have no illusion about this. If you think it is a life in which you are going to make a great name, and be praised, and one in which you are going to be made wonderful, you may as well stop at this point and go back to the beginning, for he who would enter by this gate must say goodbye to self.

Studies in the Sermon on the Mount, ii, pp. 224–5

Stoicism, in the last analysis, was profound pessimism. It really came to this, that this world is hopeless, that nothing can do any good, that the thing you have to do therefore is to get through life as best you can and just refuse to let yourself be hurt by it. The Eastern religions are, of course, entirely pessimistic. They regard matter in itself as evil, they regard the flesh as essentially evil; everything, they say, is evil, and the only thing to do is to get through life with a minimum of pain and to hope that in some subsequent reincarnation you will be rid of it altogether and at last be absorbed and lost for ever in the absolute and the eternal, and cease to be a separate personality.

Now that is the very antithesis of the Christian gospel which is . . . essentially positive . . . we reject the negative view *in toto* supremely for this reason, that it fails to give the glory and the honour to the Lord Jesus Christ. . . . Paul wants us to see that his victory is based upon his association with Christ . . . that Christ infuses so much strength and power into him that he is strong and able for all things. He is not left to himself, he is not struggling alone and vainly against these mighty odds. . . . 'In this', says Paul, 'I am able for anything'.

. . . This is surely one of the most glorious statements he ever made. Here is a man in prison, a man who has already suffered a great deal in his life, a man who knows what it is to be disappointed in so many ways—persecuted, treated with derision and scorn, even disappointed sometimes, as he tells, us in his fellow workers,* there in prison in conditions calculated to produce dejection in the stoutest heart, facing perhaps a cruel martyrdom—yet he is able to send out this mighty challenge. 'I am able to stand, to bear all things in the One who is constantly infusing strength into me.'

Spiritual Depression, pp. 293–4

* Philippians 1:15–17

December 4   *Wherefore if any man is in Christ, he is a new*
                   creature: the old things are passed away;
                   behold, they are become new
                                            (2 Corinthians 5:17)

[The Beatitudes] remind us of certain primary, central truths about the whole Christian position. . . . The Christian gospel places all its primary emphasis upon being, rather than doing. The gospel puts a greater weight upon our attitude than upon our actions . . . on what you and I essentially are rather than on what we do. Throughout the Sermon our Lord is concerned about dispositions. Later He is going to talk about actions; but before He does that He describes character and disposition. . . . A Christian *is* something before he does anything; and we have to *be* Christian before we can act as Christians. . . . Being is more important than doing, attitude is more significant than action. Primarily it is our essential character that matters . . . it is an entire fallacy to . . . say, for example, 'To be truly Christian I must take up and use Christian teaching and then apply it'. That is not the way our Lord puts it. The position rather is that my Christianity controls me; I am to be dominated by the truth because I have been made a Christian by the operation of the Holy Spirit within. . . . You cannot read these Beatitudes without coming to that conclusion. The Christian faith is not something on the surface of a man's life, it is not merely a kind of coating or veneer. No, it is something that has been happening in the very centre of his personality. That is why the New Testament talks about rebirth and being born again, about a new creation and about receiving a new nature. It is something that happens to a man in the very centre of his being; it controls all his thoughts, all his outlook, all his imagination, and, as a result, all his actions as well.

Studies in the Sermon on the Mount, i, pp. 96–7

His love in time past forbids me to think
                                  He'll leave me at last in trouble to sink

All things may seem to be against me 'to drive me to despair', I do not understand what is happening; but I know this, I know that God has so loved me that He sent His only begotten Son into the world for me, I know that while I was an enemy, God sent His only Son to die on the Cross on Calvary's Hill for me . . . that at the cost of His life's blood I have salvation and that I am a child of God and an heir to everlasting bliss. I know that. Very well, then . . . Faith says, 'I cannot believe that He who has brought me so far is going to let me down at this point. It is impossible, it would be inconsistent with the character of God. . . .'

And then the next step is that faith applies all that to the particular situation. Again, that was something [that the disciples, during the storm on Galilee] did not do, [Luke 8: 22–25] and that is why our Lord puts it to them in this way: 'Where is your faith?'—'You have got it, why don't you apply it, why don't you bring all you know to bear on this situation, why don't you focus it on this particular problem?' . . . I do not suggest that you will be able to understand everything that is happening . . . but you will know for certain that God is not unconcerned. That is impossible. The One who has done the greatest thing of all for you, must be concerned about you in everything, and though the clouds are thick and you cannot see His face, you know He is there. . . . Nothing can happen to you but what He allows, I do not care what it may be, some great disappointment, perhaps, or it may be an illness, it may be a tragedy of some sort . . . but you can be certain of this, that God permits that thing to happen to you because it is ultimately for your good.

Spiritual Depression, pp. 144–5

Here the fair tree of knowledge grows,
And yields a free repast;
Sublimer sweets than nature knows
Invite the longing taste

The Bible is quite explicit in saying that there is only one way of arriving at a knowledge of ultimate truth, and that is to accept the revelation which is given in the Bible. The Bible is truth given by God. . . . Someone may ask, 'But is not this intellectual suicide?' The answer is that it is not. It is the following-out of what Pascal says about the supreme achievement of reason and the limit to reason. . . . Once we have done this, once we submit to the revelation . . . once I have seen the truth as the result of the operation of the Holy Spirit on my mind (and I can do nothing without that), then I begin to use my reason in a manner that I have never been capable of before. I now use it at full stretch, and I begin to see reason and meaning in everything.

This is not theory; it is something which can be illustrated in practice. Take the Apostle Paul, for example, and read his epistles. Nothing strikes you so much as the element of reason, and logic, and argument, and his mighty grasp of truth . . . you do not reason yourself into truth, you come into truth by accepting the revelation; but then you begin to reason and to understand and to possess. Consider men like Paul, Augustine, Thomas Aquinas, Luther, Calvin, Pascal again, and others. These are some of the giant intellects of the centuries, and they are giants because they had the wisdom to see how far reason could take them, and then to submit themselves to the revelation. They were lifted up and enlightened by the Spirit of God, and their minds and gigantic reasoning powers then began to demonstrate themselves. . . . It is only in the light of the teaching of the Bible that I really understand myself. . . . Here alone do I see any real meaning in life. Here alone am I given any teaching in respect to death. Here I have an understanding of history— the meaning of history, the goal of history, the end of history, it is all here.

The Approach to Truth: Scientific and Religious, pp. 23–5

O give us hearts to love like Thee,
Like Thee, O Lord, to grieve
Far more for others' sins, than all
The wrongs that we receive
(Edward Denny)

Look at Him there upon the cross, who never sinned, who never did any harm to anyone, who came and preached the truth, who came to seek and save that which was lost. There He is, nailed and suffering agonies on that cross, and yet what does He say as He looks upon the people who are responsible for it? 'Father, forgive them.' Why? 'For they know not what they do.' . . . Now you and I are to become like that. Look at Stephen the martyr attaining to that. As they are stoning him, what does he say? . . . 'Lay not this sin to their charge.' 'They do not know what they are doing, Lord', says Stephen; 'They are mad . . . they do not understand me as Thy servant; they do not understand my Lord and Master. . . .' He has pity upon them and is merciful with respect to them. And that, I say, is to be the condition of every one who is truly Christian. We are to feel a sense of sorrow for all who are helpless slaves of sin. That is to be our attitude towards people.

I wonder whether we have recognized this as the Christian position even when people were using us despitefully and maligning us. . . . They are to be pitied. Look at the things about which they get angry, showing that their whole central spirit is wrong; so unlike Christ, so unlike God who has forgiven them everything. We should feel a great sorrow for them, we should be praying to God for them and asking Him to have mercy upon them . . . all this follows of necessity if we have truly experienced what it means to be forgiven. If I know that I am a debtor to mercy alone, if I know that I am a Christian solely because of that free grace of God, there should be no pride left in me . . . no insisting upon my rights. Rather, as I look out upon others, if there is anything in them that is unworthy . . . I should have this great sorrow for them in my heart.

Studies in the Sermon on the Mount, i, pp. 103–4

The Christian way of life is difficult. It is not an easy life. It is too glorious and wonderful to be easy. It means living like Christ Himself, and that is not easy. The standard is difficult— thank God for it. It is a poor kind of person who wants only the easy and avoids the difficult. This is the highest life that has ever been depicted to mankind, and because of that it is difficult, and it is strait and narrow. 'Few there be that find it.' Of course! There are always fewer consulting doctors of medicine than general practitioners; there are never as many experts as there are ordinary workers. . . . When you come to the topmost level in any walk in life the company is always smaller. Anybody can follow the ordinary; but the moment you want to do something unusual, the moment you want to reach the heights, you will find that there are not many trying to do the same. It is exactly the same with respect to the Christian life; it is such an exalted life and such a wonderful one, that there are but few who will find it and enter it, simply because it is difficult. . . . Consider what we have been told as we have gone through the Sermon in detail. Look at this kind of life as our Lord has depicted it, and you will see that it must be narrow because it is so difficult. It is the highest, it is the acme of perfection in living.

Studies in the Sermon on the Mount, ii, pp. 225–6

The Apostle Peter realizes that we need to 'grow in grace, and in the knowledge of our Lord and Saviour Jesus Christ' (2 Peter 3:18), but before we can grow we must be born. It is only a living child who can grow. There can be no growth where there is no life. The very notion of growth and development and perfection presupposes a life already in existence. Exactly the same point is made by Paul at the beginning of 1 Corinthians 3. He complains that the Corinthians are still babes, that he cannot write to them as men because they are not yet in a condition to receive it. But remember, they are already Christians, 'called saints'; they are born again, they have believed in 'Jesus Christ and him crucified'. They are on the one and only 'foundation' already. But that does not mean that they are complete. They need to be taught. This knowledge needs to develop and to grow; there are aspects of it they have not yet understood.

At the end of Hebrews 5 the author makes the same complaint about his readers that he cannot feed them with 'strong meat' but can give them only 'milk'. He would like to tell them about the wonderful doctrine of Christ as Melchisedec, but he cannot. Yet the life is there; they have believed the truth; they have laid hold of the 'first principles', the elements of the gospel of Christ. The writer's concern is that they should not 'slip away' by believing false teachers. At the same time he wants them to 'go on to perfection'.

The Basis of Christian Unity, pp. 37–8

. . . our Lord clearly chose these Beatitudes carefully. He did not speak haphazardly. There is a definite progression in the thought; there is a logical sequence. . . . 'Blessed are the merciful.' What a searching statement that is! What a test of each one of us, of our whole standing and of our profession of the Christian faith! Those are the happy people, says Christ, those are the people to be congratulated. That is what man should be like—merciful. This is perhaps a convenient point at which to emphasize the searching character of the whole of this statement which we call the Beatitudes. Our Lord is depicting and delineating the Christian man and the Christian character. He is obviously searching us and testing us. . . . How are we reacting to these searching tests and probings? They really tell us everything about our Christian profession. And if I dislike this sort of thing, if I am impatient with it, if I want instead to be talking about communism, if I dislike this personal analysis and probing and testing, it simply means that my position is entirely contrary to that of the New Testament man. But if I feel, on the other hand, that though these things do search and hurt me, nevertheless they are essential and good for me, if I feel it is good for me to be humbled, and that it is a good thing for me to be held face to face with this mirror, which . . . shows me what I am . . . in the light of God's pattern for the Christian man, then I have a right to be hopeful about my state and condition. A man who is truly Christian, never objects to being humbled. The first thing that is said about him [in the Beatitudes] is that he should be 'poor in spirit', and if he objects to being shown that there is nothing in him, then that is not true of him. So these Beatitudes taken as a whole do provide a very searching test.

Studies in the Sermon on the Mount, i, pp. 95–6

The secret of power is to discover and learn from the New Testament what is possible for us in Christ. What I have to do is to go to Christ. I must spend my time with Him, I must meditate upon Him, I must get to know Him. That was Paul's ambition—'that I might know Him'. I must maintain my contact and communion with Christ and I must concentrate on knowing Him.

What else? I must do exactly what He tells me. I must avoid things that would hamper . . . I must not eat too much, I must not get into an atmosphere that is bad for me, I must not expose myself to chills if I want to be well. In the same way, if we do not keep the spiritual rules we may pray endlessly for power but we shall never get it. There are no short cuts in the Christian life. If in the midst of persecution we want to feel as Paul felt, we must live as Paul lived. I must do what He tells me, both to do and not to do. I must read the Bible, I must exercise, I must practise the Christian life, I must live the Christian life in all its fullness. In other words, I must implement what Paul has been teaching in verses eight and nine [of Philippians 4]. This, as I understand it, is the New Testament doctrine of abiding in Christ. Now the word 'abiding' makes people become sentimental. They think of abiding as something passive and clinging, but to abide in Christ is to do what He tells you, positively, and to pray without ceasing. Abiding is a tremendously active thing.

Spiritual Depression, pp. 298–9

December 12 Here are no fair false promises,
But the sharp comfort that doth spring from truth

[The Christian life] always involves suffering, and . . . when
it is truly lived, it always involves persecution . . . 'so persecuted
they the prophets which were before you'. They have always
done that, the world has always persecuted the man who follows
God. You see it perfectly in the case of our Lord Himself. He
was rejected by the world. He was hated by men and women
because He was what He was. 'Yea', says Paul 'and all that will
live godly in Christ Jesus shall suffer persecution.' But who
likes being persecuted? We do not like to be criticized or to be
dealt with harshly. We really do like all people to speak well
of us, and it is very galling to us to know that we are being
hated and criticized; but Christ has warned us that we will be,
if we come into this narrow way. It is strait and difficult; and
as we enter, therefore, we must be ready for suffering and
persecution.

You must be ready to be misunderstood, you must be ready,
perhaps, even to be misunderstood by your nearest and dearest.
Christ has told us that He came 'not to send peace, but a sword',
a sword that may divide mother from daughter, or father from
son, and those of your own household may be your greatest
enemies. Why? Because you have been set apart . . . and have
entered by this strait gate that does not admit us by families,
but one by one. It is very hard, it is very difficult. But the Lord
Jesus Christ is honest with us; and if we see nothing else God
grant that we may see the honesty and the truthfulness of this
gospel which tells us at the very outset that . . . you can only
come one by one, for it is a strait and narrow gate.

Studies in the Sermon on the Mount, ii, p. 226

The Apostle [Paul] is concerned about the 'development' of that which is already in existence, rather than about arriving at something which is hitherto non-existent. . . . Perhaps the clearest statement of the point is . . . in Philippians 3:10, where he says that his greatest desire is 'that I may know him'. Does he mean by that, that he did not know Him at all, and that he is longing to have a knowledge of Christ? Of course not. What he is saying is this: 'I do know Him, but I want to know Him much more, I want to have a deeper knowledge.' He longs for an 'increase' and for the perfecting of the knowledge he already has.

To put the matter finally beyond dispute we may turn to the paradoxical statement of Philippians 3:12–15. Paul begins, 'Not as though I had already attained, either were already perfect'; and then continues, 'Let us therefore, as many as be perfect, be thus minded' (v. 15). . . . There is no real contradiction, of course. What he means is that all true Christians already have the knowledge essential to salvation and are perfect in that sense. . . . So he says, 'Let us therefore, as many as be perfect, be thus minded'. Then he goes on to say, 'If in any thing ye be otherwise minded, God shall reveal even this unto you'. There are still aspects of the faith and of the truth which we do not yet know; they will be revealed to us. As regards the faith we have, and our present position on the foundation, Christ Jesus, there is a sense, therefore, in which we are already perfect. But we must also go on to perfection. We have not arrived, have not 'already attained' (v. 12). We are now growing in this knowledge that we have. We are now coming into it. It is because we are in it already that we can grow and develop in and through it.

The Basis of Christian Unity, pp. 38–9

[The Christian life] is not only strait at the beginning; it continues to be strait. It is not only a strait gate, it is a narrow way also. The Christian life is narrow from the beginning to the end. There is no such thing as a holiday in the spiritual realm. We can take holiday from our usual work; but there is no such thing as a holiday in the spiritual life. It is always narrow. As it starts, so it continues. It is a 'fight of faith' always, right to the end. It is the narrow way, and on each side there are enemies. There are things oppressing us and people attacking us all along to the very end. You will have no easy pathway in this world and in this life, and Christ tells us that at the beginning. If you have an idea that the Christian life is going to be difficult at the commencement and that later it becomes quite easy, you have an entirely false view of the teaching of the New Testament. It is narrow all the way; there will be foes and enemies attacking you right to the last minute.

Am I discouraging? Does anyone feel like saying: 'Well, if it is like that, I am going back'? But I would remind you before you decide to do that, that we are told something about the end to which this road leads. Yet apart from that, is it not the most glorious thing to go on following Him? Even so, let us be under no illusion; the wrestling against principalities and powers, against the darkness of this world, and the spiritual wickedness in high places, continues while man is in this life and world. There will be subtle temptations on the road of life, and you will have to watch and be on guard, from the beginning to the end. You will never be able to relax. You will always have to be careful; you will have to walk circumspectly, as Paul puts it; you will have to watch your every step. It is a narrow way; it starts as such and so it continues.

Studies in the Sermon on the Mount, ii, pp. 226–7

Why should [righteousness] be the greatest desire of every one of us? I answer the question in this way. All who lack this righteousness of God remain under the wrath of God and are facing perdition. . . . That is the teaching of the Bible. . . . It is only this righteousness that can fit us to be right with God and to go to heaven and to be with Him and to spend eternity in His holy presence. . . . How amazing it is that this is not the supreme desire in the life of everybody! It is the only way to blessing in this life and to blessing in eternity. Let me put to you [also] the argument of the utter hatefulness of sin, this thing that is so dishonouring to God. . . . If only we saw the things of which we are guilty so continually in the sight of God, and in the sight of utter holiness, we should hate them even as God Himself does. . . .

But I put it in a positive form. If only we knew something of the glory and the wonder of this new life of righteousness, we should desire nothing else. Therefore let us look at the Lord Jesus Christ. That is how life should be lived, that is what we should be like. . . . Look at the lives of His followers. Wouldn't you really like to live like those men, wouldn't you like to die like them? Is there any other life that is in any way comparable to it—holy, clean, pure, with the fruit of the Spirit manifesting itself [Galatians 5:22, 23]. What a life, what a character. That is a man worthy of the name of man; that is life as it should be. And if we see these things truly, we shall desire nothing less; we shall become like the Apostle Paul and we shall say, 'That I may know him, and the power of his resurrection, and the fellowship of his sufferings, being made conformable unto his death; if by any means I might attain unto the resurrection of the dead'. Is that your desire? Very well, 'Ask, and it shall be given you . . .'

Studies in the Sermon on the Mount, i, pp. 93–4

'It is good for me to draw near to God: I have put my trust in the Lord God, that I may declare all thy works' [Psalm 73:28]. Now this is a very vital addition. This is the point at which we should all arrive. His final reason for determining to keep near to God is in order that he might glorify God, in order that He might declare all His works. I imagine his argument was something like this: if I keep near to God I shall be blessed, I shall experience His salvation, I shall have this great and marvellous sense of security. And of course that will immediately lead me to praise God and to magnify God and to glorify God before others. I am going to keep near to God in order that I may always praise Him, and as I praise God I will be testifying about Him to others. That is a point at which we must all arrive.

You remember that the first question in the Shorter Catechism of the Westminster Confession of Faith is, 'What is the chief end of man?' And the answer is that, 'Man's chief end is to glorify God, and to enjoy Him for ever'. Now the Psalmist puts it the other way round. He puts enjoyment first only because he is dealing with the matter experimentally. He had been deeply unhappy himself, so he comes down to our own level and he says: Keep near to God and you will be happy, you will enjoy God and you will glorify Him. These two things must always go together. 'Man's chief end is to glorify God, and to enjoy him for ever.' Yes, says this man, I am going to keep near to God in order that I may glorify Him as well as enjoy Him. He is the great Lord God Almighty, and the tragedy of man and the tragedy of the world and of history is that the world does not know that. But my business is to tell people about Him. I will do so in my life, I will do so with my lips. The whole of my life shall be to the glory of God; and I cannot glorify God unless I am near to Him and experiencing Him. But as I do so I shall reflect His life.

Faith on Trial, pp. 123–4

The gospel of Jesus Christ . . . is something that demands a decision and a committal. . . . It is not a philosophy that you look at and compare and contrast with other philosophies. . . . It is, of course, a wonderful philosophy, but the temptation is to regard it as just that, as something to be read about, and to be interested in. But the gospel refuses to be taken like that; it is essentially something that comes to us demanding to control our lives. It comes to us in much the same way as our Lord Himself approached men. You remember how, as He walked along, He came across a man like Matthew, and said to him, 'Follow me', and Matthew got up and followed Him. The gospel does something like that. It does not say: 'Consider Me; admire Me.' It says: 'Follow Me; believe Me.' It always calls for a decision, for a committal.

This is obviously something that is quite vital. There is no purpose in describing the glories and the wonders and the beauties of that narrow way if we are still going to look at it only from a distance. It is a road that is to be trodden; it is something we are to enter into. . . .

So we ask ourselves a very simple question. . . . Have I committed myself to this way of life? Is it the thing which controls my life? . . . This, of course, involves a very definite act of the will. It calls upon me to say, 'Recognizing this as God's truth and as the call of Christ, I am going to give myself to it, come what may. I am not going to consider the consequences. I believe it, I will act upon it; this henceforth is going to be my life'.

There was a time when some of our forefathers used to teach that it was a good thing for every Christian to make a covenant with God . . . they would sit down and solemnly write out on paper the covenant which they made with God, and they would put their signature to it. . . . There is something to be said for that. . . . The Christian life demands a decision.

Studies in the Sermon on the Mount, ii, pp. 229–30

Let us go on with our practical efforts and let us go on with our study, but God forbid that we should rely upon them. . . . But, in the name of God, let us not stop at that. Let us realize that even that, without the authority and the power of the Spirit, is of no value at all . . . It does not matter who I am or what I may do: it will get me nowhere. It is the authority of the Spirit that alone avails.

Now this is what grieves me. I very rarely hear any Christians today, even Evangelicals, praying for revival. . . . They pray for their own organized efforts. . . . When did you last hear anyone praying for revival, praying that God might open the windows of heaven and pour out His Spirit? When did you last pray for that yourself? I suggest seriously that we are neglecting this almost entirely. We are guilty of forgetting the authority of the Holy Spirit . . . we have forgotten the one thing that can make us effective. By all means let us continue to pray for the particular efforts, for the minister, and his preaching every Sunday, for all essential organizations. . . . But before it all, and after it all, let us pray and plead for revival. When God sends revival He can do more in a single day than in fifty years of all our organization. That is the verdict of sheer history which emerges clearly from the long story of the Church.

This is the greatest need today, indeed it is the only hope. Let us therefore decide that day by day . . . we will spend our time before God pleading for revival. . . . Let us remind ourselves that the God who in the past has come suddenly and unexpectedly upon the dying Church and has raised her to a new period of life and victory can do the same still, that His arm is not shortened, nor His power in any sense diminished.

Authority, pp. 92–3

The greatest inducement of all, however, to enter in at the strait gate and to walk the narrow way, is this. There is Someone on that road before you. You have to leave the world outside. You may have to leave many who are dear to you, you have to leave yourself, your old self, and you may think as you go through that gate that you are going to be isolated and solitary. But it is not so. There are others on this road with you. . . . There are not as many as there are on the other way, but they are a very choice and separate people. But above all look at the One who is treading that road ahead of all, the One who said, 'Follow me', the One who said, 'Let him deny himself, and take up his cross, and follow me'. If there were no other inducement for entering in at the strait gate, that is more than enough. To enter this way means to follow in the footsteps of the Lord Jesus Christ. It is an invitation to live as He lived; it is an invitation to become increasingly what He was. It is to be like Him, to live as He lived whose life we read of in these Gospels. That is what it means; and the more we think of it in that way the greater will the inducement be. Do not think of what you have to leave; there is nothing in that. Do not think of the losses, do not think of the sacrifices and sufferings. These terms should not be used; you lose nothing, but you gain everything. Look at Him, follow Him, and realize that ultimately you are going to be with Him, and to look into His blessed face and enjoy Him to all eternity. He is on this way, and that is enough.

Studies in the Sermon on the Mount, ii, pp. 235–6

People usually want a clear answer to a specific question, but the Bible does not always give us what we desire in this respect. It does, however, teach us a method. . . .

(a) *Stop to think.* . . . The first thing is to think instead of speaking. 'Be swift to hear,' says James, 'slow to speak, slow to wrath' (Jas. 1:19). Our trouble is that we are swift to speak and swift to wrath, but slow to think. According to this prophet [Habakkuk], however, the first thing to do is to ponder. Before expressing our reactions we must discipline ourselves to think. . . .

(b) *Re-state basic principles* . . . you must not begin with your immediate problem. Begin further back. . . . We must first remind ourselves of those things of which we are absolutely certain, things which are entirely beyond doubt. Write them down and say to yourself, 'In this terrible and perplexing situation in which I find myself, here at least is solid ground'. When, walking on moorlands, or over a mountain range, you come to bogs, the only way to negotiate them is to find solid places on which you can place your feet. . . . So, in spiritual problems, you must return to eternal and absolute principles. . . .

(c) *Apply the principles to the problem* . . . problems are capable of solution only if they are put into the right context.

(d) *If still in doubt, commit the problem to God in faith.* . . . If you are *still* not clear about the answer, then just take it to God in prayer and leave it there with Him. That is what [Habakkuk] did in 1:13. In the preceding verse and in the early part of v. 13, the prophet was clearly still perplexed, so he took the problem to God and left it there.

Once we have the right method we can apply it to any problem: to God's strange dealings with a nation, to problems in the world, or equally to personal difficulties.

From Fear to Faith, pp. 25–8

What is mercy? I think perhaps the best way of approaching it is to compare it with grace.... The best definition of the two that I have ever encountered is this: 'Grace is especially associated with men in their sins: mercy is especially associated with men in their misery' . . . while grace looks down upon sin as a whole, mercy looks especially upon the miserable consequences of sin. So that mercy really means a sense of pity plus a desire to relieve the suffering. That is the essential meaning of being merciful; it is pity plus the action. So the Christian has a feeling of pity. His concern about the misery of men and women leads to an anxiety to relieve it . . . to have a merciful spirit means the spirit that is displayed when you suddenly find yourself in the position of having in your power someone who has transgressed against you.... Are you going to say, 'Well now . . . this person has transgressed against me; very well, here comes my oppprtunity'? That is the very antithesis of being merciful.... Or, again, we can describe it as inward sympathy and outward acts in relation to the sorrows and sufferings of others.... The great New Testament illustration of being merciful is the parable of the Good Samaritan. On his journey he sees this poor man who has been in the hands of robbers, stops, and goes across the road to where he is lying. The others have seen the man but have gone on. They may have felt compassion and pity yet they have not done anything about it. But here is a man who is merciful; he is sorry for the victim, goes across the road, dresses the wounds, takes the man with him and makes provision for him. That is being merciful. It does not mean only feeling pity; it means a great desire, and indeed an endeavour, to do something to relieve the situation.

Studies in the Sermon on the Mount, i, pp. 99–100

*Do the duty that lies nearest thee. Thy
second will already have become clearer*
(Thomas Carlyle)

What a wonderful idea! This is a kind of spiritual blood transfusion—that is what Paul is teaching here. Here is a patient who has lost much blood for some reason or another. He is faint and gasping for breath. It is no use giving him drugs because he has not enough blood to absorb them and use them. The man is anaemic. The only thing you can do for him is to give him a blood transfusion, infuse blood into him. That is what Paul tells us the Lord Jesus Christ was doing for him. 'I find I am very feeble,' says Paul, 'my energy seems to flag and sometimes I feel I have no life blood in me at all. But . . . because of this relationship, I find He infuses it into me. He knows my every state and condition, He knows exactly what I need. Oh, how much He gives me! He says, "My grace is sufficient for thee", and so I can say, "when I am weak then I am strong". Sometimes I am conscious of great power; there are other times when I expect nothing, but He gives everything.'

That is the romance of the Christian life. Nowhere does one experience it more than in a Christian pulpit. . . . I ascend the pulpit stairs Sunday after Sunday; I never know what is going to happen. I confess that sometimes for various reasons I come expecting nothing; but suddenly the power is given. . . . Thank God it is like that. I do my utmost, but He controls the supply and the power. . . . He is the heavenly physician and He knows every variation in my condition. . . .

That, then, is the prescription. Do not agonize in prayer beseeching Him for power. Do what He has told you to do. Live the Christian life. Pray, and meditate upon Him. Spend time with Him and ask Him to manifest Himself to you. And as long as you do that you can leave the rest to him. He will give you strength—'as thy days so shall thy strength be'.

Spiritual Depression, pp. 299–300

Look . . . at that worldly life which those people live who are on the broad way. . . . Look at the life and analyse it. What is there in it ultimately . . . ? Can you imagine anything that is so utterly empty finally? What real satisfaction is there in such a life? . . . What is the gain? . . . What is there uplifting and ennobling in dressing in a particular way and having their photographs in the so-called society papers, in being known for their fashionable attire or personal appearance, or for the figure they cut . . .? Look at the people who live for such things, analyse their lives, and especially their end. . . . As the hymn puts it,

> Fading is the worldling's pleasure,
> All his boasted pomp and show.

How empty it is!

. . . Then look at the other life and see how essentially different it is in every respect. The broad way is empty and useless, intellectually, morally, and in every other respect. It leaves man with a nasty taste in his mouth even at the time. . . . But look at the other, and immediately you see a striking contrast. Read the Sermon on the Mount again. What a life! Take this New Testament. What food for your intellect! Here is something to engage your mind. . . . Can you imagine a higher intellectual occupation, apart from anything else? Here you have something to think about, something to grapple with intellectually, something that gives you real satisfaction. How ethical, how uplifting, how large and noble it is.

The trouble ultimately with all who are not Christian is that they have never seen the glory and the magnificence of the Christian life. How noble and pure and upright it is! But they have never seen it. They are blind to it . . . once a man gets a glimpse of the glory and majesty and privilege of this high calling I cannot imagine that he would ever desire anything else.

Studies in the Sermon on the Mount, ii, pp. 232–4

We must get rid of this spirit of fear, this lurking pride, this inferiority complex, this tendency to apologize for the Word of God and its blessed Truth. . . . We must have confidence and assurance! In what? In the Bible as the Word of God. Why? Because it is God's Word, because it is God's revelation; because it is not the theories and the ideas of men with respect to Truth. . . . It is what the Living God has revealed to men . . . and has commanded them to preach. [Martin Luther] puts it like this: 'Philosophy has to do with what can be known by human reason. Theology has to do with that which is "believed", with that which is apprehended by faith.'

This is God's Word, this is God's Truth. This is from Heaven, not from men and it is therefore invincible. We must learn to say what [Paul] said in his Epistle to the Galatians in the first chapter. . . . 'I marvel that ye are so soon removed from him that called you into the grace of Christ unto another gospel: which is not another; but there be some that trouble you, and would pervert the gospel of Christ'. 'I certify you, brethren, that the gospel which was preached of me is not after man. For I neither received it of man, neither was I taught it, but by revelation of Jesus Christ.' 'A dispensation of the Gospel', he says to the Corinthians and to others has been 'committed unto me.' This was his whole position and it must be ours. This is the Word of God! This is Revelation! This is infallible because it is God's! This is the first weapon of our warfare. This is something which is to be proclaimed; not to be defended, but to be proclaimed; to be spoken with a holy boldness; to be 'declared' unto men. We do not need 'dialogues'; we need 'declarations'.

The Weapons of our Warfare, pp. 20–1

. . . what God wants, and what our blessed Lord wants, above all, is ourselves—what Scripture calls our 'heart'. He wants the inner man, the heart. He wants our submission. He does not want merely our profession, our zeal, our favour, our works, or anything else. He wants *us*. . . . God does not want our offerings; He does not want our sacrifices; He wants our obedience, He wants *us*. It is possible for a man to say right things, to be very busy and active, to achieve apparently wonderful results, and yet not to give himself to the Lord. He may be doing it all for himself. . . . And that is finally the greatest insult we can offer to God . . . to say, 'Lord, Lord', fervently, to be busy and active, and yet to withold true allegiance and submission from Him, to insist upon retaining control of our own lives, and to allow our own opinions and arguments, rather than those of Scripture, to control what we do and how we do it . . . whatever else we may do—however great our offerings and sacrifices, however wonderful our works in His name—it will avail us nothing. If we believe that Jesus of Nazareth is the only begotten Son of God and that He came into this world and went to the cross of Calvary and died for our sins and rose again in order to justify us and to give us life anew and prepare us for heaven—if you really believe that, there is only one inevitable deduction, namely that He is entitled to the whole of our lives, everything without any limit whatsoever. That means that He must have control not only in the big things, but in the little things also. . . . We must submit to Him and His way as He has been pleased to reveal it in the Bible; and if what we do does not conform to this pattern . . . it belongs to this type of conduct that makes Christ say to certain people: 'Depart from me, ye that work iniquity.' . . . He calls them [this] because . . . they were doing it to please themselves and not in order to please Him. Let us solemnly examine ourselves in the light of these things.

Studies in the Sermon on the Mount, ii, pp. 281–2

December 26   *Christianity isn't for anything . . . except the love and worship of Him.*

. . . a very common danger at this present time is to be interested in the social and general rather than in the personal aspects of Christianity. This has been particularly important in the present century. Many people today, confronted by the problems of this country and of society, are saying more and more that what is needed is biblical teaching and a Christian attitude towards these national and social problems. Watch the statesmen, and the politicians—even some of the leading ones. Although one is given to understand that they practically never attend a place of worship on a Sunday, they are using increasingly the words 'religion' and 'Christian'. They seem to think vaguely that Christian teaching can help to solve the problems of State. Though they are not active and practising Christians themselves . . . and are not giving any personal obedience to the Lord, they seem to think that Christianity can be of help in a general way. We are always on dangerous ground when we begin to talk about 'Christian civilization' and 'Christian' or 'Western' values. . . . I refer particularly to the tendency to regard Christianity as if it were nothing more than anti-communist teaching. This can be seen in the way in which Christian organizations sometimes advertise, and in their use of slogans such as 'Christ or Communism?', etc. . . . It works in a very subtle way. A man persuades himself that, because he is an anti-communist, he must be a Christian. But it by no means follows. . . . The substitution of the social and general for the particular and personal in Christian matters is always a terrible danger. . . . If I find my interest tends to be more and more general, or social, or political, if that is increasingly my main interest in Christianity, then I am in an extremely dangerous state because I have probably ceased to examine myself.

Studies in the Sermon on the Mount, ii, pp. 286–7

There can be no doubt at all that the commonest cause [of misinterpreting the Bible] is our tendency to approach the Bible with a theory. We go to our Bibles with this theory, and everything we read is controlled by it. . . . There is a sense in which it is true to say that you can prove anything you like from the Bible. That is how heresies have arisen. The heretics were never dishonest men; they were mistaken men. . . . they have been some of the most sincere men that the Church has ever known. What was the matter with them? Their trouble was this; they evolved a theory and they were rather pleased with it; then they went back with this theory to the Bible, and they seemed to find it everywhere. . . . There is nothing so dangerous as to come to the Bible with a theory, with preconceived ideas, with some pet idea of our own. . . .

Now this particular danger tends chiefly to manifest itself in the matter of the relationship between law and grace. . . . Some so emphasize the law as to turn the gospel of Jesus Christ with its glorious liberty into nothing but a collection of moral maxims. It is all law to them and there is no grace left. They so talk of the Christian life as something that we have to do in order to make ourselves Christian, that it becomes pure legalism and there is really no grace in it. But let us remember also that it is equally possible so to over-emphasize grace at the expense of law as, again, to have something which is not the gospel of the New Testament.

Studies in the Sermon on the Mount, i, pp. 11–12

December 28   *Man looketh on the outward appearance, but the Lord looketh on the heart*

[The disciples] had been sent out to preach and to cast out devils, and had been highly successful. [Luke 10.] They came back full of pride because of the things that had happened, and our Lord said to them in effect, 'Did I not tell you in the Sermon on the Mount that people who are outside the kingdom can preach in my name, and cast out devils and do many wonderful works? Do not be misled by these things; make certain of yourself. It is your heart that matters. Is your name written in heaven? Do you really belong to me? Have you this holiness, this righteousness which I am teaching? "Not every one that saith unto me, Lord, Lord, shall enter into the kingdom of heaven; but he that doeth the will of my Father which is in heaven".' The way to test yourself, the way to test any man, is to look below the surface. Do not look at the apparent results, do not look at the wonders and the marvels, but discover whether he conforms to the Beatitudes. Is he poor in spirit; is he meek; is he humble; does he groan in his spirit as he sees the world; is he a holy man of God; is he grave, is he sober; does he say with Paul, 'We that are in this tabernacle do groan, being burdened'? Those are the tests, the tests of the Beatitudes, the tests of the Sermon on the Mount—the man's character, the man's nature. Not the appearances only, but the reality itself alone counts with God.

Studies in the Sermon on the Mount, ii, pp. 270–1

How do I keep near to God? . . . First of all by a life of prayer. . . . If I realize truly who He is, I shall want to talk to Him. The man who really keeps near to God is the man who is always talking to God. We must resolve to do this; we must decide that we will not allow the world to control us any longer, but that we are going to control it, and our time, and our energy and everything else.

Then in addition to prayer, there is Bible reading . . . read and study the Scriptures.

Next comes public worship. It was when he went into the sanctuary of God that [the Psalmist—Psalm 73] found peace and rest for his soul. And we have often had the same experience. If we want to keep near to God, we must not only pray in private, but also with others, we must not only read and study the Word in private but also come and do so with others. We help one another, we bear one another's burdens.

Then there is meditation and taking time to think. Throw the newspaper on one side and think about God and your soul. . . . We do not talk enough to ourselves. We must tell ourselves that we are in His presence, that we are His children, that Christ has died for us and that He has reconciled us to God. We must practise the presence of God, and realize it, we must talk to Him, and spend our days with Him. . . .

The final thing, of course, is obedience, because if we disobey Him we break contact. Sin always means a breaking of the connexion, it means going far away from God. So the two rules are, to seek God and then to obey Him. And if we should sin, so breaking the contact and communion, we immediately re-establish it by confessing our sins, knowing that 'the blood of Jesus Christ his Son' cleanses us from all unrighteousness. . . . 'For me, nearness to God is good for me.' May we know Him and dwell with Him and spend the remainder of our days . . . in the sunshine of His face.

Faith on Trial, pp. 124–5

. . . he faces the whole of [the teaching of the Sermon on the Mount]. He does not pick and choose, he allows every part of the Bible to speak to him. He is not impatient. He takes time to read it, he does not rush to a few favourite Psalms and use them as a kind of hypnotic when he cannot sleep at night; he allows the whole Word to examine him and to search him. Far from resenting this searching, he welcomes it. He knows it is good for him, so he does not object to the pain . . . the true Christian humbles himself under the Word. He agrees that what it says of him is true. Indeed, he says, 'it has not said enough about me'. He does not resent its criticism, nor that of other people, but rather he says to himself, 'They do not say the half, they do not know me'. . . . He immediately conforms to the Beatitudes because of the effect of the Word upon him, and then, because of that, he desires to conform to the type and pattern set before him. Here is a very good test. Would you *like* to live the Sermon on the Mount? Is that your true desire? Is that your ambition? If it is, it is a very good and healthy sign. Any man who desires to live this type and kind of life is a Christian. He hungers and thirsts after righteousness; that is the big thing in his life. He is not content with what he is. He says, 'O that I might be like the saints I have read about, like Hudson Taylor, or Brainerd, or Calvin. If only I were like the men who lived in caves and dens and sacrificed and suffered everything for His sake. If only I were like Paul. O that I were more like my blessed Lord Himself.' The man who can say that honestly is a man who is building on the rock. He is conforming to the Beatitudes. Observe the nature of the test. It is not asking whether you are sinless or perfect; it is asking what you would like to be, what you desire to be.

Studies in the Sermon on the Mount, ii, pp. 312–13

Faith always shows itself in the whole personality. We can summarize it all in the words we find in the first and second chapters of John's first Epistle, where we read, 'If we say that we have fellowship with him, and walk in darkness, we lie, and do not the truth.' 'He that saith, I know him, and keepeth not his commandments, is a liar, and the truth is not in him.' We can see where those have gone astray who hold that the Sermon on the Mount cannot apply to us, but only to the disciples of our Lord's own day, and to the Jews of some future kingdom which is yet to come. They say it must be so, otherwise we are put under the law and not under grace. But the words just quoted from the first Epistle of John were written 'under grace', and John puts it like that specifically: If any man says, 'I know him'—that is your faith, believing in the grace of Christ and the free forgiveness of sin—if any man says, 'I know him, and keepeth not his commandments, (he) is a liar.' That is simply repeating what our Lord says here about those who shall enter the kingdom of heaven: 'Not every one that saith unto me Lord, Lord . . . but he that doeth the will of my Father which is in heaven.' And it is the message of the whole of the New Testament. He 'gave himself for us', says Paul to Titus, 'that he might . . . purify unto himself a peculiar people, zealous of good works'. We have been saved 'unto holiness'. He set us apart in order to prepare us for Himself, and 'every man that hath this hope in him purifieth himself, even as he is pure'. That is the doctrine of the Bible.

Studies in the Sermon on the Mount, ii, pp. 310–11